Human Geography in the Making

Series Editor:

ALEXANDER B. MURPHY

Department of Geography,
University of Oregon, USA

For Grace and Simon

SERIES PREFACE

To understand the rapidly changing world in which we live, the study of geography is essential. Yet the nature and importance of a geographic perspective can easily be misconstrued if geography is seen simply as a set of changing patterns and arrangements. Like the world around it, the discipline of geography itself has undergone sweeping changes in recent decades as its practitioners have confronted and developed new concepts, theories, and perspectives. Placing the contributions of geographic research within the context of these changes is critical to an appreciation of geography's present and future.

The *Human Geography in the Making* series was developed with these considerations in mind. Inspired initially by the influential 'Progress Reports' in the journal *Progress in Human Geography*, the series offers book-length overviews of geographic subdisciplines that are widely taught in colleges and universities at the upper division and graduate levels. The goal of each of the books is to acquaint readers with the major issues and conceptual problems that have dominated a particular subdiscipline over the past two to three decades, to discuss and assess current themes that are shaping the evolution of the subdiscipline, and to highlight the most promising areas for future research.

There is a widely recognized gap between topically focused textbooks and narrowly defined scholarly studies. The books in this series move into this gap. Through analyses of the intellectual currents that have shaped key subdisciplines of geography, these books provide telling insights into the conceptual and empirical issues currently influencing research and teaching. Geographic understanding requires an appreciation of how and why ideas have evolved, and where they may be going. The distinguished contributors to this series have much to say about these matters, offering ideas and interpretations of importance to students and professional geographers alike.

Alexander B. Murphy
Series Editor
Professor of Geography
University of Oregon

TITLES IN THE SERIES

Making Political Ecology
(Roderick P Neumann, Florida International University, USA)

Making Political Geography
(John Agnew, UCLA, USA)

Making Development Geography (forthcoming)
(Victoria Lawson, University of Washington, USA)

Making Population Geography

ADRIAN BAILEY

University of Leeds, UK

Hodder Arnold

A MEMBER OF THE HODDER HEADLINE GROUP

Distributed in the United States of America
by Oxford University Press Inc., New York

First published in Great Britain in 2005 by
Hodder Education, a member of the Hodder Headline Group,
338 Euston Road, London NW1 3BH

www.hoddereducation.co.uk

Distributed in the United States of America by
Oxford University Press Inc.
198 Madison Avenue, New York, NY10016

British Library Cataloguing in Publication Data
A catalogue record for this book is available from the British Library

Library of Congress Cataloging-in-Publication Data
A catalog record for this book is available from the Library of Congress

ISBN-10: 0 340 76264 0
ISBN-13: 978 0 340 76264 6

1 2 3 4 5 6 7 8 9 10

Typeset in 10½ on 14 Gill Sans by Phoenix Photosetting, Chatham, Kent
Printed and bound in Great Britain by CPI, Bath.

What do you think about this book? Or any other Hodder Education title?
Please send your comments to the feedback section on www.hoddereducation.co.uk.

CONTENTS

PREFACE

Barbara Benish's reworking of Dürer's *Death of the Virgin* calls to mind key topics in population geography like mortality, conception and fertility. It also suggests that social institutions (in this case, religion and medicine) shape population events and our beliefs about them. Along with mobility and migration, fertility and mortality affect how quickly populations grow and decline, how they are distributed geographically and how this affects social progress. Theorizing the connections between population, geography and social change has been at the heart of research debates in population geography for much of the last 500 years. The belief that population plays *some* role in the growing gap between the world's rich and poor and contributes to environmental damage in many parts of the world has lent credibility and timeliness to this quest.

While the field's research debates continue to address how and why the geographical organization of population matters to society, its ways of understanding – that is, *knowing* the world – have shifted. The field's different research perspectives reflect different philosophical beliefs about knowledge and how the world works. Beliefs about knowledge that arose as part of the (European) Enlightenment have affected the intellectual, economic and military projects of western society for over 500 years. These Enlightenment beliefs themselves arose as a critique of 'Dark Age' views on religion and society. Indeed, key Enlightenment thinkers like Albrecht Dürer (whose woodcut *Death of the Virgin* appears in 1510) promulgated new ideas about the relationship between the individual, religion, rationality and science.

The growth of rational and 'scientific' approaches to knowledge helped sponsor western mercantilism, industrialization and colonialism and, more recently, globalization. The accompanying growth of nation states, in turn, changed the relationships between individuals and society and created new demands for knowledge. As nation states gained the authority to be generally responsible for society, the field of population geography came to understand populations as groups 'made' by and for states. Populations worked, they consumed, they formed cohesive social groups and communities, they served in armies and they built political communities. Populations constituted states and were made by states.

The criteria used by states to make populations often reflected their strategic interests in linking knowledge and power. When the Third Reich sought to consolidate power in Germany in the 1930s, it 'created' two populations as enemies of the state, demonized them and ultimately perpetrated the mass extermination of the 'races' it had created, Jews and Gypsies. Other 'political technologies', like slavery, apartheid, segregation and ethnic cleansing, evidence how state interests have been variously served by the creation and maintenance of population groups using strategic classifications. Interested in subjugating and expropriating resources from colonial holdings, colonial states sought to define distant 'native' populations as different from themselves, and thus in need of protection and administration. Racial, occasionally environmental and increasingly ethnic hierarchies were used in this process to make populations. Through promoting certain forms of knowledge, including geographic knowledge, states exerted their power.

Population, then, has been a concept used by states to identify groups who had intrinsic characteristics that helped, hindered or had some systematic bearing on national goals. Populations were or needed to be made useful. When geography, and latterly population geography, itself began contributing specific 'disciplinary' knowledge at the turn of the last century, the usefulness of population was often defined economically. Economists noted that population growth affected economic growth, and demographers revealed the mathematics of that growth. Geography combined these insights from economics and demography with an in-house focus on proximity and context. By defining populations in demographic terms, looking at where they were and predicting how fast they were growing, an emerging field of population geography could be seen to serve the national interest. As national interests became increasingly concerned with issues like social provision, international relations, urbanization and suburbanization and ageing, the field's research *debates* shifted topical focus. Its research *perspectives* remained largely untouched.

Yet, like all scientific fields, population geography has to change its questions and concepts as the authority of different ideologies and belief systems wax and wane. Benish's art reminds us of this. Her reworking of Dürer questions his – and the Enlightenment project's – assumptions about knowledge. Dürer believed that his work could best serve the social good by faithfully recording the world as it appeared to him. This he famously accomplished by placing his subjects in spatial settings that provided clues about meanings. In *Death of the Virgin*, the placement of the body of the virgin in a room redolent of a medical institution assesses the relationship between medicine, rationality, religion and the human condition.

Dürer also meticulously constructed sight lines to provide the viewer with an architecturally accurate representation of a scene, with objects positioned in space according to exact mathematical principles. By zooming in and disrupting the subject–setting relationship, Benish asks if a subject can be satisfactorily 'understood' with reference to the contents of its setting. By superimposing red sight lines over Dürer's invisible graticule, Benish suggests a danger in assuming that mathematical conventions of the world are neutral.

Just as Benish is keen to expand the Enlightenment idea of history (and geography), this book explores how the field of population geography is being remade by expanding its perspectives on population and geography. Population geography now discusses such 'post'-Enlightenment beliefs and what they mean for research perspectives and research debates. A good deal of this rethinking is linked to globalization. This is changing the links between states, population and social progress in several ways. Global capital mobility has been accompanied by global labour mobility: both undermine the security of the nation state. Neo-liberalism has had a profound effect on public services and the ways that states support different groups like the elderly, children and unmarried mothers. Globalization is also associated with the emergence of other bodies, which play an increasingly important role in affecting social progress. These include supra-national entities like the EU and NAFTA, multinational companies, non-governmental organizations, cooperatives and community groups. The changing research agendas of population geography reconsider how and why the geographic organization of population matters to society.

Thus, the goal of this book is to explore the intellectual development of population geography as a field of scholarship: this is a book about how the field of population geography is made. Its basic premise is that the field is made and remade by conditions within academia and conditions in broader society. As a system of ideas, a field acknowledges prevailing philosophical beliefs about knowledge and how to collect and make sense of knowledge. As a contemplative and sometimes critical account of a history of ideas, the book aims both to take stock of the nature of population geography and point towards areas of further growth. Using contemporary examples, I also illustrate what lies behind the perspectives of population geography and why these perspectives remain so productive for contemporary society.

A large number of people have directly and indirectly shaped the ideas in this book, although their appearance in this list (ordered somewhat chronologically) should in no way implicate them in what follows. I extend my appreciation to John

Odland, George Stolnitz, Dennis Conway, Rshood Khraif, Mark Ellis, Tom Cooke, Brigitte Waldorf, Richard Wright, Jennifer Dahlstein, Richard Morrill, David Lanegran, Martha Sharma, George Demko, Ellen Kraly, Damaris Rose, Dusan Drbohlav, Alison Mountz, Danny Dorling, Allan Findlay and Jan Monk. The series editor, Alexander Murphy, provided consistent encouragement; Abigail Woodman at Hodder managed the process professionally; Jen Dickinson provided timely research assistance; Barbara Benish produced something wonderful.

I am indebted to a number of people whose various interventions have enabled the making of this book. To Mum and Dad, thanks for always believing. To my children, thank you for accepting all those trips to Hastings. Megan Blake lent her intellectual nourishment and – in consigning me to the garden shed as the final deadline loomed – gave me what I needed most: discipline.

8. Figure 4.4: Constructing Remittances, reprinted with kind permission from Brac Bank (www.bracbank.com).

Every effort has been made to trace copyright holders and obtain appropriate permissions. The author and publisher will gladly receive any information enabling them to rectify any error in subsequent editions.

Adrian Bailey
Ilkley, West Yorkshire
16 July 2004

INTRODUCTION

Population geography studies the geographic organization of population and how and why this matters to society. This often involves describing where populations are found, how the size and composition of these populations is regulated by the demographic processes of fertility, mortality and migration, and what these patterns of population mean for economic development, ecological change and social issues. For example, suburbanization in the developed global North has been linked back to the migration decisions of many families who leave central cities and relocate on the urban fringe. This type of metropolitan decentralization matters because it contributes to the pressures on rural and 'green-field' land, the underfunding of inner-city schools, the continuing segregation of groups in society and the difficulties some 'suburban' housewives encounter in finding jobs. Similarly, Malthus's argument that the size of a population grows more quickly than its food supplies also used the idea that the geographic organization (in this case, the setting) of population could be used to 'diagnose' deeper structural problems in society, namely overpopulation and scarcity, and to justify appropriate social and political interventions, namely moral restraint and the reduction of government social support to the poor. The regular historical sequencing of patterns of population growth and decline across northern Europe supported the demographic transition diagnosis that population change was scientifically related to modernization, industrialization and urbanization. In turn, this led to the idea that best-practice (European-experienced) low growth rates could be rationally exported to the global South with government interventions like family planning.

While still important, this is not the only view of how the geographic organization of population matters to society. A number of alternative views address the increasingly diverse and complex links between governments (states) and populations. This enlarged perspective is associated with globalization in several ways. First, states assume different roles and functions under globalization. The footloose nature of some employment opportunities, neo-liberalism and increasing global interdependence all affect how governments think about populations. States have an increasingly problematic relationship with immigrant populations. While many states encourage immigration because immigrants fill jobs nobody is able or prepared to do, cultural insecurities have led to the demonization of some immigrant groups – more often than not dark-skinned and Arabic – and stretched to breaking point government models of inclusion, incorporation and membership in a national community. Second, globalization has availed the state – and other actors, including corporations, non-governmental organizations and trafficking networks – of a new range of technologies, strategies and practices that achieve political, economic and cultural ends through population means. Third, these strategies – and ways to read them – have been enabled by a critique of Enlightenment knowledge, another hallmark of globalization.

Population geography, like other social sciences, has been profoundly affected by these developments in contemporary economic, political and social life. In short, to understand the changing relationships between states and populations, the field has enlarged its focus. Rather than view population groups as the end product of individual demographic events, population geography examines the two-way relationships between the acts, performances, social institutions and discourses that make up these groups and their geographic organization. These enlarged views augment the traditional assumption that population groups are best under-stood when they are studied as the aggregate outcomes of individual population events, including fertility, mortality and migration. What this has meant in practice is that geography no longer just contains or reflects populations, it also helps create them. This book is about how population geography adds value to our understanding of society by studying both how populations are organized *in geography* and how populations are organized *by and through geography*.

Consider retirees, an increasingly influential population. The traditional UN definition of this group is based on an age, 65, the age at which state retirement benefits have been made available. A comparison of the ages of retirement for women reveals geographic differences reflecting the demographic supply of workers and the availability of pension funds. While the use of an age concept to define and understand this population group is statistically convenient, an enlarged view of the retired population shifts attention away from this demographic life-course event and considers how later life groups balance the acts of working, home life and leisure through their relationships with places. Accordingly, to be retired is to change the balance between acts of working and acts of not working, that is to change the relationship an individual has between their work life and their home life. Some locales actively enable work lives through subsidized mass transit, permissive attitudes and non-ageist employment practices. Technologies like telecommuting have also opened up new possibilities for combining – and blurring – home and work life. Moreover, at a local and regional scale, the concentration of later-life adults in affinity communities has greatly expanded leisure activities and further undermined the absolutist, age-based approach to retirement.

In common with other areas of human geography, population geography is busy reinventing itself. The second goal of *Making Population Geography* asks what is new in the field. I explore the proposition that the spatial turn widely observed across the social sciences and humanities has touched population geography. Recent views on how geography matters acknowledge the diversity and complexity of relationships between populations and states under conditions of globalization. The following vignettes, culled from news stories appearing in mid-May 2004 introduce some of the contemporary concerns of the field. They also suggest how ideas about geography and population are shifting:

Israeli security forces continued to demolish selected houses in the Gaza community of Rafah that they said contained tunnels under the border with Egypt. This occurred against the backdrop of Israel's planned withdrawal from this part of the Occupied Territories of Gaza and the West Bank, land it had acquired militarily in 1967. For Israel, the elimination of these particular Palestinian settlements was necessary to protect its own national security, as it claimed militant groups including Hamas were using the cross-border tunnels as key supply routes for arms. For Palestinian residents, and much of the Arab world, the Israeli actions were another symbol of continuing Israeli aggression toward, and non-recognition of the human rights of, a dispossessed population. This case – often described as the world's most intractable geopolitical crisis – shows how geographic perspectives on population are an essential component of what at first appears as a political issue concerning where to draw boundaries. When the 'political' creation of Israel was brokered in 1948, the act of drawing boundaries created new populations and divided others. Specifically, the displacement of thousands of residents of the former Palestine and the wholesale destruction of over 500 Arab villages 'created' a refugee population that is, today, the world's largest (over 4 million) and longest lasting, comprised of over two generations. Palestinian refugee communities – including Rafah, and like other refugee populations worldwide – lack access to 'taken-for-granteds' like human rights, protection, territorially rooted homelands and land that can support reasonable livelihoods. Refugee populations are some the world's poorest, most insecure, most fragile and most dependent communities. While poverty and endemic insecurity characterize Palestinian refugees – ironically, similar experiences have applied to large parts of Jewish history – the contemporary Israeli state is both threatened by the co-presence of this refugee community and complicit/active in its maintenance, through acts such as the above. Not unconnected to their economic and political disempowerment, the growth rate of the Palestinian population in the Occupied Territories exceeds that of the Israeli population, prompting Israel to project this differential growth rate as part of its ongoing security concern in the area and promote the construction of new Jewish settlements in Gaza and the West Bank (the doctrine of 'Judaification', Agnew 2002: 31). The fate of many recent Jewish settlements in Gaza and the West Bank appears today as another stumbling block in the peace process. Understanding the location, growth and economic and cultural characteristics of populations tells us much about the antecedents of geopolitical conflicts and may flag new routes to peace.

Tuberculosis (TB) was a leading cause of death among young men and women in many North American cities at the turn of the twentieth century. Medical discoveries about the spread of the disease and childhood vaccinations helped arrest TB and case mortality rates declined steadily during the century. However, by the early 1990s, figures from the Centers for Disease Control (CDC) suggested that TB had re-emerged in many inner-city areas of the USA. Decomposing these figures by place of birth suggested that foreign-born persons were eight times more likely to die from TB than native-born Americans. Immigrants from Mexico, the Philippines, Vietnam, India and China had the highest case mortality rates of any 'population' group. CDC data suggested that while immigrants accounted for more than 50 per cent of TB deaths in just four states in 1992, they accounted for more than 50 per cent of TB deaths in 22 states in 2002. The deepening association between TB and immigration was most starkly illustrated in the seven states where 70 per cent of all TB deaths were of immigrants: California, Colorado, Hawaii, Idaho, Massachusetts, Minnesota and New Hampshire. Media concerns have been raised about how increased global interconnectedness and mobility is contributing to the rapid spread of TB and other infectious and parasitic diseases (IPDs) like HIV-AIDS, SARS and the Ebola virus. By studying the geographic context of disease, it becomes apparent that TB is less a marker of immigration than it is of poverty (Farmer 1999). Rising TB levels in areas of the former Soviet Union and Haiti suggest that unemployment, poor access to underfunded health care systems and stress all elevate risk. Rather than 'blame' immigrants for bringing IPDs to the shores of the USA, causality may be reversed and immigrants may be developing TB once inside the USA. Geographic perspectives on 'biomedical' characteristics of populations place disease – and health and wellness more generally – in its economic (for example, access to jobs), social (for example, access to health care) and political (for example, anti-immigrant rhetoric) setting. Concentrations of TB among immigrants in non-traditional destination states may suggest poor agricultural working conditions, barriers to accessing health care and concentrations of refugee groups in unhealthy areas.

On 1 May 2004 the European Union enlarged to include ten 'new' members: Estonia, Latvia, Lithuania, Poland, Slovakia, Hungary, Cyprus, Malta, Slovenia and the Czech Republic. Overnight, this additional 75 million people created the world's most influential (in terms of purchasing power) consumer market of over 500 million persons. Media coverage of this newly created population focused on the extent to which impoverished and unskilled young adults from Central and Eastern Europe would cross into the old West seeking jobs and social support and overwhelming local resources. On the flip side, the media spotlight also fell on those trained as dentists, nurses and teachers in countries like Poland, who could help countries like Britain meet sectoral shortages of suitably qualified workers. Political entities create populations to solve economic problems. On one level, allowing labour mobility (within the Eurozone) is argued to be in Europe's overall advantage by smoothing out labour supply and demand. At another level, however, 'old' Europe was reacting to an impending population crisis in a particularly geographic way. Demographic ageing was leading to a shrinking supply of new workers in key industrial nations, including the big four, Italy, Britain, France and Germany. Seen as a demographic crisis, the response of recruiting guest workers from former colonies had exacted a very high political price, which included anti-immigrant rhetoric and the growth of far right movements. By enlarging in the geographical (and historical) direction it did, Europe was able to welcome a new generation of young (and European) workers to its labour force without further worsening its growing identity crisis. This case illustrates the importance of demographic interdependence, with patterns of population demand (consumption) and supply (labour force entrants) linked to fertility, immigration and ageing. It also suggests that previous population fixes, like guest worker programmes, combined with the historical tactics that governments have used to maintain such population groups (through national membership models of assimilation and pluralism) may constrain future political possibilities. Geographic perspectives on population thus highlight demographic and historical interdependencies.

Same-sex marriage became legal in the Commonwealth of Massachusetts. As such, this US state recognized that gay and lesbian partners who married each other could expect the same legal rights as heterosexual partners. This meant equal treatment regarding the adoption of children and equal accessibility to benefits payable to one partner on the death of the other. Gay marriage is part of the diversification and pluralization of household forms and structures underway in contemporary society. Gay marriage also asks us to rethink the basis of family life as one not only defined around natural sex and reproduction but also based on the commitment of partners to one another (i.e. from the biological to the social). Both candidates for the US presidential nomination publically expressed their opposition to the Massachusetts legislation. Geographic perspectives illuminate this case study in several ways. Here the state is trumping biological over social bases of relationships. There is a geography to same-sex marriage legislation. Massachusetts, San Francisco and the Netherlands have all witnessed attempts to legalize gay marriage. All have concentrations of gay and lesbian groups in positions of economic and political power. An emerging global geography reflects not just factors of absolute location but relative location as well. The Australian prime minister firmly identified with George Bush's opposition to the legislation, saying that what was important was to recognize Australia's long history of heterosexual marriage as a building block of society. While the opposition shared the same view, queer groups said opposition to gay marriage amounted to a new apartheid based on sexual preference. Taiwanese legislators have seen the debate differently. Keen to appear as a modern and cosmopolitan member of the global community, support for same-sex marriage here references the desire to protect basic human rights (such as being in a consensual relation-ship). While local and national governments continue to debate who gets what rights, many employers have already extended in kind benefits and rights (for example, insurance policies, pensions) to their same-sex partnered employees. The multinational reach of large employers further complicates the geographies of same-sex marriage and suggests that players other than states are increasingly involved in population matters.

Michelle Smith, a high school girl living in the English East Midlands, had a chemical abortion. While a major event in her life, this type of population act rarely makes the news. On this occasion the 14-year-old had received abortion counselling in her school and decided against informing her mother of her decision to abort. An abortion was then arranged for her. Maureen Smith, her mother, did not find out about the termination until after the event. Abortion is an emotive issue and this story raises questions about rights: of the unborn child, of the mother and father, of the parent, of the school and of the government. Should a parent have the right to know about the advice being given to a dependant for whom they are legally responsible? Does a teenager have a right to withhold information from a parent and, if so, in what circumstances? These questions about rights in turn raise issues about the definition and meaning of population performances, including parenthood and childhood/ adolescence. Once based on biological relationships defined by a parent–child bond and age, both parenting and childhood are increasingly understood in social terms. The case illustrated how it was not Michelle's age that mattered, but her social maturity. Geography again matters as population performances like parenting and childhood/adolescence are being renegotiated in contemporary society. *Where* these renegotiations take place is crucial. Michelle received and acted on advice in the familiar surroundings of her school. Britain has the highest rate of teen pregnancies in Europe and a policy to provide health care counselling to teens in those places seen as the heart of their communities, including schools. The strategic 'placing' of information and advice, with knock-on effects for the relationship between the government, parents and teens, represents another dimension of state influence over population matters.

The moderate Islamic Sudanese government had just signed a long-awaited agreement to end years of conflict with rebel groups in the dominantly Christian south of the country. The civil war had uprooted millions of Sudanese and created the largest population of internally displaced persons – groups deserving of refugee status but who remain within a national border and thus out of reach of international intervention – during the late twentieth century. While many were justifiably heralding the new peace, charities, aid agencies, Amnesty International and the UN continued to report an impending humanitarian disaster in the western Sudan region of Darfur. Here, nomadic pastoralist 'Arab' groups were allegedly being backed by Sudanese army special forces in their ongoing skirmishes with 'black African' farmers.

Local Arab militias, known as *janjawid*, were said to have adopted a scorched earth policy, razing entire African villages to the ground, raping women, killing over 10,000 and displacing between 1 and 2 million persons; 22 per cent of the region's children under five had already developed acute malnutrition as crops had either not been planted due to the instability or had failed as water systems were compromised. Some in the international community accused the Sudanese government of cynical contempt for its population, as it collected accolades for its new policy towards the south on the one hand, but turned a blind eye to or, worse, actively supported repression in the west. Others turned the blame on an international system of protection that had failed Sudan's already large internally displaced population; the same system that had similarly failed the 800,000 Rwandans massacred exactly ten years before and that seemed to be about to fail the millions already displaced in Darfur. The case also reveals how governments wage war against populations inside their borders by emphasizing religious differences (Islamic and Christian beliefs in the southern dispute), racial and ethnic differences between groups (brown-skinned Arabs and black-skinned Africans in Darfur), by destroying environ-ments which support population livelihoods and by destroying the places and settlements which define the cultural homes of (pastoral) populations. While debates continue about the extent to which the Darfur crisis is an example of a race-based genocide, an example of ethnic cleansing or the latest round in an ongoing dispute between contrasting ways of life, the case again highlights how states variously create and react to their own, and global, population issues.

Several themes emerge from these situations. Population issues continue to matter to society, in ways that touch upon geopolitics, economic expansion, liveli-hood systems, consumption, social structures and cultural transformations. Contemporary population topics are often framed in geographic ways. Geography can be seen both as a location where events occur and a context which defines the nature of the issue. An important part of the field's reinvention involves the rewriting of what is meant by the terms geography and population. Thus, as the usage of the term 'geography' expands, the term population is also enlarged to:

- refer to groups, sometimes externally defined (Palestinian refugees, those internally displaced in Sudan, teenagers), sometimes self-defined (Israeli settlers) and the demographic events that make them (for example, fertility, mortality, migration);

refer to the acts and performances of individuals in groups that help constitute and give meaning to populations (including childhood, parenthood, retirement, being a student, being internally displaced and so on);

refer to the social institutions (work, home, family and so on) and discourses (ageism, sexism, racism, sedentarism and so on) that affect the formation and maintenance of populations by variously enabling and constraining population acts and performances.

The reinvention of contemporary population geography gives clues about *how* fields and sub-disciplines make and remake themselves. How and why fields of knowledge like population geography are made and remade is important because the research agendas that make up these fields inform the ways we build society. Therefore, my third goal addresses the mission of the *Human Geography in the Making* series and reflects on how the field is made. What are the internal and external drivers of change? Where is the field going?

Before exploring how population geography is made, it is helpful to consider what is meant by the notion of a field, or a sub-discipline, in the first instance. What are the necessary ingredients? I introduce three prevailing interpretations by comparing the field to Motown. There is some geographic irony here, as population geography was itself 'founded' at about the same time and only a few miles away from Detroit. Technically minded purists and industry buffs might define Motown as a set of recordings released on the Motown record label between the late 1950s and 1980s. Almost as if to anchor this aesthetic, early Motown record labels featured a map of the eastern USA with a red star placed over 'motor town' (Detroit: see figure 1.1). Similarly, many population geography textbooks argue that University of Wisconsin professor, Glen Trewartha, gave birth to the field in 1953 when he called for the establishment of a specific subfield in an impassioned speech at the Association of American Geographers conference in Cleveland. However, more than a handful of contemporary geographers would argue that the introspectives and critiques of the field in the 1990s (White and Jackson 1995) signalled the end of a recognizable, credible or authorized sub-discipline called population geography.

A second way of viewing population geography focuses on its scholarly outputs rather than its administrative structures. Artists like Mary Wells, Marvin Gaye, The Supremes and Stevie Wonder variously wrote, produced and performed 'Motown' music, and gave Motown a particular sound, style and musical genre.

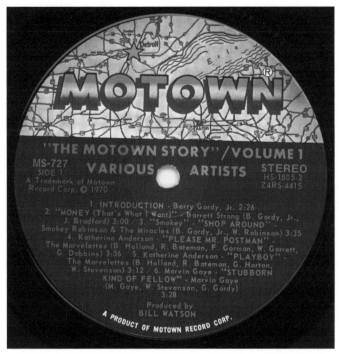

Figure 1.1 Placing Motown

Similarly, population geographers developed, between the 1950s and the 1990s, a diverse set of ideas, models and theories about population phenomena. Scholars continue to contribute to research agendas on the causes and consequences of migration, racial and ethnic segregation and the relationship between economic modernization and birth and death rates, for example. According to this notion, to be a population geographer means to contribute to these outputs.

A third approach to population geography recognizes that, like Motown, its legitimacy is both internally and externally regulated. That is, the record-buying public, music critics, popular culture, and even place marketers all have a role in validating and authorizing what is understood as Motown. Similarly, the users of population geography knowledge – society at large – play a key role in legitimizing the field. In this book I argue that population geography's 'negotiated' legitimacy comes from the way it connects population matters to society through the evolving concepts of space, environment and place.

The field of population geography thus covers knowledge produced and circulated by those:

from the corporate label (for example, an active member of a population geography interest group);

responding to the internal debates of the field;

taking a geographic perspective on population matters.

To summarize, in this book you will learn about three aspects of population geography. First, how does population geography add value to our understanding of society? Connected to this, I will overview the research debates within contemporary population geography. Second, what ideas has the field used to reinvent itself? To support this, I will introduce the research perspectives used in the field. Third, how do fields of knowledge change in response to shifting political and cultural imperatives? The various answers to this question – which I will show are place and time specific – tell us about the personalities of the researchers involved, their professional identities, funding priorities, the state of the academic discipline of geography, national pride and what society believes to be important and how we might know this (i.e. philosophy). My argument is that these various contexts play a complex role in continuing to shape the making of population geography and thus influence the questions that have been asked and, as importantly, the silences and the questions that are yet to be asked.

The four main chapters of the book describe the making of population geography in the following ways. Chapter two discusses how national governments became key producers and consumers of population knowledge. It traces how geography grew as a discipline that informed state agendas through the concepts of space, environment and place. Three vignettes explore the relevance of geography to contemporary population issues surrounding ageing, trafficking and HIV-AIDS.

Having set up the basic framework, the next three chapters show how specific research poles emerged from changes in external and internal contexts. Chapter three describes the heady days of the new sub-discipline and its rise to academic prominence between the 1950s and the late 1970s. A key theme is how political and social events and academic debates informed the way in which the new field represented itself; that is, were it to have been constituted at an earlier date, one might suspect a very different intellectual trajectory. This is not to downplay the significant role of individual researchers, and I reference signal speeches which quite literally did change the direction of the sub-discipline.

Chapter four continues the intellectual history (and geography) up to the near-present day. While the early growth I describe in chapter three had meant convergence around positivism and a full deployment of spatial perspectives, the 1980s and 1990s witnessed a growing plurality of approaches that rediscovered place and environment (although in different guises). The field felt somewhat insecure and, at times, apologetic for its continuing applied focus. The reasons for these shifts can be traced to transformations in (global) society, particularly the roles of migration and ageing, and the circulation of new beliefs about knowledge. As it became apparent that the nation was no longer the sole arbiter of links between population and social progress, many of the field's core assumptions – particularly demographic ones – were exposed. Links with other areas of geography, particularly social, urban and medical/health geography, strengthened. The lack of consensus over an intellectual core, and the clear differences between those occupying continuity, pluralist and critical positions meant the field had a new shape.

Emerging research agendas continue to share a commitment to rubbing together the terms population and geography to inform society. Chapter five explores how work on transnational geographies, the geopolitics of population and activism both reflects and critiques the changing relationships between states and populations. Attention is paid to the ways that security concerns and neo-liberalism affect how the geographic organization of population matters to society. While not meant to predict future agendas or to suggest that the activities of chapter four have waned, introducing such emerging agendas shows how the field balances cultural and material concerns and generates insights of interest to society.

chapter 2
KNOWLEDGE, GEOGRAPHY AND POPULATION

This chapter establishes the overall framework for the book by considering:

- How society's beliefs about knowledge have changed.
- Who is interested in knowledge about geography and population, and for what reasons?
- What are the perspectives that population geography carries to population matters? I explore why the field asks some questions, but not others, and link this to the development of geography as an academic discipline in Europe and North America, beginning around the eighteenth century.
- What relevance does contemporary population geography have?

Enlightenment beliefs

All societies need knowledge and all societies create knowledge. 'Scientific' knowledge about population geography is one example among many of a system of ideas that can shed light on how societies function. As such, knowledge has a tendency to reflect and reinforce the belief systems and philosophies of those with power and influence. Population geography emerged as a distinct set of ideas in an industrializing Europe during the early part of the nineteenth century. Its appearance and development has been strongly influenced by the underlying beliefs of what many philosophers of science term 'Enlightenment' society (Gregory 1996).

Three sets of Enlightenment beliefs shape the intellectual and political possibilities of population geography knowledge. The first belief is that knowledge is power (Foucault 1977). As power – the ability to influence others – is key to social progress, knowledge production is carefully authorized. For example, who has the power (moral authority? legitimacy?) in society to create knowledge? How did these groups acquire this power, on what basis and using what claims? How do they retain this power? More broadly, how does the way these groups create and exchange knowledge affect the basis of, or redistribution of, power within society?

In a decisive break from the norms of medieval Europe, where religious elites dominated knowledge production, Enlightenment society placed knowledge production in the hands of the state and its agents (notably, academia), and ceded the realm of spiritual reflection to religion. The imperial and colonial ambitions of European and North American states that underpin the contemporary world order assumed that states were in the business of making knowledge. Thus, social progress was less a matter of fate, divine intervention and faith, and more a question of state arbitration through the production of appropriate knowledge. The belief in state-mediated 'progress' emerged as a strong Enlightenment norm.

A second element of Enlightenment thinking held that, sooner or later, every-thing that was worth knowing could be known. Enlightenment views of society consisted of two parts: a world of 'order' that could, through the application of systems of scientific reason and logic, be communicated through knowledge; and a world of uncertainty that was beyond order, beyond knowledge, and thus counter to the desire for progress and understanding. Objectivity facilitated the search for single and universal truths in the world of order. Doctrine, spiritualism, tribalism, mysticism and other knowledge systems were associated with the world of uncertainty and were not only different, but also inferior and anti-progress.

A third Enlightenment perspective that informed the development of population geography argued that social and geographic setting (that is, context) belonged to the world of order and, as such, could eventually yield truth. In this search for truth context was a worthy intellectual enemy. Context was a kind of intellectual dragon to be slain with the sword of simplifying assumptions (for example, a flat isotropic plain), the sword of mathematical relationships (for example, distance decay) or the sword of proximity (for example, by arguing that close objects are similar objects). Early statements about geography – including those by Kant (1791) – saw its contribution to society's knowledge project as centred on ideas about context. Geographic perspectives variously tackled social context by developing ideas about 'space' (a dimension of reality that presented and described proximity relations), 'environment' (the absolute and physical characteristics of these spaces) and 'place' (the ways that ecological and cultural processes came together in certain spaces and environments to influence the choices individuals make about their ways of life). Space, environment and place became some of the 'master concepts' through which geography 'dealt with' context, at least as Kant had bequeathed it.

While these and other Enlightenment beliefs have shaped society's views of itself and its worlds, a series of recent critiques have opened up new possibilities for knowledge, its production, circulation and role in furthering social progress. Post-Enlightenment thinking often takes a 'relational' view of knowledge that replaces the notion of absolutes (like order and disorder) with a belief that parts of concepts only exist in relation to each other. For Jacques Derrida and others, disorder should not be seen as separate from (and less than) order, but as a term which brings the characteristics of 'ordering' into focus (Derrida 1991).

A relational ontology has transformed how social science knowledge is being made in a number of ways. First, it questions epistemologies and methodologies that assume observers are neutral and separate from the objects of their inquiry. Indeed, outside philosophy, developments in quantum physics and string theory have also suggested that subjects and objects are mutually constitutive. Relational ontology unsettles the traditional authenticity claims of the academy and opens up new possibilities for the shared creation of knowledge. Rather than being construed as passive objects of inquiry, individuals and groups become active participants – knowledgeable subjects – who both create and are constituted by knowledge. Of keen interest to geographers, context is no longer 'out there', and something to be dealt with, but an integral part of the nature of society. Indeed, the related development of new ways of thinking about space and spatiality has greatly increased the profile of geographic scholarship across the contemporary social sciences. Henri Lefebvre's (1991) treatment of the production of space – taken forward by key thinkers in geography like David Harvey, Ed Soja, Neil Smith and Sallie Marston – argues that space (and space-time/scale) is socially created as part of the ongoing capitalist project. Populations are important not as static objects and disinterested categories, but as active participants in this process of production and becoming. Furthermore, the unsettling of binaries present in dialectical thinking implies the rethinking of time-honoured categories like race, nation, family, gender, sexuality and class. These developments suggest a diverse setting for research, activism and politics.

Enlightenment beliefs in knowledge as power, authorization, objectivity, the worlds of order and disorder, progress and the nature of context have underpinned the development of geographical perspectives and shaped what inter-sections were and are now possible between geography and the study of popula-tions. Key to understanding these intersections is an appreciation of *why* geographic knowledge about population was needed at this time and in these places. In turn, this prompts a brief discussion of *who* sought knowledge about population.

Players

States have played and continue to play a key role in producing and consuming knowledge about population. Why this keen interest? For starters, the notion of a state implies the presence of people in a given territory. The Kurds are frequently described as a 'stateless' nation precisely because the 30 million members of the imagined Kurdish 'nation' are dispossessed of any specific territory in which they have been able to form a majority (state) political system. States also pay close attention to the size, growth rates and distribution of their populations, particu-larly in times of generalized conflict and geopolitical uncertainty, when the continued existence of the state in its current form may be threatened by neighbours. For example, with Polish independence at the end of the Great War of 1914–18, Romer produced an atlas that literally 'placed' Poland in Europe by mapping its borders, establishing the internal distribution of its population and locating the ethnic structure of the population over space. The more recent Judaization of the West Bank, discussed in chapter one, shows how the presence of appropriately classified and organized 'settler groups' in a politically claimed territory can lend legitimacy to a political project. The power of corporeal presence may also be transmitted through technology and symbols. While the North American lunar landing in 1969 did not involve a group of settlers as such, it illustrated how American ideological (cold war) ambitions were serviced by the conquest of space (in both senses) by NASA technology, and evidenced through TV images of the placing of the US flag on the moon.

States also monitor relationships between population and social, economic and cultural progress. Greek society incorporated Plato's ideas about an optimal (stable) population size (5,040 persons) and geographic distribution (urban concentration) into his city-state model of geopolitical organization. German Johann Peter Süssmilch believed that eighteenth-century Prussia's mercantilist project could be enhanced by a growing population. However, the more recent examples of the Suaharto regime in 1950s Indonesia and Singaporean population policy in the 1990s remind us that pro-natalist visions are not restricted to particular stages in development or specific cultures. The Soviet Union aligned acts of fertility and performances of motherhood with state ideology by awarding women medals based on the number of children they 'produced' (figure 2.1).

Taxation and revenue collection requires information about the location and characteristics of the population. The eleventh-century Domesday project demonstrated the English monarch's appetite for information about 'populations as producers' and served as a precursor to modern censuses. As interaction within and between societies intensified, the breadth and depth of desired information about populations has grown, and from the nineteenth century countries began conducting regular censuses of their population. Furthermore, the expansion of mercantilism and overseas trade, colonialization, empire building and

Figure 2.1 Motherhood medal, Soviet Union

colonial management and subjugation all required information about economic and political opportunities and threats. The production of population maps that could depict the size and location of potential political threats and inform decisions about trade and economic exploitation became key accoutrements to colonial and imperial projects.

State ambitions and projects – be they military, economic, cultural or political – have frequently been supported by the organization of populations into particular groups. Age norms are used to identify groups with particular functions, like armies and students. For Marx, the interests of capital (via the state) in the production of a docile, pliant and well-disciplined labour force was advanced by a class-based division of population groups. As these groups evidenced the fundamentally flawed nature of the circulation of economic power in society, coalitions around class-based consciousness could unsettle and undermine the inherent capitalist structures in society. Foucault argues that 'populations' are constituted by states through, for example, legal requirements (including conscription and systems of education), social support, acculturation and surveillance. Examples include social classes, ethnic communities, urban and rural residents, the homeless and immigrants. Hannah Arendt's discussion of the Holocaust identifies how the 'radical' totalitarian strategy of dehumanization used racial and ethnic hierarchies to suggest that groups and individuals were enemies of the state who needed to be eliminated (Arendt 1966).

States, however, have neither a monopoly on the need for population knowledge, nor on its mediation. As European mercantilism internationalized and formed the basis of a geographically expansive capitalist world system in the latter part of the second millennium, an ever increasing share of commerce, broadly defined, traded on population knowledge. Often pejoratively referred to as applied knowledge, facts and figures about the locations and characteristics of populations formed a key part of commercial geography. Today, similar information about populations as producers (for example, the operation of the internal labour markets of multinational companies whose size often exceeds that of labour markets in US states) and populations as consumers (for example, the location and preferences of consumers) has stimulated the growth of business opportunities (for example, geodemographics). Many concepts developed in the private sector have infused and prompted debates within the academy and blurred the lines between 'pure' and 'applied' knowledge. The definition of population groups has moved beyond a reliance on traditional academic constructs (race, ethnicity, class, age) to encompass measures of lifestyle and consumption choices.

Perhaps reflecting more contemporary bases of affinity and connection, such lifestyle clusters are not only (reverse) applied to academic debates on gentrification and household organization in space, but also spur new debates about the nature of consumption in society.

Other groups with interests in populations include faith communities. Religious elites have long recognized the value in influencing the behaviour of their members – and groups within their communities – to achieve particular ends. Theocratic states (including those in medieval Europe and China at different periods) used religious texts (including Judeo-Christian and Confucian teaching) to argue for specifically pro-natalist policies. Belief systems also guided the depiction of world maps and the placement of key populations in key locations. NGOs, community groups and activists who organize around population issues like environmental health, labour rights and access to health care resources and treatments groups also contribute population knowledge. Their strategies often make use of horizontal technologies (including the internet) and lead to a system of knowledge circulation that contrasts with the vertical hierarchies of many states and businesses.

Acts of knowledge

Having briefly explored changing belief systems and the motives of those interested in population, this section explores how population geography was made in academic contexts. Drawing both on Haggett (1990: 122) and Gregory (1996), I recognize four such institutional phases, or acts, of creating knowledge. In pre-Enlightenment knowledge, Act I, geographically (and historically) isolated scholars worked through particular practical issues in ways that reflected religious and political ideology. In Act II, knowledge makers were woven into groups and societies, and produced and deposited empirical geographic knowledge on a near continuous basis. Act III knowledge emerged from a tightly woven enterprise often located within state-funded tertiary education institutions, with scholars contributing to accounts and theories which were national and increasingly international in scope. Post-Enlightenment Act IV knowledge is contributed by and circulated between more diffuse groups and questions approaches that assume researchers are objective and stand outside the research process.

Classical knowledge was created in the context of top-down, centre-to-margins 'sovereign' power. In many cases, ontology referenced scripture and religious texts that codified traditions, norms of behaviour and belief systems. In this system of knowledge, ruling monarchs were often seen as the holders of accumulated knowledge (wisdom), and bore the right and responsibility of passing this commodity down through bloodline and ancestral linkages for the benefit of subsequent generations. Knowledge production and circulation acquired a strong sociobiological structure which, in turn, supported a naturalized view of this form of social stratification and organization. When early universities were founded and received charters they often drew legitimacy to their enterprise from referencing such monarchs or classical thinkers: Charles University (Czech Republic), established in 1348, was named for King Karlov, while St Catharine's College, Cambridge (UK), established in 1473, referenced the authority of St Catharine of Alexandria. In some cases – as with religious beliefs about the shape of the earth and the relative status of Jesus Christ and Muhammad – knowledge became fixed as doctrine in a way that not only maintained cultural continuity but also re-inforced social stratification in society. Histories of science are replete with examples of societies vesting knowledge production in the hands of elite classes. Many classical thinkers since labelled as proto-geographers – Strabo, Erastothenes, Ptolemy, Ibn Khaldun – all appeared to occupy somewhat privileged and separated positions within their societies. Likewise, luminary figures in population thought – Goodwin, Malthus, Condorcet – claimed membership in social/occupational classes that facilitated and legitimated their knowledge claims.

The European-centred Enlightenment project was predicated on a shift in the knowledge-power nexus of the classical age to a formation that accompanied the rise of mercantilism and capitalism. Descartes' argument that the world could be split into a realm of order and certainty and a second realm of disorder and uncertainty was not only consistent with religious treatments of notions of good and evil, but also implied that disorder and uncertainty had a limited and negative role in knowledge production. This thinking privileged certain epistemologies that valued the making of order and certainty from disorder and uncertainty. It also facilitated the blurring of lines between discovery, expedition, exploration, exploitation, imperialism, conquest and colonialism in the European (and later North American) imaginary. Thus, the adoption of this binary approach to knowledge production and circulation was consistent with the political and economic ambitions of an imperial and colonial Europe that wished to apply power beyond its borders by bringing (political and economic) order to the world of non-reason.

However, as Kant acknowledged, the use of this ontology demanded the development of specific ideas and theories of knowledge that could organize and order physical objects (including rivers, resources, populations, etc.) and that could clarify the relationship between such objects and the knowing (European) subjects (i.e. researchers). The (re)emergence of philosophy helped connect up the Enlightenment ontology to epistemologies that sought to describe order and accumulate these descriptions, and methodologies that provided legitimate tools (for example, map) and techniques (for example, empirical observation and experimentation) for accomplishing this.

The institutional form of an 'academy', with disciplinary specialization and a strong internal division of labour, began to take shape. Kant (1791) argued for a division between 'logical' subjects, which discovered order in disorder by grouping subjects according to their similarity and difference on a conceptually derived scale (anthropology used racial hierarchies), and two 'physical' subjects (geography and history), which contributed to knowledge products by classifying like objects on the basis of proximity in space and time respectively.

Within this evolving institutional structure, the discipline of geography was ceded a generalist role that would help society understand the meaning of context and proximity. It often did this by borrowing intellectual frameworks from other subjects. Widely regarded as the first European formulation of a disciplinary geography, Freidrich Ratzel (1882) tellingly referred to the earlier label 'anthropo-geography' in deference to the anthropological underpinnings of his project. The overseas activities of European powers had sought and acquired much empirical evidence about the wider world and anthropogeography provided an appropriate racial and sociobiological framework for ordering this knowledge. Indeed, the nascent geography discipline drew strength from and co-opted the work of individual (state-sponsored) explorers and natural scientists. Specialized clubs were bringing those with similar interests together: in London, the Association for Promoting the Discovery of the Interior Parts of Africa had been established as early as 1788. It was the merging of this and similar clubs in 1830 that led to the creation of the still influential Royal Geographic Society (RGS). In Washington, DC, the National Geographic Society (NGS) was formed in 1888 to 'increase and diffuse geographic knowledge'. The NGS now boasts 15 million members, a TV channel and has the status of a global brand. The original missions of both the NGS and RGS reflect the strong state commitment to ordering (geographic) knowledge.

This academic production of knowledge about geography and population became increasingly professionalized as it underwent a kind of nationalization in the last decades of the nineteenth and the first half of the twentieth century (i.e.

early Act III). Germany invested in its first endowed chair of geography in 1874, and by the turn of the century many German universities had functioning geography departments. In the UK, a major round of university building was co-funded centrally and locally and led to the appearance of red-brick universities, including those at Manchester, Leeds, Bristol and Edinburgh. This institutionalization of knowledge production in the colleges and universities of the tertiary sector was in the state interest for a number of reasons:

- Institutes of higher education could supplement primary and tertiary education and extend the duration of educational provision for members of the population.

- The needs of an increasingly specialized academy were served by the economies of scale of agglomeration (shared access to libraries, technical facilities, classrooms etc.).

- Clustering could enable academic exchange and debate, and foster the growth of team and eventually interdisciplinary research.

- Universities served as 'frontier posts' (the phrase belongs to Haggett 1990), from which new knowledge was to be 'pushed forward'. It is apparent that such a mission would be directed not only at fellow academics and students, but also at colonial holdings, as the expansion of British universities in Nigeria, Uganda and Ghana in the colonial 1940s shows.

- Universities could also serve as 'district hospitals', ready and waiting to be called up by the community to problem solve for society.

- Universities derived and continue to derive symbolic capital for states. By acting as ordered repositories of what was to the Victorians 'exotic' knowledge, universities and colleges showed how the Enlightenment commitment to progress and modernization overcame the disorder of the traditional, the unclean and the past through libraries, collections, courses, degrees and experts. More recently, local areas and regions derive symbolic capital from the presence of international/global research universities that participate as cultural industries in what some call the symbolic economy.

A key consequence of this institutional arrangement was the development of so-called national schools of thought in many disciplines. As many universities were founded and funded by states, political expedients could directly influence academic agendas. Following the rise of communism in the 1930s Soviet Union, some nascent subjects, including demography, were seen as ideologically unsound and not supported: this is thought to have delayed the development of Soviet demography by 30 years. In the 1970s, the Chinese state required inputs to models of population distribution that could inform centrally planned economic resource allocation.

In other instances, the locational isolation of academics seemed to keep national schools of thought apart. Within geography, Richard Hartshorne's (1939) work on areal differentiation was widely circulated in the USA, but was much less influential in British geography. Australian geographer Griffith Taylor continued to espouse environmental determinist views in 1950 Australian geographic discourses, four decades after Ellen Semple (1911) had herself popularized this view in the USA, and two decades since many US geographers had disavowed the view. The development of French population geography in the 1950s also illustrates how language can promote the nationalization of academic debate. Here, the work of Pierre George sparked a turn towards demography and away from both the French geographic tradition of Vidal de la Blache and the growing prominence of North American approaches to spatial science. For others, inattention to scholarship from outside the 'Enlightenment orbit' smacked of cultural imperialism. Western scholars paid little heed to the development of population thought within the non-metropolitan periphery (Underhill-Sem 2004).

Nationalization was also facilitated when disciplines formed nationally based professional groupings. In geography, these include the Association of American Geographers (founded in 1905), the Institute of British Geographers (1933) and the Institute of Australian Geographers (1960). To pursue their cross-cutting interests in geography and population, some members of these professional associations also formed specialized research groups. A number of groups formed to pursue their simultaneous interests in geography and population: the Commission for Population and Urban Geography (founded in the USSR in 1945), the Population Geography Study Group (UK, 1963) and the Population Geography Interest Group, later renamed the Population Specialty Group (US, 1980). These groups provided escalators for some academics (at least three presidents of the Association of American Geographers were active members of the Population Specialty Group) and launched specialized journals (the UK-based PGSG founded the *International Journal of Population Geography (IJPG)* in 1991).

These academic communities existed alongside a growing range of state-funded institutes, agencies and centres. Emerging scholarship was also influenced by national institutions that specifically concerned themselves with demographic issues and the production of population statistics. For example, long concerned with its declining population, France set up the now world-renowned Institute National d'Etudes Démographiques (INED) in 1945 to pursue population research and sponsor publications. The Netherlands Interdisciplinary Demographic Institute (NIDI), based in The Hague and now a leading centre of life-course research, has a similar vintage. In the USA, the premier centre for population scholarship, the Population Studies Center at Princeton University, was commissioned in the 1940s by the League of Nations (the forerunner to the United Nations) to undertake a worldwide study of the question of population growth in Europe (the resulting report by Frank Notestein (1945) popularized the notion of the demographic transition). Although its funding model differed from its European rivals, the Princeton centre served to consolidate US demography and population studies, at least in the decades following World War II. National Census Bureaus and Agencies, National Statistical Offices, Mapping Agencies, Planning Agencies and other more specialized centres all provided resources (data), training and expertise for population geographers, albeit in an explicitly national rubric.

The growing interest of bodies like the League of Nations and the United Nations in population issues evidenced a more general internationalization of knowledge that intensified with post-World War II reconstruction. This affected the development of population scholarship in geography in several ways. For example, the efforts of the United Nations to standardize and harmonize the collection and release of national census data facilitated cross-national comparative analyses and, for the first time, the production of a meaningful world population map. Indeed, the prospect of the latter product galvanized the members of the International Geographical Union (IGU) to form a Commission to take national census data from the 1950s and 1960s and work towards this end. The UN began publishing its Demographic Yearbook (UNDY) in 1949 which, together with the release of increasingly detailed national and sub-national population data, sparked a major wave of population mapping. The establishment of the UN Population Division offered an international venue for population training and facilitated the diffusion of what were increasingly technical demographic approaches. Other international agencies – including the UN High Commission for Refugees (UNHCR), the World Health Organization (WHO) and the International Organization for Migration (IOM) – all provided harmonized data and training that promoted international research.

Much internationalization occurred as a result of the import and export of scholars and their ideas. International organizations, including the Ford and Rockefeller Foundations and the Marshall and Rhodes Scholar programmes, financially supported academic exchanges. Nigerian academic Akin Mabogunje, whose work is reviewed in chapter three, recently described how his exposure to geographic scholarship, particularly that of the quantitative revolution, at Northwestern University in 1963 prompted him to return to his home institution at the University of Ibadan and subject its British-inspired curriculum to 'drastic reform'. With departmental support, a programme of scholar exchanges subsequently brought leading geographers from the USA, Sweden, Australia and Britain to Ibadan, where they had a 'significant' impact on geographic discourse among the department's students and, eventually, across Nigeria, as new departments were established (Mabogunje 2004). More commonly, national meetings of geographers drew increasingly international audiences and new international conference series were established to further promote academic exchange. These included meetings sponsored by geographic organizations like the IGU, and demographic organizations, including the International Union for the Scientific Study of Population, established in 1928.

As it internationalized, geography's interests in population topics reflected their global provenance. One barometer of this changing interest is the topical choice made by the specialized Commissions of the IGU. Accompanying dramatic out-migration from southern and eastern Europe, the 1891 commission focused on emigration. In a similar vein, commissions that focused on settlement (1928), overpopulation (1931), rural settlements (1934), population problems (1949), the world population map (1956) and, more recently, migration and gender (1997) all pointed up the cross-boundary nature of many population issues.

Internationalization was one factor that encouraged the development of more theoretical approaches to questions about population. Distinctive national schools of thought gradually disappeared as academic discourse converged around a series of key debates that played out in internationally circulated journals and books, and at international conferences. While these debates tackled topics of mutual international concern, like urbanization and counterurbanization, the internationalization of the field has meant more recently that critiques of Enlightenment systems of knowledge have spread quickly and decisively to help set new agendas. One such agenda now expands the demographic basis of the field by questioning the authority of phenotypical hierarchies used to define race and ethnicity, and examining how population differences are socially produced. While some argue

25

that the institutional legitimacy of population geography may be undermined, it also seems that both geography and population are being remade in exciting ways. Not only has the political been reclaimed through the stories of people's everyday lives and communication technologies have enabled isolated groups to form new 'horizontal' coalitions, but opportunities for dissemination through online journals are also increasing (for example, the first internet geography journal, *ACME*, was launched in 1999).

Covalence: space, environment and place

As the fledgling discipline of geography emerged against the context of Enlightenment thinking, geographic perspectives on population matters coalesced around the concepts of space, environment and place. Kant had given geography 'special status' when he cast it as a 'physical' discipline that was authorized to group together objects on the basis of their spatial proximity. This meant that geography could 'service' other sciences, by showing proximity and thus similarity, but could not be relied upon to generate its own explanations. In short, it would need academic partners to help make sense of and explain context and proximity.

At the time, eligible partners included biology, economics, linguistics and the mathematical and physical sciences. Demography appeared as a science much later, partly explaining why population geography was one of the last sub-disciplines of geography to develop. These eligible partners often made reference to their own conceptual frameworks as ways of recovering and reorganizing order from the world of 'reason' in ways that legitimized colonial ambitions and the commitment to progress. Anthropologists categorized human populations on the basis of skin colour and phenotype. They used racial and ethnic hierarchies to differentiate European society (superior) from other societies (inferior), and lend intellectual sponsorship to programmes of exploitation-by-any-other-name. After Linnaeus, botanists adopted a taxonomic system of classification that 'naturalized' species distinctions between plants and animals. Ricardo's and Smith's treatises on economic rationality and marginalism provided economics with a particularly persuasive device for making sense of the increasingly complicated and abstract economic world. Durkheim similarly focused on the 'rational and moral basis' of consensus in society as a frame for locating social order (Gregory 1996). Demographers drew on formal mathematics to derive a stable population theory that continues to underlie accounts of population structures today (Henry 1976).

Geography worked hard to couple with these sciences. But unlike the strong commitment to 'holism' seen in Humboldt's *Cosmos* and Ritter's *Erdkunde*, the new disciplines of anthropology, sociology, economics and demography pushed for specialism and separation. A similar tension between geography as a unifying, integrative and holistic enterprise and geography as a specialized spatial science persists today. Geography's commitment to integrative accounts of the physical and human environment also proved increasingly burdensome as the sheer volume of knowledge to be processed increased rapidly. The emerging discipline developed an intellectual tool kit – and informed the study of population – by preserving its commitment to integration and nature–society links, and by stressing the development of empirical generalizations, which could begin to build geographic theory. Meanwhile the growth of commercial geographies also meant that geographic perspectives could not just present difference (i.e. us and them) to the Euro-American mind, but also were charged to develop conceptual frameworks that explained how such difference had arisen, explained how such difference made Euro-American society better than the foreign other and, most generally, informed the Enlightenment commitment to progress. The emerging perspective turned on three key concepts.

Space

Geographic thinkers used the concept of space in a number of ways. Most significantly, space located objects in a Euclidean metric that could be relied upon to yield a measure of association (namely proximity). 'Space as container' thus enabled scientists to order their accounts of the human and physical world and to suggest differences between one location and another. Furthermore, space as container enabled geographers to freeze-frame complex and dynamic social, economic and cultural processes as meaningful snapshots that could promote reflection and conceptualization of the nature of society. A second epistemological use of space was to group like objects together in the form of regions. 'Regionalization as classification' enabled geographers to simplify and order otherwise complex landscapes. Regionalization also supported a third view of 'space as codex', that is, a landscape to be decoded on the basis not only of proximity, but also inherent physical laws.

A good deal of geography's long-standing and cross-cultural intellectual commitment to space had deployed the space-as-container approach. For Greek (Strabo, Erastothenes), Roman (Ptolemy) and Arab (Ibn Khaldun) geographers, space and the organization of society in space enabled the local accomplishments of civilization and empire projects to be framed and appreciated in a broader context. Indeed, as European states of the eighteenth and nineteenth century formed increasingly imperial and colonial ambitions, this use of space as container provided a necessary intellectual backing for projects that sought first to legitimize colonialism in moral terms, and later to suggest ways of exerting more power and control. The space-as-container view underpins population maps used by states and regional governments to visualize differences between one political system and another. Nineteenth-century European town plans often used a nearby hill as a vantage point from which to view and sketch the totality of a well-organized, clearly defined urban area that was itself surrounded by a relatively untamed, natural, non-urban (i.e. rural) world. The map conveyed a dual message: urban and rural are different (the urban world of order is defined as 'not rural'); progress is advanced in the urban, not the rural. Still earlier maps of unexplored territories and new frontiers similarly used empty spaces and fanciful monster icons to suggest the superiority of an enlightened colonial society over a soon to be tamed other.

The production of technically competent cartographic depictions of the size, characteristics and location of populations was the lifeblood of many early attempts to fuse population and geography. Often, the availability of recently released data from national censuses prompted geographers to publish population maps, such as Frère de Montizan's population distribution of France (1830) and Harness's population density map of Ireland (1837). While population size, distribution and density were the most common map subjects, increased concern about the integrity of the nation state also spawned the production of maps depicting the distribution of the ethnic characters of populations, at first in Nazi Germany and the Soviet Union, but latterly in colonial holdings (Kosiński 1984). As biologically derived markers of phenotype legitimized the use of racial systems to differentiate western society from non-western society, population maps of empire increasingly concerned themselves with the distribution of population races as a way to constitute difference between colonial and non-colonial society. The empiricist methodologies of spatial differentiation were further extended with attempts to describe the within-national and between-national variations in 'naturalized' characteristics of populations.

Other geographers applied the epistemology of space as container to freeze-frame complex cultural and economic processes and launch geographic accounts of these societies. For example, in *Die Geographie*, Alfred Hettner (1927) provided possibly the earliest and certainly most succinct justification for geographic considerations of population. Arguing that geographic inquiry should proceed from a population map, Hettner believed that population issues affected all areas of geographic inquiry and should have equal status with the other branches of geography, including settlement geography, economic geography and investigation of the state (political geography). Crucially, Hettner connected population activities to these other branches by simultaneously conceptualizing populations as producers and consumers. The logical implication is that population becomes an integrative element in geography through its attention to, for example, both production and consumption issues. Although Hettner himself was not to make such links explicit, Glenn Trewartha's later (1953) call for a sub-discipline of population geography did make more than passing reference to this insight. What Hettner did contribute, however, was the notion that population geographies should combine static descriptions and profiles of biological and social character-istics with dynamic accounts of population growth (including migration) over space. Hettner's work would prove important because he implied the study of population was not just an end in itself and progress in studying areal differentia-tion could be enhanced through acknowledging the productive and consumptive nature of society.

A similar approach – albeit in a different national setting – permeated the intersection of geography with population in the Soviet Union. Here, Soviet geographers drew on Marx's notions of historical materialism to see population distribution as reflecting the underlying territorial organization of economic production: populations were producers. Earlier, in his 1926 contribution *Ekonomicheskaya Geografiya* (subsequently much revised and eventually translated into English in 1956 as *Economic Geography of the USSR*), Baranskiy had seen the geography of population as an independent discipline because of its breadth of focus and its concern with both economic and non-economic spheres (that is, the natural environment and the cultural environment). The significant redistribution of population in the Soviet Union, growing urbanization and shortages of labour in certain places and industrial sectors kept population geography in Soviet minds during the coming decades. By the 1950s, Pokshishevskiy occupies similar ground to Hettner (ideologically unlikely) by focusing on both productive and con-sumptive elements of population geographies:

> Distribution of population over a country as a whole, and its regions, always is determined by the character and geography of production. However, changes in the settlement process and in the materialised forms of settled places very often do not

catch up with changes in the geography of population. . . . Any cluster of population creates a node of consumption, therefore the geography of population discloses places of considerable concentration of separate branches of economy which belong to the consumers' 'side' of social production process . . . (quoted in Melezin 1963: 146–7)

Thus, for Pokshishevskiy, population enters the society-space equation through its appearance in territorial nodes, themselves jointly conditioned by production and consumption.

While population maps serviced colonial and national projects, some geographers argued that maps of populations were a basis for regionalization as classification. For Isaiah Bowman (1921), population maps could be aggregated to reveal the 'environmental' structures of regions by looking at key organizing factors, such as the natural environment, and sequentially identifying subregions on basis of additional factors. Here, the regional distribution of races was seen as an important marker of regional distinctiveness. However, it was Landry whose adoption of this epistemology was to yield the most far-reaching implications for contemporary scholarship. In his 1934 *La Révolution Démographique*, Landry sought to position low French birth and death rates within a more general regional system. Accordingly, he regionalized countries of the world according to then current rates of population growth. His 'contemporary' region – which included much of Western Europe – had low or zero growth because of a raft of public health interventions that had reduced mortality. Reductions in fertility were traced to the widespread practice of birth limitation that families used across the region. The trigger of areal differentiation, the identification of a range of inter-dependent factors (operating through the coincidence of birth and death rates), and the end goal of regionalization would underpin what eventually took shape as the demographic transition model. Meanwhile, another French scholar, Pierre George (1959), contributed a book-length geographic study of the world's population that also relied on regionalization to order his observations.

Indeed, a growing number of researchers argued that both the proximity and the structure of objects in space could be construed as code that, once read, would yield clues as to underlying process and causality. The space-as-codex epistemology took a number of forms. In a now infamous map of the distribution of reported cholera cases around a series of water pumps in central London, John Snow (1965) not only identified a source of infection (a specific water pump) but, by drawing on Pasteur's continuing work on bacteriology, was also able to comment on how cholera spread. This type of thinking served as an entrée to the rapidly developing field of epidemiology. Ravenstein's so-called Laws of Migration offered revealing empirical insights into the rural-to-urban population redistribution that Britain had experienced with the intensification of industrialization in the late nineteenth century. He suggested that the discrete points of economic opportunity (i.e. jobs) in space exerted a pulling force on populations. Ravenstein noted that the majority of moves took place over short distances, and, as the distance between two places increased, the frequency of moves decreased. Migration responded both to absolute location (i.e. the characteristics of places) and to relative location (i.e. the spatial structure of settlements). He also observed that migration tended to occur 'up' the settlement hierarchy, that is from village to small town and small town to city (Ravenstein 1885).

Ravenstein's studies of internal migration foreshadowed some of the most significant early work on urban sociology that emerged from the Chicago School in the early twentieth-century USA. Ernest Burgess and Robert Park shared a concern with how social processes like migration unfolded systematically over space and time in the context of growing industrialization. But unlike England in the 1860s and 1870s, where urbanization and industrialization generally involved internal population movements, Chicago's industrial growth in the 1910s and 1920s involved both large numbers of immigrants from southern and eastern Europe and significant cohorts of African Americans from the US South. Drawing on Durkheim's notions of social morphology and Darwin's use of ecological principles, sociologists Burgess (1924) and Park et al. (1925) sought to describe and understand the nature of the new industrial community in terms of its spatial and social ecology. They not only described the areal differentiation of population groups in Chicago, but also linked these *spatial* (neighbourhood) ecologies to underlying *social* ecologies. While neo-Ravensteinians would soon evoke Newtonian physics to relate regularities in migration behaviour to laws of gravity and the conservation of mass, social ecology was able to draw on Darwinian notions of competition and succession to sketch a sophisticated conceptual super-structure that lay behind the drift towards the suburbs of assimilating immigrants in Chicago.

Environment

A second and at times closely related geographic concept ordered society on the basis of the absolute (site) characteristics of the natural environment. While the use of this concept can be traced to the formative contributions of Ratzel (1882),

US geographers, including Ellen Semple, directly linked environmental attributes to racial and ethnic hierarchies. Semple (1911) asserted that 'man is a product of the earth's surface' and argued that racial distinctiveness arose from environmental exposure. The link between environment and society was taken further in Huntington's 1924 book, *Civilization and Climate*, where an environmental determinist argument links racial traits of populations to the group's physical environmental context. Others linked skin colour variations between races to regional variations in temperature and believed that indigenous populations tended to maintain close (dependent) relations with their environment. When superimposed on biological hierarchies of species separation, this implied that close links to environment (perhaps being in balance with the surroundings) could be read as non-mastery of the environment, which in turn helped set natives apart from western civilized man who had achieved environmental mastery. Such a discourse functions in the same way as the urban-rural constructions of nineteenth-century city plan maps above. Indeed, Winchester et al. (2003) argue that this thinking 'was used as justification for dispossession, extinction, or exploitation of indigenous people by the supposedly superior races' (12).

While geographers incorporated notions of the environment into aggregate and synthetic views of the world, demographers and economists treated the intersections between population and environment using more specialized frameworks, including theories of rationality and economic marginalism (Weeks 1999). While many geographic accounts of the environment tended to be static, population economists focused on how changing population conditions mediated environment–society links over time. Thus, population issues became central to questions of social progress, economic modernization and development. Indeed, the view that population was a change agent for society came to affect the development of neoclassical economics and, through the debate about population and resources attributed to Thomas Malthus, came to dominate large tracts of demographic and popular debate in the twentieth century. Before Malthus, economist François Quesnay argued that the best response to rising poverty in mercantilist France was to 'extend' the land resource by expanding free trade. Accordingly, neither trade protectionism nor population policies were appropriate. Such a *laissez-faire* view of social progress was also important in the influential work of Adam Smith. Although he countered the physiocratic privileging of the land resource with his belief that labour power added the essential value to resources on which social progress would be supported, he continued to believe that manipulating population numbers was not the answer. Left to its own devices, population would reach a level commensurate with the underlying level of economic development.

Adam Smith's writings influenced Malthus' own take on population. Malthus – and other scholars of the late eighteenth century, including Townsend and de Condorcet – seeded the influential and controversial concept of overpopulation. This implied that a relationship existed between a population and a resource base (natural environment) *over* time and *in* an environment with a particular resource base. For Malthusians, natural resources were fixed in space, but population numbers and growth rates were variable over time. As a moment of overpopulation was approached, the onus was on the population to demand less (fewer mouths to feed). In practice, Thomas Malthus's 1798 *Essay on the Principle of Population* had tied population growth to the mean of subsistence, which in the eighteenth-century English context of the author meant the ability of the arable production system to provide sufficient food. Thus, for Malthus, the physical environment played a decisive, self-evident processual 'link' role, but a limited conceptual one. Indeed, Joseph Townsend had already drawn a wider net around 'environment' to incorporate what he believed as the potentially ameliorating effects of long-distance trade on food supply. This trade was itself facilitated by a stable market and favourable geopolitical conditions and thus pointed to the interplay of the geo-economic with the physical. While acknowledging the singular role of the environment, both commentators went on to discuss how governments were involved in the environment–population nexus. But both men were skeptical about the role of state welfare. Malthus thought the English Poor Laws had the effect of prolonging the lives of the working classes, with a detrimental knock-on effect for the development of society. He argued that natural selection would, left to its own devices, provide a positive check on the further expansion of population numbers in areas where the land's carrying capacity had been exceeded. Finally, both analyses recognized how the social institution of marriage acted as a proximate determinant of fertility and would further complicate the relationship between environment and population growth.

Many of the conceptual elements that would characterize the intellectual development of population geography were already present in this debate. Societies had 'group attributes' (for example, an increasing working-class population that was impoverished) that had implications for the world around them (overpopulation and resource depletion). The setting could – through famine and plague – shape the development of these population groups. So, too, could political (the role of state laws) and cultural factors (marriage norms) affect the size and growth rates of population groups. In turn, size and growth depended on births, deaths and migrations, making further knowledge on these 'proximate determinants' socially useful. Developing a demographic language to address the population/resource debate meant that the classist bias in Malthus's work could be disguised. Of course, Malthus was not alone in developing the liberal position. While economist John Stuart Mill believed that gender equality, among other individual circumstances, would prompt formerly growing populations to maintain a population size that was most likely to yield increases in the overall cultural, social and moral development of society, such contributions showed how the emerging discipline of economics was already developing a more credible and integrative approach to population/environment questions than the static doctrine of environmental determinism.

Place

Proximity and context were also enlivened by new ideas about place. Ratzel saw landscapes as organic wholes whose true nature exceeded the sum of their constituent (physical and human) parts. Quintessentially integrative, and developed most forcefully by the French *géographie humaine* school, this strong commitment to holistic thinking frequently elevated regions as the tool of choice for geographic thinking. However, this use of 'region as synthesis' (or 'region as place') differs from the regionalization-as-classification technique described above. While *geographie humaine* has often been labelled *geographic regionalism*, the moniker region is misleading, as some accounts (including Landry's early demographic transition regionalization) had already applied the idea of regionalization in an explicitly spatial way. Thus, when describing the development of geographic scholarship on place, it is important to distinguish between the complex physical and cultural interdependencies that emerged through space and time and which expressed themselves in the forms of particular 'ways of life' (*genres de vie*), and the more generic term region that continues to reference aggregates of geographic phenomena. While regions could be studied and organized independently of the ways of life/ways of being that they supported, and vice versa, places could not be so disassembled.

The epistemological commitment within *géographie humaine* responded both to the integrative ambitions of the nascent discipline and the desire to keep nature and society hitched together in their accounts. Place acts as much more than space as a container or space as regionalization in the accounts of the school's

34

most well-known savant, Paul Vidal de la Blache (1922). A place's *genre de vie* brings economic (production) and cultural (consumption) performances into focus. As these performances are framed by the possibilities of the current environmental context and the past cultural context, place is shaped by experiences of the past and the present, and in turn moulds social progress. Indeed, for Vidal, population was a key but not overdetermining factor in the emergence and maintenance of place.

While *géographie humaine* supported an interdependent view of population and society, its early applications somewhat betrayed this potential by privileging the cultural treatment of places and landscapes. Bruhnes treated population geographies as settlement geographies, which were themselves one component of human geographies. It was only through the cultural landscapes of places as settlements that population issues were brought into play: 'It is in the connection with the house, the village, and the city that the questions of the distribution of the population must be examined – under its real and logical aspect' (Bruhnes 1910: 67). In this view, culture (as opposed to environment, or economic production) underlay settlement.

Earl Shaw's reading of Newfoundland's population illustrates an approach which attempted to balance the environmental/ecological (ecumene) with local cultural factors. A graduate of the same department where Semple worked and a Ph.D. programme still strongly associated with nature/society research (Clark University), Shaw's selection of population distribution and density as both his entrée to and end point of analysis immediately betrays his allegiance to a more synthetic geography. However, it is apparent that Shaw is not interested in the idiosyncracies of the world's tenth largest island for the sake of it, but rather in adding to specific knowledge about island geographies in general, and to a greater conceptual understanding of how ecumene and culture are useful tools in understanding particular places. Thus, the research question is 'to analyze the influence of fishing, and that of other factors as well, upon the population pattern and population problems of Newfoundland' (Shaw 1938: 239). Just as much (around 70 per cent) of the world's population is concentrated within 1000 km of the sea, so, too, did the majority of Newfoundlanders (90 per cent in 1935) live on the 'sea-facing fringe' (figure 2.2).

Shaw's account began by linking population distribution to the development of Newfoundland's economy. As early as the fifteenth century, European colonists were aware of significant fishing grounds to the east of the island. However, exploitation of this resource was guided by the seasonal availability of the cod

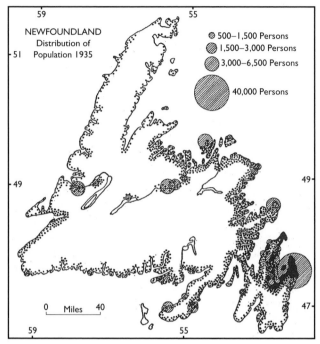

Figure 2.2 Population distribution, Newfoundland.
Source: redrawn from Shaw (1938: 239)

stock (restricted to the summer months), a need to provide regularized training for British seamen through annual voyages and the high costs (financial and other, including the French claim to the western interior) of settling what looked to the colonial mind like inhospitable interior lands. In short, the British actively dissuaded permanent settlement on the island for the next 300 years: those towns that were constructed were coastal and colonial-facing. Natural features, in particular the presence of sheltered harbours, meant that over time the coastal fringe would be characterized by pockets of population density against a general backdrop of sparsity (Shaw records 1300 fishing outports along 9000 km of coast). Mining and agricultural opportunities were generally limited and, where practised, tended to further concentrate coastal settlements, as goods flowed out through Newfoundland's main ports as exports.

Shaw continues by linking the island's settlement patterns to its declining growth prospects by examining how isolation affects the cultural system. In some areas (notably the western fringe), up to three-quarters of the population received government unemployment payments. Many Newfoundlanders had already emigrated, although depression-era economic conditions in Canada and the USA meant this was not the safety valve it had been. Key to the island's overpopulation was not the simple ratio of people to resources, but the geographic organization of the population and how this affected local cultural patterns. The general isolation of the settlement pattern was responsible for problems with civil administration, education, health, marketing and transportation. This led to a still deeper sense of geographic isolation, evidenced in some rural hamlets by practices of intermarriage between as few as two or three families. At this juncture, a more deterministic shadow falls over the analysis:

> That isolation may affect one's philosophy ... is a belief generally accepted by most geographers. But not until a few weeks' contact with people along the north-western coast of Newfoundland did the writer suspect that isolation could compete with climate in developing a mañana or procrastinating attitude ... No doubt cold, snowy winters, the prevalence of fog, and the whole complex of a difficult environment also encourage a postponing attitude ... (Shaw 1938: 249)

While this extreme and facile interpretation of culture resonates with the then persisting trope of environmental determinism, Shaw concludes by arguing that cultural systems provide the key to solving overpopulation. He dismisses birth control as 'Newfoundlanders take their religion very seriously and no doubt the majority of the people would oppose such a solution' (252). He also doubts that emigration is a long-term solution, as it tends to select 'the most ambitious', precisely those most needed on the island. Going beyond demographic solutions, he calls for the adoption of new practices in the cod-fishing industry. In pointing to the need for fish to be caught using larger schooners, for the curing process to be standardized across the large number of outports and for new markets to be researched and targeted, Shaw implies that it is the cultural isolationism and conservatism – manifested and reinforced in the settlement pattern – that is the limiting factor to greater prosperity and social progress in Newfoundland.

How space, environment and place still matter

Geography's emergence as a discipline was predicated on the development of concepts including space, environment and place. Geographic perspectives on population were – and still are – greatly informed by these concepts. This chapter closes by showing how three contemporary population issues (fertility decline and ageing, the global sex trade and HIV-AIDS) can be illuminated in a productive and vital way using a geographic perspective based on the concepts of space, environment and place.

Fertility, demographic momentum and ageing

Since the early 1970s, China has been well known for its attempts to reduce population growth by limiting fertility. Known as the 'one-child policy' because, in some urban areas, women have been strongly encouraged (many argue, coerced) to have no more than one child, in practice, China has followed many policies which have dramatically different meanings and consequences across the country.

In 1970 the crude birth rate in China was 33 live births per 1000 of the population. In 2000 the crude birth rate had fallen to 14 live births per 1000 of the population.

Annual growth rates for the Chinese population have steadily declined from 2.3 per cent in the 1960s to 1.8 per cent (1970s), 1.5 per cent (1980s), 1.0 per cent (1990s) and 0.6 per cent (current decade). The growth rate is suggested to average 0.0 per cent between 2030 and 2040.

Despite these declines in growth rate, the Chinese population still added 440 million persons between 1970 and 2000, a total that exceeds today's combined population of the USA, the UK, Canada and Australia.

China's decline in population growth rate is credited with delaying by two years the moment when the world's total population reached 5 billion persons.

Over the period 1970–2000, China's economy grew substantially (in per capita terms, at a rate similar to that of the USA). Furthermore, over this period, the crude birth rate in the USA and China actually witnessed similar percentage reductions. The USA accomplished economic growth and reductions in birth rate without state population planning interventions. Some argue that China's falling birth rates are likewise a function of its economic growth.

Vignette 1

Population policy in China

Governments and coalitions of leaders continue to debate the purpose, design and implementation of population policy, as they have done ever since groups of people became populations and societies. For much of the latter half of the twentieth century, the developed regions of the world believed that population growth had negative or, at best, neutral consequences for economic development. While clearly outside the capitalist orbit, China's socialist regime generally shared this view. Vice Premier Chen Muhua argued in 1979 that population control was needed in China on account of the negative relations between rapid population growth and capital accumulation, educational levels and innovation and standard of living improvements. Indeed, since the revolution of 1949, China witnessed strong population growth, and the regime believed that its earlier 1971 policy of 'later, longer, fewer' [wan xi shao] needed to be revised.

The first phase of the 'one-child policy' was introduced in 1979. This attempted to convince parents not to have a third child but, instead, to regard a one-child family as the new 'social norm'. Propaganda, local activism, direct coercion, increased use of contraception and a system of economic benefits for those meeting the target and disincentives for those exceeding the target were variously used to pursue this one-child objective. Given long-standing son preference norms in many societies, including China, those designing the policy were aware from the outset that limiting families to first-borns could put severe pressure on parents, foetuses known to be female and first-born daughters. Although such pressure was meant to be dealt with through ideological means, in practice, female foetuses were aborted and many daughters were abandoned, given up for adoption or murdered.

Evidence of these responses is largely indirect, taking the form of sex ratios. In most societies, the ratio of male babies to female babies hovers around 105 males per 100 females. In the years after the policy was introduced, the reported sex ratio in Chinese cities was 110, in towns 113 and 114 in rural counties (home to three-quarters of the population).

This policy originally applied equally to all Han-Chinese couples, although it did acknowledge geographic context. In urban areas, parents who had limited their offspring to one child and who could demonstrate continued use of appropriate contraceptive technology were eligible for childcare subsidy benefits, had some preferences in access to housing, education and employment opportunities for their child and were promised larger pensions. In rural areas, couples with one child were eligible for larger income payments and avoided heavier taxes that were levied for second and subsequent children.

However, active resistance to the new measures was strong. Greenhalgh and Li (1995) note that, with the advent of decollectivization in the rural Shaanxi province in 1982–3, peasants were able to resist the provisions in several ways. These included: refusing to pay fines; temporary migration and re-registration in another city to give birth; removing or not using contraceptives; concealing pregnancies. Such resistance, combined with an acknowledgement that local cadres may have lost some of their power and influence after decollectivization, and initial evidence that rates were not continuing to decline at the steep rates seen in the 1970s, led the central government to stress in 1983 a 'New Mobilization' for comprehensive planned reproduction. At the local level, state policy thus became renegotiated by party workers, parents and communities. At least in the Shaanxi villages of their study, two-child families were now tolerated. Indeed, national policy reluctantly changed to recognize this and was rewritten in 1984. The 'kai xiaokou du dakou' slogan ('open a small hole to close a big hole') enabled local provincial officials to permit two-child families where the first-born was a daughter.

By the late 1980s it had become apparent to the central state policy makers that fertility was not declining, but had increased by as much as 10–20 per cent, and more in some rural areas. Provincial governments were instructed to standardize and coordinate their policies so that couples with first-child sons had no more children. The only two-child families permitted were those with first-child daughters and they were made to wait four years between births. These stricter laws continued to drive the sex ratio at birth upwards, transform adoption into a one-gender activity (males being seen as too precious to be adopted) and even change the use of traditional practices like breastfeeding, with sons given more nipple time. By the close of the 1990s, estimates of the total fertility rate (a measure of the number of children born to a woman over her reproductive years) stood at 1.7, well below the theoretical level of replacement at 2.1. Between 1970 and 2000, China did reduce its fertility rate and it did make strides with economic and social development. Commentators pose at least two questions about this experience: to what extent did population policy drive (or react to) development? Was it worth it?

A geographic perspective informs this case study in at least three ways. First, the design, meaning and implications of China's one-child policy varied enormously from one part of China to another. Spatial variations in policy incentives and disincentives took account of the different structure of employment, housing and educational opportunities in rural and urban China. Strategies of resistance reveal that the policy was not interpreted and understood by individuals in social isolation. Rather, partners, parents, families and party workers (to name a few population groups) learned about and reacted to the policy in the context of their local communities. As places with particular and dynamic social and cultural values and norms, these communities and their populations are an integral part of any meaningful account of why it was that one of the most centralized and occasionally violent regimes repeatedly modified its one-child policy in the 1980s. Accounts of China's recent history of population policy are made richer when spatial variations in fertility, family, gender and sexuality are linked to the environmental context and the biography of the places where people live and work.

Second, attention to the geographic context of population changes shows how state actions taken in the national interest involved the discursive creation of a population group of 'offenders', who subsequently experienced cultural and economic marginalization. In the late 1970s, Chinese socialists linked the economic development and future prosperity of China to reductions in population growth. Once it had named the problem as a population one, Chinese demographers then embodied the state agenda by identifying what – and crucially who – had to change. As the abstract demographic analysis suggested that it was the long-standing cultural practice of giving birth to two, three or more children that had to disappear, and such practices were most entrenched in rural areas, women living in rural communities became marked out as a key non-compliant population group. This embodiment and emplacement of state policy contributed to the further economic marginalization of rural women by encouraging some expectant mothers to move temporarily to urban areas, where conditions of poverty drove some among this group to enter the informal sector as sex workers and the like.

Because the one-child policies have had such a dramatic impact upon the fertility outcomes of a large group of people over several decades, the case also illustrates the need to examine how demographic interdependencies will affect different parts of China in different ways. For example, the desire to escape detection by party workers in rural areas has contributed to the growth of temporary migration in China. Moreover, an analysis of birth order data from the Hubei province in central China suggested that temporary migrants who move from a rural origin are more likely, all else being equal, to give birth to a second child. This may be due to detachment from local social norms, running counter to the one-child policy, and is greatest among temporary migrants moving from rural to rural areas.

Falling fertility levels have meant that China now faces demographic ageing and a new pattern of households (see figure 2.3). Both will be mediated geographically according to where fertility fell and what kinds of knock-on effects this has had for population migration. As the demand for food increases on a per capita basis in smaller families, China will also face geographically variable demands for food. Most generally, demographic ageing affects the funding and provision of pensions and support for the elderly. For example, the ratio of persons aged 15–64 to persons of retirement age and over is projected to fall from 5.0 in 1975 to 2.3 in 2025 (Adamchak 2001). Putting the case in its international context, will China seek replacement workers in the same way that Europe (and, to a lesser extent, North America) currently does? Is it possible that China will become a net importer of migrants?

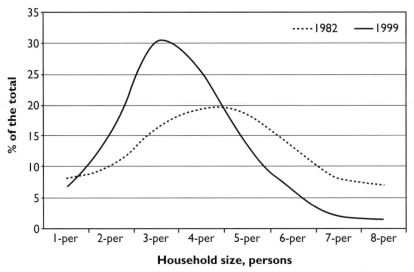

Figure 2.3 Household change, China. Source: redrawn from Hussain (2002: 1832)

Sexual dealing and children

Between 1 and 4 million persons are trafficked every year. Most are children and women under the age of 25.

50,000 persons are trafficked in to the United States every year. Most come from Russia, Ukraine, Poland, Latin America and South East Asia.

During the Atlantic Slave Trade an estimated 15 million black Africans were forcibly relocated to the Caribbean and North and South America in the 150 years leading up to 1850. Thus, the current annual volume of human trafficking exceeds an annual measure of the slave trade by between 10 and 40 times. A number of commentators compare the contemporary trafficking of women and children to this 'slave trade'.

The first international agreement to address trafficking was the 1904 International Agreement for the Suppression of the White Slave Traffic. The most recent agreement was the 2000 International Convention against Organized Transnational Crime that was signed in Palermo, Italy. This was signed by 124 of the 189 member states of the United Nations (Potts 2003).

Vignette 2

Janie

The streets and neighbourhoods around the central London district of Paddington witness multiple stories of contemporary world cities under globalization. Being close to the upmarket consumption venues of Kensington, Fulham and Chelsea, and on the doorstep of Hyde Park and museum land, the area is a popular base for foreign tourists, a good number of them overseas students studying in London. Many of Britain's Arab communities have made homes here, and the whole area has a multicultural, cosmopolitan feel commensurate with its position in Britain's most global city. At the heart of the area, Paddington station is also the destination of commuter trains from the leafy-laned and mock-Tudor suburbs to the west of London, and the constant toing and froing of workers adds to the vibrancy. The recent addition to Paddington's train services of the Heathrow Express, a high-speed shuttle linking London with the world's busiest airport in just 15 minutes, adds to the area's global status.

Janie lived and worked in Paddington as a teenager. However, she did not arrive here on the Heathrow Express. Having grown up in post-communist

Albania, Janie worked in a Paddington brothel, having sex with her commuter and tourist clients for up to 16 hours a day. She told journalist Sophie Arie (2003) that, on one night, she had 26 customers. Each paid between £30 and £50 per half-hour, depending on what was required. The oversized white T-shirt she was asked to wear reminded her of a nurse's uniform. Arie wrote 'After work, the pimps would rape her one by one, tie her down and use her naked belly to snort cocaine. One day another of the girls, who cried too much and put her customers off, had the fingers of one hand crushed in a door and her hair shaved off as a punishment. "We had no one to talk to. I had nowhere I could go. I had no one I could trust"'.

The circumstances that led to Janie's imprisonment in the Paddington brothel illustrate the extent to which human trafficking is a product of poverty. Like many sex workers she grew up in poverty, one of eight children living in a household headed by an older sister's husband on account of their father being shot over a property dispute. Struggling economically, the husband beat and abused Janie. After she had attempted to take her own life she was befriended by a neighbour, who said he had fallen in love with her, and smuggled out of Albania into Greece and, eventually, Italy. Here the boyfriend met up with Albanian colleagues in Turin and beat Janie until she agreed to work the streets as a child prostitute. When she was not working she was locked in a flat, unable to reach friends or make contact with her family back in Albania. Eventually, increased police activity and falling custom led the gang to relocate to Brussels. But here the continued beatings aroused police suspicion and her pimp was arrested.

This was not, however, the end of her European tour. While on the surface she was now 'free' of her Albanian handler, Janie had no resources of her own to make the trip back to her family. Moreover, she knew that if she were to return she would be ostracized as a sex worker. Worse, her former pimp or his gang would have every chance of enslaving her again. Faced with these non-choices she fled, in the back of a truck, across the English Channel, and was again rehoused as an asylum seeker in England. To support herself she began working in a London café. Here she attracted the attention of a group of Albanian boys and, after their persistent entreaties, she was enticed back to their flat. The current chapter closes with her deportation from England after the Paddington brothel was raided by police. In early 2003 she returned to her small town as a 20-year-old with a London accent, a desire to go back and an interrupted childhood.

44

Trafficking is a generic term used to refer to trade which is illegal and/or immoral. Trafficking generates between $5 and $7 billion revenues worldwide every year. As such, the economic importance of the trafficking industry exceeds the gross national product of Zimbabwe in 1999. The rich lexicon of terms associated with such trade – smuggling, bootlegging, moonshining, racketing, pushing, gun-running, rum-running and fencing, to name a few – belies trafficking's cross-cultural and often romanticized nature.

However, human trafficking is becoming a reality for many impoverished children and teens. There is a distinctive geography of sex trafficking. This reflects the networks of gangs and traffickers and the routes they use to cross borders and escape detection. A German police psychologist described his country's border with the Czech Republic as 'Europe's biggest brothel', attracting as many as 100,000 German sex tourists every year.

The geography also reflects that of poverty and powerlessness in many regions of the world, including countries in the orbit of the former Soviet Union like Albania. One of the triggers of Janie's flight – the inability of the environment to support a family livelihood – makes trafficking an attractive economic strategy, for pimps and many prostitutes alike.

Sex trafficking is also placed in very important ways. For example, studies of the emergence of the mail-order bride industry (see chapter four) suggest that brides-to-be are often marketed in culturally specific ways that reference places of origin. The growth of the sex trade between the Philippines and Japan, which accounts for over 100,000 Filipinas travelling to Japan annually, is one flow that turns on place-based constructions of sexuality.

Place context also affects the ways that states can intervene in the trafficking business. While Janie had returned (for a while) to her village in Albania, in reality the majority of trafficked children are unable to return to their former homes because their participation in unsanctioned sexual activity is deemed to have broken the place-based cultural codes. States who simply return such children to their homes are making an already difficult situation worse.

Child trafficking specifically, and human trafficking more generally, raises further questions about the nature of vulnerability in populations under globalization. Does trafficking illustrate the impotency of the state to protect those it should be protecting, or is participation in prostitution a viable economic strategy and one condoned by individuals, families and communities (Kempadoo and Doezema 1998)?

HIV-AIDS

- 40 million persons worldwide were living with HIV-AIDS in 2001.

- 14 million children had lost one or both of their parents to HIV-AIDS and were living as AIDS orphans. While 80 per cent of these children live in sub-Saharan Africa, over 500,000 live in the Caribbean and Latin America.

- School enrolment has been up to 36 per cent lower in parts of southern Africa, with girls and AIDS orphans most affected. Gender disparities in education are set to increase.

- The number of HIV-AIDS deaths in South Africans aged between 15 and 34 will peak in 2010–15 at a level four times higher than it was in 2000.

- The price of an anti-retroviral drug regimen in Uganda declined from $12,000 per year in 1998 to $350 per year at the end of 2001.

- The cost of a global response to HIV-AIDS is estimated at $1000 per infection saved. Few sub-Saharan African countries have a per capita GNP that can afford this cost.

Vignette 3

HIV in Botswana

The southern African nation of Botswana is an important case study because it exhibits some of the highest occurrences of HIV-AIDS and its experiences seem likely to be repeated in other countries. Without the disease its population could have expected one of the highest life expectancies in Africa (70 years). With HIV-AIDS, the life expectancy is estimated at 39 years. Figure 2.4 depicts Botswana's missing population.

While acute, the epidemic does not yet appear to have peaked. Among all pregnant teens, 28 per cent tested positive in 1997. The same figure for women pregnant and living in urban areas was 39 per cent. By 2001, this had further increased to 45 per cent.

Of all Botswana's children, 10 per cent are AIDS orphans. As the epidemic spreads, this figure will increase to 20 per cent by 2010. Because parents, aunts and uncles are dying in such large numbers, the traditional child-fostering system that relied on extended family networks to care for those orphaned is breaking

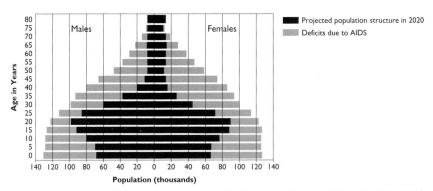

Figure 2.4 Missing population, Botswana. Source: *UNAIDS-WHO (2002)*

down. Evidence from elsewhere in the region suggests that impoverished children enter informal employment in urban areas, frequently as sex workers, and further increase their own exposure to HIV-AIDS. The loss of a generation means that one in four Botswanan families will lose an income earner and, nationally, 30 per cent of the labour force will have been lost to AIDS by 2020.

At least one of the traditional explanations for the spread of the disease does not seem to apply. For example, rates of polygamy – often associated with increased transmission – are low relative to the region. However, lack of employment opportunities meant that men had a tradition of long-distance commuting and circulation to South Africa to work in the mines. Indeed, mineworkers were identified as a high-risk group in the late 1980s. Personal political leadership and consistent government funding for health outreach and, more recently, multisectoral programmes have had important effects. For example, the rate of female condom use (75 per cent) is one of the highest in Africa. Up to 70 per cent of women have taken medical advice and replaced breastfed milk with free formula to cut the 30 per cent risk of mother-to-child infection. Another group frequently recognized as in a high-risk category, the armed services, have access to free, confidential and voluntary AIDS screening, are not required to leave the service if they test positive and are guaranteed full benefits for themselves and their families. Indeed, had the government not embarked on an aggressive programme to combat malnutrition in the 1970s and 1980s, many feel that the current rates of stunted growth among children (22 per cent), while high, would have been much higher.

Geographic perspectives inform our understanding of HIV-AIDS in a number of ways. Identifying where (urban versus rural) risks are higher can illuminate how the disease spreads. Similarly, appreciating the geographic behaviour of groups in space (like mineworkers and sex workers) can also deepen our understanding of how these groups are vulnerable and what outreach activities are required. A number of geographic approaches to HIV-AIDS have also cast it as a diffusion process, that is, a disease that spreads systematically over space. In the USA during the early 1980s, HIV-AIDS spread from a few large urban centres (including New York and San Francisco) down the urban hierarchy, before continuing its outward spread more locally through daily commuting fields. Diffusion approaches argue that commuting and migration serve as key geographic vectors in the transmission of infection. The 'truck-town' hypothesis also suggests that the movement of truck drivers in and through Uganda and their contact with sex workers is responsible for the hierarchical diffusion of HIV-AIDS in East Africa.

Critics of this approach worry that the model of agency is oversimplistic and that the identification of an origin hearth could promote dangerous general- izations about cause and effect. Craddock (2004) warned that diffusionist rhetoric about HIV-AIDS tended to blame the victim. For example, a *Time* Magazine February 2001 cover story on HIV-AIDS in Africa described AIDS as a 'spark in the dry timber' of African societies (i.e. an accident waiting to happen), and ventured into 'the heart of the heart' of the epidemic where 'ignorance, promiscuity, and denial help generate' transmission (Craddock 2004: 3).

Recent work on HIV-AIDS variations has also suggested a role for environ- mental context. Foster (2004) argues that the trace element selenium is largely absent in the soils of a number of countries with high HIV-1 prevalence (Uganda, Tanzania, Congo, Kenya), but present in the marine-deposited soils of Senegal, a country with a lower HIV-1 prevalence rate. Citing a similar association between the absence of soil selenium and HIV-1 prevalence in African Americans in the USA, he argues that individuals with selenium deficiencies are more likely to spread HIV-1, and, because HIV-1 is in turn associated with increasing selenium deficiency, there is a damaging positive feedback between the two.

Other perspectives have stressed the role of place context in shaping sexual practices. Investigating condom use, sexuality and HIV-AIDS in Botswana and across southern Africa, Susser and Stein (2004) note that women see themselves as active participants in negotiating sexual practices. However, these practices

> are shaped by historical and cultural perceptions of the bounds of the human body. Among some groups . . . a woman can insist a man uses a condom and she can with- hold sex if he refuses. Among other groups, a woman's request that her partner use

a male condom is seen as a challenge ... [in these cases] a woman has the right to use a female condom ... (143)

In this example, place-based cultural and economic factors have framed the positive choices women make about sexuality in a way that suggests that the wide-spread distribution of the female condom will be a useful government-led initiative.

Taken together, these vignettes suggest that a geographic perspective can inform contemporary population issues. On the surface, geographic perspectives on population continue to focus on demographic processes like fertility, population composition and ageing, migration, population growth and decline and morbidity/mortality. However, the changing involvement of key players in these cases – including governments, trafficking networks and drug companies – set against the increasingly interdependent context of globalization implies that both this geographic perspective and what has been meant by population will continue to evolve. This, then, is the continuing task and nature of any 'population geography.'

Summary

Early population geographies described areal differentiation in populations. Concepts of space, environment and place were variously used to inform a geographic perspective that attempted to maintain a commitment to an integrative geography that fused nature-society. Many geographic accounts used these descriptions of populations to highlight differences between the West and the rest and, as such, to legitimize the imperial and colonial ambitions of the state. Geographers also sought to hitch population to their own accounts of space, environment and place in order to develop their nascent discipline.

Many of the key conceptual models in contemporary population geography – including the demographic transition, stable population theory, the gravity model of migration and assimilation – have an intellectual pedigree that connects them with much older knowledge projects. However, the connection between their emergence in the nineteenth and twentieth centuries, and their continued circulation today is anything but a linear and straightforward one, as the next two chapters suggest. To begin with, while the conflation of space with nation had served some interests, the widespread discrediting of such *geopolitik* thinking meant that attempts to develop a spatial epistemology, particularly one linked to 'social' (anthropological, sociological and economic) theory, were stifled. When it was crudely operationalized using racial hierarchies, environmental determinism offered a transparent legitimizing function for colonialism and repression that has become untenable. The lack of a conceptually defensible epistemology, combined with the subsequent ideological appropriation of determinism by Haushofer, consigned geographic treatments of environment to the margins of the discipline for over 50 years. Likewise, place-based perspectives were increasingly at odds with extant discourses, both within and beyond geography.

Writing after the Great Depression, Hartshorne (1939) called for a back-to-basics empiricism that returned geography to its comfort zone of areal differentiation. Space was to be rebranded and redeployed as a container which revealed society, and its properties and processes, in a systematic and meaningful way. Against the gathering pace of disciplinary specialization in the mid-twentieth century, geography's stripped-down view of the world was a 'unique' one that cast it as one of three 'spatial' sciences and distinguished it from its partners (astronomy and geophysics) by the self-evident idea of scale. With the need to formulate a credible epistemology again highlighted after World War II, geography looked beyond the social sciences towards the physical sciences (particularly physics and mathematics) to (re)energize its 'inner' spatial perspective. Population geography was about to assume a very specific institutional identity.

chapter 3

THE RISE OF A MODERN POPULATION GEOGRAPHY

This chapter reviews the emergence and development of population geography as a field within human geography. I consider:

- How did the role of states in the changing international context influence research agendas?
- What intellectual visions were proposed for the field, and how durable did they prove?
- How did the turn to positivism influence the growth of the field?
- How did specific poles of research reflect the changing external and internal context?

The 1950s to the 1970s was a formative period in the development of ideas about population geography for at least two reasons. First, a number of geographers made expansive conceptual statements about what population geography could be. The three authors discussed here are Glenn Trewartha, Jean Beaujeu-Garnier and Wilbur Zelinsky. Running through each of their statements is the notion that population geography should exist as a separate sub-discipline. Second, and following on from the agendas sparked by these foundational statements, this was also the period when a number of influential texts were written about population geography. These included (listed by date of first publication): John Clarke, *Population Geography* (1965), Louis Henry, *Population* (1976), Gary Peters and Robert Larkin, *Population Geography* (1979), William Hornby and Melvyn Jones, *An Introduction to Population Geography* (1980), George Demko et al., *Population Geography* (1970), Huw Jones, *A Population Geography* (1981) and Robert Woods, *Theoretical Population Geography* (1982). These texts presented a remarkably uniform view of the field to its students and shaped the agendas of the following generation of researchers.

Population and the changing international context

This section examines the changing ways in which states were interested in population matters. The three decades following World War II witnessed a profound series of transformations in the nature of society and the roles of states. Examples come from the spheres of geopolitics (for example, the cold war, independence of many former colonial holdings), economics (for example, the growth of the US economy and international trade), culture (for example, the rise in secularism) and social relations (for example, the growing incidence of urban unrest and participation of women in paid employment). As many of these transformations appeared to be accompanied by noticeable changes in the size, growth and behaviours of population groups, the study of populations rose to prominence.

Cold war ideologies superimposed a distinctive East-West (communist, non-communist) axis to international relations over the period. Societies and their populations were transformed both by the competing communist and non-communist ideologies themselves and by the geopolitical conflicts to stem from these alternative approaches. In the communist orbit, Marxist-Leninist theory emphasized the needs of collective production over social provision. However, the translation of these ideas into a series of five-year plans illustrated that population growth and distribution, and the institutions that mediated it, were crucial elements of the production complex (Pokshishevskiy 1962). State programmes for urban housing provision, rural collectivization and the provision of family planning and childcare all responded to particular bottlenecks in production by promoting the supply of populations. The same measures also fostered demographic responses (particularly low birth rates) that would, in time, undermine economic output and the demand for goods.

While the Soviet system was actively promoting and enabling the participation of women in the labour market, many women in the USA were struggling to re-enter the labour force after having relinquished wartime employment activities to returning servicemen. Fertility levels rose sharply for at least 15 years after the war as the 'All-American/Leave-it-to-Beaver' family formation became associated with not just this demographic generation, but this generation placed in suburbia. Family planning methods illustrate another example of how population behaviours diverged across the ideological divide, with the pill favoured in Europe and North America, and legalized abortion the most prevalent technique in the Soviet Union.

Population issues also came into sharp relief as a consequence of the territorial and ideological wars between the superpowers. The spatial logic of partition gave rise to parallel international systems of migrations that interconnected the West and the East (at least within Europe), but which ruptured long-standing flows between the two. In some cases, like the completion of the Berlin Wall around the enclave of West Berlin in August 1961, the demographic response was immediate. But just as population issues became emblems of the independence and difference of communism and capitalism, issues surrounding population movement also emerged when antagonisms between the East and West surfaced. The enthusiasm European powers showed in the 1960s for refugees fleeing Hungary and escaping communism may have been propelled by a sense of ideological one-upmanship as much as by a deep sense of humanitarianism (Loescher 1993). Persistent conflict between the superpowers generated a significant number of refugees in Asia (Vietnam and Afghanistan in the 1960s and 1970s), Africa (Angola in the 1970s) and Latin America (Cuba in the 1960s and Central America in the 1970s). It was migration that symbolized the fall of the cold war, with its stark images of the dismantling of the Berlin Wall and the surge of East Berliners west through Checkpoint Charlie.

Industrialized nations continued to invest economically and politically in the international system of politically independent, sovereign and freely trading nation states. In many regions this involved profound transitions from colonialism to 'independence'. Civil war, genocide and partition resulted in catastrophic loss of life, both among combatants and the wider civil population, as food supplies and infrastructures were disrupted, in many cases, for over a decade. Geopolitical conflict generated large and enduring communities of refugees, notably Palestinians. In addition to the direct demographic impacts of loss of life, states also had to contend with indirect demographic impacts, through uneven sex ratios, boom-bust cycles of fertility, labour force shortages and large internal movements of displaced persons, frequently to primary cities.

This system of trading between nation states became associated with an international division of labour. The most industrialized nations coordinated production onshore but sourced materials and, as necessary, skilled (brain drain) and unskilled (guest worker) migrants from the global South. While most industrializing countries responded to labour shortages by promoting temporary immigration that reinvented neocolonial and neo-imperial relations between, for example, Algeria and France, Turkey and Germany, the 'British' Caribbean and the UK, and Mexico and the USA, Japan did not, at least not in public. Other regions – notably the Gulf oil states – recruited both skilled and unskilled temporary workers *en masse* as oil production increased in the 1960s. Following the oil crisis of 1973, temporary workers were released. This was, then, a period when the relationships between population and resource issues occupied both national and international stages.

The management of increasingly visible and disruptive population issues proceeded at two levels on the assumption, at least in the West, that the ideal of nation-state sovereignty represented the best geopolitical and geo-economic strategy for a new, post-World War II international order. First, specifically tasked supranational bodies devised, and in some cases implemented, plans of action to respond to what were increasingly seen as pressing international issues. Public concerns about the relationship between population growth, resources, environmental impacts and economic development surrounded the 1974 International Conference on Population and Development (ICPD) held in Bucharest. Progress was difficult partly because such bodies tended to be narrowly focused to reflect agency interests: the later UN Conference on Environment and Development which covered similar material paid much less attention to demographic aspects of interrelations. Furthermore, national agendas continued to politicize many plans of action.

This politicization is evident in the well-known debate between neo-Malthusians (including Garett Hardin, Donella Meadows and the Club of Rome group), who argued that rapid population growth contributed to ecological decline and reduced levels of development, and more *laissez-faire*, neoclassical economists, like Julian Simon, who emphatically argued that population was either neutral or a positive asset (*à la* Boserup) for national economic development. Two talismanic figures in this debate, Garrett Hardin and Julian Simon, both of whom were born in New Jersey in 1953, placed a bet in 1980 as to the accuracy of their perspective for predicting the price of resources ten years later. Simon won the bet, the battle and, noting the rise of neo-liberal economics in the 1990s, many would say the war. The subsequent 1984 ICPD was influenced by Reagan–Thatcher ideology, itself reflective of Simon's perspective.

The fortunes of another UN agency concerned with population matters, the High Commission on Refugees (UNHCR), further illustrates how international cooperation and coordination during the period was swayed by national political interests. Formed in 1951 as a response to the large numbers of political refugees that had been 'created' by war, the demands on the UNHCR increased greatly over the period as the number of nation states increased with the independence of many former colonies, and economic dysfunctions within these nations intensified further political instability. Despite some notable modifications that include the Organization of African Unity agreement (OAU) and a regional accord signed in Cartagena, this regime of protection for those fleeing with well-founded fear of persecution remains in place today (Loescher 1993). It faced financial pressures as the number of refugees increased and their geographic destinations were areas least well equipped to respond (notably, south-west Asia and sub-Saharan Africa). The international refugee regime also faced political and ideological pressures as refugees were increasingly drawn from non-communist states. Thus, while the USA had welcomed with open arms refugees from communist Cuba in the 1960s, those fleeing civil war and political persecution in US-leaning countries like Nicaragua and El Salvador were denied refugee status in the 1970s and 1980s.

The World Health Organisation (WHO) and the United Nations Fund for Population Activities (UNFPA) were tasked to deliver western best practice in the areas of mortality and morbidity and fertility. Over time, the success of the WHO, together with the diffusion of public health systems and steady increases in water access and quality, put pressure on the latter agency to help deliver lower fertility levels and slow population growth.

Globally, population growth emerged as a key population matter for at least two reasons. First, in the eyes of national and international communities, the apparent unevenness of population growth began to threaten economic recovery and social progress. Several nations within Europe, including France and East Germany, were aware of their slow or even stationary population growth. Earlier population-based answers to the problem of a shrinking labour force, namely the recruitment of foreign-born guest workers to staff key industrial sectors, quickly became part of the perceived problem. Second, and related, the economic fortunes of the global South were very much the business of the increasingly interdependent North. Family planning norms from secular industrial society began to diffuse to the global South on the back of cultural messages about modernization and progress. China strengthened its own commitment to its one-child policy.

Questions of internal population distribution also rose to prominence as key issues for individual nations. Following the economic disruptions of World War II, the USA (and to some extent Japan) promoted geopolitical stability by investing in significant reconstruction projects, both at home and across the developed North. While the Marshall Plan sparked the redevelopment of many European areas devastated by war, US domestic policy targeted transportation and accessibility improvements (for example, the Interstate Highways Act of 1957), housing supply (for example, the establishment of the Federal Housing Authority that, among other activities, underwrote mortgages for returning servicemen) and the growth of the service economy (for example, the decentralization of many government research and development activities to the US South and West).

In many places, this significant dose of supply-side Keynesian investment fostered the necessary conditions for a radical restructuring of space economies. Economic growth and recovery was concentrated in key regions (including the US Sunbelt and the European Golden Triangle). Internal migration flows followed this growth pattern: in the USA, the deindustrializing Midwest began to empty as young workers sought opportunities in California, Texas and Florida. Britain's north-south divide reinvented itself, with London and the south-east emerging as an economic and demographic core. As much of this service-oriented growth centred on metropolitan areas, a profound decentralization of economy and population unfolded, particularly in the USA and Canada. Indeed, the growing suburbanization of the population became at once consequence and cause, as new investment followed families out of the inner-city areas. However, in other areas, decentralization was resisted. In Europe, some nations put the brakes on decentralization partly because many of their post-war central cities contained recently bombed-out building sites that were available for redevelopment, and partly because central city property holders actively opposed new, out-of-town developments.

Reconstruction, broadly writ, meant that states were involved in new ways in population matters. Charged to protect and nurture economic recovery, national and local governments became keenly interested in questions of unequal population growth and population distribution. While post-war recovery was associated with increasing fertility levels in many countries, and resulting baby booms (and, when fertility returned to earlier levels, baby busts), the medium-term implications of this temporal unevenness in growth were overshadowed by the immediate issues that the sudden arrival of migrants brought with them. Because those moving were more likely to represent particular parts of the population – young, educated and, in the case of suburbanization, white – there were immediate implications for the areas they left and the areas they moved into. Regional migration led to acute housing shortages in destination areas for single workers, but disinvestment from origin areas as consumption levels fell back. More local patterns of residential mobility created difficult conditions for the supply of education. In areas where education was largely funded locally, the suburbanization of white middle-class families alongside the consolidation of non-white neighbourhoods in inner-city areas meant a deficit of funds for central city schools. Furthermore, and reflecting the integrationist agenda, some cities bussed suburban children to inner-city schools to maintain a white/non-white demographic balance. However, the problems of inadequate infrastructure provision were particularly pronounced in those parts of the world experiencing the most rapid rises in population numbers. As political and economic power consolidated and centralized in many former colonial holdings, already dominant urban areas like Rio de Janeiro, Lagos, Dar es Salaam and Mexico City attracted many young rural-to-urban migrants. This had the effect of boosting local fertility rates and further increasing the rural/urban population growth differential. Both capitalist (the development of Brasilia as a counter to Rio) and Maoist (the designation of Dodoma as Tanzania's national capital) ideologies responded geographically to what was understood as a problem of population distribution.

Perhaps because population issues were such a visible icon of economic growth, an increasing number of 'solutions' or 'fixes' to economic problems revolved around the manipulation of populations and population behaviours. An expanding economy demanded a growing labour market that could supply both skilled and unskilled workers. The speed, scale and periodicity of economic growth (including the boom-bust cycles of recession) meant that new recruits had to be located and productively integrated into the economic and political life of the nation. The apartheid regime in South Africa represented one extreme model. Based on a doctrine that some groups (whites and Afrikaners) were superior to other groups (Cape coloureds and black Africans) and that social harmony was most likely when these different groups were spatially segregated (literally, apart-heid as set aside), black African men were forcibly recruited to work in the mines, but expected to live in temporary camps, returning once or twice a year to their permanent homeland settlements.

Indeed, the same assumption about the temporariness of residence of workers permeates the Bracero Agreement signed by the USA and Mexico in 1942 to legalize the semi-permanent importation of agricultural workers, and the guest worker programmes of France and Germany from the same period. The geographic distribution of temporary workers showed both regional concentration (linked to, for example, the availability of agricultural employment in California, the distribution of auto-manufacturing employment in France and Germany and the need for transportation workers in cities like London) and local concentration and segregation. However, structural decline in agriculture and manufacturing during the 1970s led to large-scale job losses and an increase in job insecurity for all workers. The geographic association between temporary workers and declining industries promoted growing resentment among local populations that economic decline had been precipitated by foreign migrants. Hate crimes and racist activities rose in areas where foreign workers were visibly concentrated. Deeper questions about the integration of foreign-born workers into host societies, many of whom had limited political rights, thus began to be framed in quite geographic ways.

The geographic framing of white–black relations was particularly prominent during this period in a number of large and deindustrializing cities. So-called race riots erupted in Detroit and Cleveland and became coded as segregation issues. In the USA, of course, Chicago School sociologists had suggested that, in contrast to a raced white norm of sedentarism in society, minority groups (immigrants and African Americans) could best assimilate (progress) by linking social mobility to spatial mobility. Amongst these groups, sedentarism and isolationism was anti-social and deviant. While the tendency of minority communities to cluster for an initial period of time in a new setting was established, the fact that many black communities continued to be segregated led to a debate between those who argued that such geographic behaviour was culturally motivated (i.e. community-led) and those who argued that persistent segregation resulted from the unequal distribution of opportunities in capitalist society. While *Brown* versus *Board of Education* (1954) had made racial segregation in US schools unconstitutional, urban school districts continued to bus white and black students across neighbourhood lines to combat what had become a *de facto* pattern of segregation. Attention turned to how segregation unfolded in the housing market, how it might be linked to migration and how public policy could better address it. This was understood as a way of taking the civil rights agenda forward, and population geographers began to contribute.

In summary, states became absorbed by population matters for a diverse set of reasons, including reconstruction, the need to foster economic and geopolitical stability and the mandate of promoting social cohesion and progression. Population geography was to emerge as a coherent field against a backdrop of increasing involvement of many levels of government in population questions. In keeping with the Keynesian spirit of much of this period, states had the authority to act on behalf of the national interest using established scientific evidence. But state involvement in social welfare sometimes turned to the explicit use of force against particular population groups: this was a period when students were shot in the Tlatelolco Massacre in Mexico City's Plaza de las Tres Culturas, Kent State's campus and Soweto's football fields. While Enlightenment norms about rationality and progress were in ascendance, an undercurrent of unrest, alternative thinking and, with the anthems of the Sex Pistols, high street anarchy also 'complicated' the relations between states and populations.

Reinventing geography

Matching changes in external contexts, geography's own place in the academy underwent significant restructuring during this period. This section describes how the discipline of geography reinvented itself by institutionalizing the ways in which population questions would intersect with space, environment and place. While geography had been established as a university discipline in Europe and the USA for around 50 years, its attempts to move beyond descriptive accounts of physical and human patterns had proved troublesome. Epistemologies that sourced their explanations from the environmental or cultural context were seen as overly simplistic on the one hand and, after the co-option of *geopolitik* thinking by the Third Reich, ideologically dangerous on the other.

Researchers interested in questions about population faced their own battles. The 'science' of demography had avoided the isolationism of geography and adopted, as appropriate, insights from formal mathematics (stable population theory), anthropology (racial and ethnic hierarchies), biology (notions of sex and age), sociology (family and kin structures) and neoclassical economics (rationality and marginalism). It had – and used – a tool kit that could make sense of ever pressing population issues, including the relative decline of the European population, the rapid growth of Third-World populations and the implication of population change for resource issues, at international and local levels. However, very few demography departments had opened and some saw the applied focus almost as a liability. Moreover, population scholars received their training in cognate disciplines like sociology and economics, as well as national institutes like INED or the UN. At the risk of oversimplifying a more complex terrain, there arose a moment when the needs of demographers to 'house' their perspectives coincided with the needs of geographers to identify partners whose work carried credibility and relevance.

The kind of alliance that geography and demography forged was very much tied up in the internal restructuring of human geography after World War II. Hartshorne's (1939) call for a reinvigorated study of areal differentiation signalled a restated commitment to an integrationist view of the world that preserved nature–society links and sought to recover order through an empiricist approach which assumed the world was as it appeared. However, the idiographic methods (thick descriptions) of the day had a tendency to create knowledge that was difficult to integrate with the dominant scientific approaches of, for example, demography, sociology and economics. Geographic empiricism steadily yielded to other philosophies of science, notably positivism but also structuralism, which stressed a nomothetical search for order in the general (some geographers also turned to humanism, which retained a commitment to the particular). For Fred Schaeffer, geography needed to avoid an outmoded exceptionalism and shift its attention towards patterns of similarity. Peter Haggett shifted his gaze away from the empirical real world and on to a geographic lens, or graticule, which could be imposed upon the real world to order it.

Freed from the obligation of linking order to the appearances of objects on the earth's surface, a more scientific geography could now fully co-opt the insights of the physical and mathematical sciences (theories of relativity and quantum mechanics), economics (principles of least effort) and sociobiology (the ecological structure of human communities), to name three. The growing use of inductive and, to a lesser extent, deductive methods became firmly associated with the application of a positivist approach to spatial differentiation. A central goal of positivism was to verify and falsify empirical observations and construct generalizable laws that informed complex models and theories with widespread (i.e. universal) applicability. This was a view of the world that discounted metaphysical input (feelings, values, experiences). It held that researchers existed apart from their subjects and were objective, disinterested and concerned only 'with the facts'.

The rise of positivism and, to a lesser extent, structuralism and humanism in human geography had important implications for how concerns with context and proximity might be informed with the concepts of space, environment and place. Two broad treatments of context emerged (see table 3.1).

Table 3.1 Geographic approaches to knowledge, 1950s–1970s.

		Power	
		Unproblematic	Problematic
Treatments of context and proximity	Passive	EMPIRICISM POSITIVISM	STRUCTURALISM
	Contingent	HUMANISM	

Empirical accounts tended to treat context passively and adopted views of space as container. While positivist accounts additionally conceptualized space as codex, it was also the case that context was there to be reduced and explained away, and existed passively and outside the research process. A family of location theories sought order by hypothesizing that underlying economic processes generated patterns on the landscape. Spatial phenomena – like the size and spacing of central places, the location of manufacturing activities and urban land uses – were outward 'morphological' manifestations of systems of relations that constituted society. Features of the environment were frequently assumed away as location theorists constructed their models on flat, isotropic plains.

The development of positivist spatial science in human geography was also predicated on simplifying assumptions about geographic actors. Sociological and anthropological treatments of population had defined actors as individuals, families, kin groups and communities. The imposition of deterministic models of economic rationality or gravitational pulls led to dehumanized accounts that failed to capture the variety of experience of individual population behaviour. So-called 'behavioural geography' developed, both to describe individual behavioural out-comes in space and to search for generalizable rules that governed information acquisition, choice assessment, decision making and actions. In the latter positivist approach, space contained environmental stimuli that prompted choices and constraints, and was regionalized and classified according to common structures of behaviour (for example, the production of maps of perceptual regions, mental maps). Informed by empiricist and positivist thinking, behavioural geography also adopted a passive view of context. Similarly, applications of Marxist thought in geography regarded space passively and theorized it as a derivative of capitalist class relations. Structuralist thought also held that environments represented generalized contexts of human action that provided specific opportunities and constraints for society. This environmental context could be ecological or political.

Geographic humanism acknowledged the situatedness and contingency of social life and ceded context a more active role in its accounts. Using literary analysis, diaries, direct observation, archival research and other techniques, humanists sought to describe an experience of the world that was intensely personal. Environment – as a constrainer and enabler of action – informs the accounts of individual life worlds. But it is the concept of place that humanist work most expanded, with sense of place linked to both individual experiences and broader economic and cultural trends in society. Humanists explored the site/situation, economic/ecologic and individual/group characteristics of settings in ways that rendered the strict divisions of the terms space, environment and place unhelpful. Attention to the recursive relations between individual feelings, intentions, constraints and landscapes helped reclaim the concept of 'place' (Bunge 1971).

Just as the diversification of geographic approaches to knowledge enlarged the treatment of context and proximity, it also broadened the ways that geographers thought about the relationship between power and knowledge (see the horizontal axis of table 3.1). While empiricist and positivist geographies focused attention on generalizable individual and group decisions, humanistic approaches to the individual proceeded from the position that knowledge was subjective. By contrast, structuralism acknowledged a link between how knowledge was produced and how power circulated in society. Many structuralist approaches held that empirical appearances obscured networks of unequal and disequilibrating structural forces and authorized the production of conceptual frameworks (extending, for example, Marx's labour theory of value) that could resonate with events in social life. Marxist ideas about uneven development (across rural–urban, regional and First World–Third World spheres) suggested that space itself was produced in a particular (uneven) way by the underlying means of production, as a necessary reflection of the contradictions inherent in the capitalist system.

Through the continuation of empiricism, and the development of positivist, humanist and structuralist approaches to knowledge production, the meaning and use of the geographic concepts of space, environment and place shifted between the 1950s and the late 1970s. In theory, the growth of a population geography could continue to utilize all three concepts in much the same way as its intellectual forerunners had. The three main protagonists of a joined up population geography all argued that the field should be underpinned by some combination of these concepts. However, joined up implied institutionalized, and this meant compromise.

Cleveland and beyond

While geography reinvented itself, three pioneering visions were proposed for the development of a sub-field that studied population. In the 1940s and 1950s, both demography and geography were keen to establish their disciplinary credentials. While population questions were increasingly connected to international processes, approaches to these questions were still often dominated by 'national' schools of thought. But with the reorganization and increasing specializations of social sciences after World War II, not to mention increasing availability of demographic data, it was strategic for many geographers interested by population to simultaneously institutionalize and internationalize their agendas. In general terms, epistemological undercurrents, the need to be relevant and credible and the growing availability of national and international statistics presented geographers with a choice between a systematic (specialized) or regional (synthetic) future. New systematic fields of geography were created when geography derived a deductive framework from a related discipline, used this to generate hypotheses about processes and tested these ideas using data on spatial variations and structures. US geographers favoured this systematic approach, but other national schools of thought – notably the French tradition – continued to develop place- and regional-based accounts. As US geography grew, the discipline quickly moved towards a systematic focus, and the now familiar fields of urban geography, political geography and economic geography established their institutional credentials.

A number of issues surrounded the emergence of a systematic field of population geography. For some, the demographic focus on population groups seemed either a self-evident component of human geography or to cross-cut all other fields in a way that elevated it to a super(synthetic)-field and argued against it standing alone as a field of inquiry. Furthermore, unlike economics, anthropology or sociology, demography itself was not an established discipline. Moreover, demography presented a narrow epistemological focus. It defined itself as the (formal) mathematical study of the human population, and/or: 'when we talk about distribution we are talking about statistics, so demography means the statistical study of population or, in other words, the application of statistics to human populations' (Henry 1976: xii). Reflective of the continuing sponsorship of the nation state, population groups were most frequently constructed at the national scale and, with a preponderance of national data, much demography was still concerned with between-nation variations, with analyses rolled out to other scales as data and applications permitted.

Demography's dual concern with the national and with change over time served to bookend the development of the field in two ways. First, and going back to Ratzel, geographers knew and were comfortable with the nation state and had already contributed to population mapping at this scale. Epistemologies of regionalization as classification meant that geographers could further extend this work to regionalize national populations or, increasingly, to divide national populations into their regional components. Of course, spatial disaggregation was a key skill that geographers could bring to the enterprise. Demographic components of change – fertility and mortality – could be mapped and described at the regional and local level. Indeed, geographers not only acknowledged that scale dependency could impact upon theory development, but actively researched the so-called 'modifiable areal unit problem'. Second, by seeing space as codex, geography could supplement the demographer's focus on change over time with a geographer's focus on change over space. Practitioners could seek process in observed spatial patterns in demographic distributions and could posit derived deductive models (for example, modernization and the demographic transition) and internal deductive models (for example, diffusion) that helped explain how fertility/mortality changed over space and time. Crucially, this concern with population behaviour over and in space focused attention on mobility and migration, considered the stepchild of demography. Those who made explicit calls for a joined up population geography negotiated these tensions in different ways.

Vision 1: A trinitarian project

The moniker of 'founding father' of population geography rests with Wisconsin geographer Glenn Trewartha. His 1953 presidential address to the Association of American Geographers in Cleveland, Ohio drew a line in the sand that initiated debate about how geographers might think collectively and internationally about population. Although Trewartha's vision was not particularly new, retaining as it did key insights from Hettner's work, the timing of his intervention was sublime. Richard Hartshorne's 1939 *The Nature of Geography* had growing support from many human geographers, who believed that the future of the discipline lay in strengthening the collaborative links with traditional (for example, economic) and emerging (for example, sociological) partners in the social sciences. Hartshorne believed that this exchange would promote geographic knowledge *both* through the development of branches of systematic geography (defined by intersections with cognate disciplines) *and* through the retention of geography's particular commitment to regional synthesis.

Trewartha was underwhelmed by Hartshorne's treatise, which, after all, had not mentioned population as a systematic subdivision. Hartshorne believed that an interchange between human geography and the biological sciences (especially human physiology) would lead to the study of 'the geography of races', alongside 'animal geographies' and 'plant geographies'. Second, Trewartha and many others in geography – especially outside the USA – were only too aware of the growing prominence of, and respect for, the field of demography. Princeton-based scholars such as Frank Notestein had recently completed (1945) what was destined to become the single most important demographic contribution in the social sciences, an account of a demographic transition in Europe. Demography was increasingly recognized as contributing to the intellectual infrastructure of reconstruction initiatives: indeed, work on the demographic transition had been commissioned by the United Nations' precursor, the League of Nations. Trewartha saw an important opportunity for geographers to contribute to and benefit from developments in demography.

In examining his corpus, with particular attention to the 1953 reprinted address, it is apparent that Trewartha danced to the drum of those who saw geography as a unitary field: 'Physical and cultural, systematic and regional, general and special, are dualisms which appear at times to fog the oneness. As geographers I believe we are committed to the study of earth regions' (Trewartha 1953: 85). Trewartha went on to argue that the prospects for a unified geography would be served through a tripartite approach to studying the key element of areal differentiation. He rejected the physical-cultural divide, in particular, because it leaves population questions in a kind of intellectual no man's land. Conceptualizing population growth in physical (environmental) terms was also difficult given determinism's low status in the discipline as a whole. But neither did the overly cultural narratives of workers like Carl Sauer or Bruhnes – who saw population phenomena as objects on the cultural lansdscape – appeal. Although he appeared unaware of the earlier contributions by Pokshishevskiy, Trewartha argued that population matters commanded equal status with the studies of the cultural earth and the physical earth (see figure 3.1).

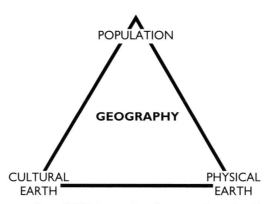

Figure 3.1 Trinitarian vision. Source: *redrawn from Trewartha (1953:81)*

What was crucial to Trewartha was the idea that population geography was on the one hand special enough to deserve relatively high status in some sub-disciplinary pecking order, but not so special as to undo the fundamentally unitary character of geography. Thus, the distinctiveness of this new field would be found in its ability to centre geography on human lives:

> The here-suggested trinomial organisation results in giving man his deservedly explicit and important position within the unitary geographic structure. The only *final* value is human life or human living, and this being the case it is difficult to understand why geographers should judge the creation of man, and the environment out of which he creates them, relatively more important than man himself . . .
> (Trewartha 1953: italics in original)

The mixing of the conceptual and the political sat uncomfortably with a model of science 'from nowhere' where 'facts speak for themselves'. However, this conviction would prove to be a harbinger of a constant thread of radicalism within the field that continues to the present in the form of debates about activism.

Trewartha's system for population geography proceeds from a description of regional variations in population distributions. These variations are linked to demographic (fertility and mortality), environmental (ecumene) and cultural (settlement systems) attributes in a way that demonstrates continuity both with Hettner and the *géographie humaine* school. Indeed, it is apparent that the geography of population characteristics affects not only population growth mechanisms (for example, areas with early ages of marriage showed higher fertility), but also how people lead their daily lives as both producers and consumers (Pokshishevskiy 1962). In aiming for such broad synthesis, which drew on geography's environment, space and place traditions, Trewartha acknowledged that off-the-shelf data produced by national governments in the form of surveys and population censuses would need, at a minimum, to be supplemented by methodological innovation and creativity.

Despite his commitment to regional synthesis, Trewartha's scheme was to lead the way for a more systematic form of study of population geography. Table 3.2 outlines an essentially descriptive approach that reached beyond demography into realms of social, cultural and economic geography. The scheme 'locates' historical population geography and medical geography, two areas of scholarship that would both struggle to define themselves in relation to population geography. While he criticizes the physical/cultural divide within geography as unhelpful, he saw the merit in both generalized and topic-focused (specialized) approaches to geography.

Table 3.2 Trewartha's vision for population geography. Adapted from: Trewartha (1953: 88)

AGENDA	EXAMPLES
Historical population geography	1. Regional variations in population growth and decline, data limitations.
Population numbers	2. Gross patterns of numbers 3. Fertility and mortality dynamics 4. Over and underpopulation 5. Gross patterns of distribution by ecumene/nonecumene, settlement type, density 6. Migration
Qualities and regional distribution	7. Physical Body Race Nationality Sex Age Health 8. Socioeconomic Religion Education Occupation Family structure Urban/rural Development Customs

While David Hooson (1960) shared a similarly holistic intellectual vision, the rapid adoption and dissemination of positivist approaches to an increasingly 'socially scientific' human geography meant specialization, not integration, guided research. Paradoxically, while Trewartha's *vision* for population geography went unheeded, his *call* was widely heard and appropriated by the very specializations he sought to avoid.

Vision 2: Populations, places and landscapes

According to Sorbonne-educated Jean Beaujeu-Garnier (1966: 3), the mission of population geography was to describe 'demographic facts in their present environmental context'. Her influential contribution to the crystallization of population geography unfolded in the opposite fashion to Trewartha's. Between 1956 and 1958 she completed a two-volume portrayal of the world's populations (*Géographie de la Population*) based on statistical data, interviews and participant observation. Then, in the 1966 *Geography of Population* she presented a 'synthesis' of 'the present state of humanity' with 'many question marks, many expressions of doubt, many pointers to further research, which will enable [the researcher] . . . to become aware of the limits and uncertainties of our knowledge and the immense task which confronts us.' Influenced by the *géographie humaine* of Paul Vidal de la Blache, and the writings of Bruhnes and Pokshishevskiy, Beaujeu-Garnier's view from Europe extends Trewartha's in three important directions.

Both authors believed that geography should be focused on the needs of society and that population geography could inform an essentially political agenda. They both held that the study of population geography was best approached inductively from the vantage point of areal differentiation. However, Beaujeu-Garnier cedes a greater role for demographic forces of change. This first difference is apparent by comparing how each author treats migration. Regarded by demographers as the most troublesome element of the balancing equation, mobility merits only a passing mention in Trewartha's agenda. Beaujeu-Garnier divides her treatment of population change (evolution of human societies) into change taking place *in situ* and change arising as a result of displacement. The second element of the 'double evolution' ultimately merits approximately 30 per cent of her discussion of the world population. Trewartha's comparable volume – *A Geography of Population: World Patterns* (1969) – devotes less than 6 per cent of its attention to the discussion of mobility. In addition to change generated as a result of migration, Beaujeu-Garnier draws on Carr-Saunders (1936), and possibly Landry's (1934) work on demographic transitions, to firmly ground her account in demographic thought.

A second difference in emphasis between the two authors is evidenced by Beaujeu-Garnier's quite explicit 'regionalization' of population using occupational structures. While her description of spatial variations in populations begins with an examination of the census-derived construct of race, she describes a three-way classification of societies into those with primitive, in transition and fully developed occupations. The demographic growth of population helps explain the emergence of these occupational types, while racial hierarchies underlie variations in demographic drivers of change of these occupational sectors.

Third, the authors differ on the role of productive relations and economy. Unlike Trewartha, who sought 'explanation' in the spatial relations revealed by population maps, or Bruhnes, who believed culturally produced settlement geographies were conceptually primate, Beaujeu-Garnier locates economy in a way resonant with Pokshishevskiy's notions of work-territorial imperatives. Unlike Pokshishevskiy, she cedes a greater role to demographic structures for mediating the geographies of work in the first place. While she does not go as far as developing a structural model of societal evolution that produces, by necessity, uneven population growth, which leads to uneven development and back to uneven population growth, she does 'connect up' and integrate economy (via occupational structure) in what was a ground-breaking way. By combining her sympathies for *géographie humaine* with demographic insights, Beaujeu-Garnier hypothesized that areal variations in economy were related to both spatial and temporal variations in underlying demography.

A key contribution from Beaujeu-Garnier recognizes that inequality is the 'fundamental basis of the relations between human societies' (353). 'Fundamental inequalities' are discerned on the basis of her regionalization and include both environmental factors like food and natural resources and productive capacity. This is the author (and the field) at its most capacious. By going on to explore how alternate population scenarios could alter and mitigate inequality, Beaujeu-Garnier has successfully linked population back to her overarching theme of the evolution of regions. Places and regions lie at the heart of this dynamic vision of population geography.

Vision 3: A systematic population geography?

Another illuminating vision of the field came from Wilbur Zelinsky. His *Prologue to Population Geography* first appeared in the same year as Beaujeu-Garnier's *Geography of Population*: 1966. Zelinsky's work appeared as a 'goad to thought' and followed from a decade of primary research, which included a 1954 jointly authored article with Trewartha on population issues in Belgian Africa, and a 1962 bibliography of population geography that (allegedly) contained 2588 items! Trained at the University of California Berkeley, Zelinsky also had extensive field experience in the Caribbean and Central America. Zelinsky's approach certainly drew on Sauerian cultural geography, but its sympathies lay more with a Hartshornian view of systematic foci, with population issues firmly connected to the economic world. For Zelinsky, population geographers studied 'the spatial aspects of population in the context of the aggregate nature of places' (1966: 5).

Widely overlooked as a think-piece on the nature of population geography, Zelinsky's almost diminutive *Prologue* has been influential in the field in at least four ways. First, Zelinsky linked population geography to broader social agendas. Whereas Trewartha and Beaujeu-Garnier had focused on the relation of population geography to geography, Zelinsky also located population geography within the science project of the 1960s USA: 'Along with other social scientists the geographer will be called upon to study the problem of population growth and rate of change, and the stresses imposed upon society and habitat by enormous increases in human numbers and appetites – practical and theoretical challenges of a completely new order of magnitude' (Zelinsky 1966: 129). Within the social sciences, disciplinary boundaries were there to be crossed (he remarked that boundaries were administrative conveniences, not barricades), and geography (the study of places) and demography (the study of populations) could and should intersect to examine population change in the context of places.

Second, Zelinsky also recognized that if population geography were to be 'useful', it needed to be 'effective'. He noted that calls for a population geography that had couched the field as a total (unmanageable) geography (i.e. Trewartha) were going largely unheeded. He was also critical of the generality of Beaujeu-Garnier's work on world populations and wished for generalizable principles (which were later contributed by Beaujeu-Garnier, but after Zelinsky's own *Prologue* went to press). For Zelinsky, an effective population geography meant a limited population geography. Although he acknowledged that population issues touch on many anthropological concepts, in practice analysis should be restricted to only those variables available in national censuses (including race, sex and nativity). In the same spirit, Zelinsky provided a concise, if not dense, definition of the field:

> Population geography can be defined accurately as the science that deals with the ways in which the geographic character of places is formed by, and in turn reacts upon, a set of population phenomena that vary within it through both space and time as they follow their own behavioral laws, interacting one with another and with numerous non-demographic phenomena. (Zelinsky 1966: 5)

Third, he believed that culture was a key element in an account of population. Unlike Beaujeu-Garnier, who keyed the economic aspects of areal differentiation, Zelinsky read culture broadly to include the general cultural configuration of the society, social disasters, social and population decisions and the structure of the economy. Citing the post-war baby boom in the USA, he accused demographers of being blind-sided by what was essentially a cultural phenomenon. For Zelinsky, the boundary between population geography and cultural geography was a particularly permeable one. His inclusion of the broad cultural milieu as a starting point for explanation is certainly consistent with his Berkeley Ph.D., where Carl Sauer cast a long shadow.

Fourth, Zelinsky operationalized his vision for population geography in strong methodological terms. He wrote:

> The population geographer is concerned with three distinct and ascending levels of discourse: (1) the simple description of the location of population numbers and characteristics; (2) the explanation of the spatial configurations of these numbers and characteristics; and (3) the geographic analysis of population phenomena (the interrelations among areal differences in population with those in all or certain other elements within the geographic study area). Ideally the geographer would look to the cartographer for maps showing the location of population features, and to the demographer for adequate accounts of their genesis. (Zelinsky 1966: 5–6)

This embrace of demography and its implied empiricism and positivism would render Zelinsky's belief in cultural explanations increasingly problematic, particularly as geography became strongly influenced by social theoretic accounts in the 1970s and after. Thus, while it was clear that population geographers would need to address the cultural context of change, the 'restriction' of methodology demanded an untenable epistemological performance. Indeed, the treatment of culture remains an Achilles heel for the field today.

Perhaps Zelinsky's most profound legacy was to clear the way for the growth of population geography as a systematic area of geographical study. Although Trewartha had acknowledged this, Zelinsky was more emphatic:

> If a regularity or pattern is suspected in certain geographic aspects of population, and if this suspicion survives trial as a working hypothesis to blossom into a full blown theory that seems to fit all known causes, then such a formulation could be extremely valuable, less as an end in itself than as a tool for grasping more fully the geographic character of the inhabited earth and its various regions. It is this understanding ... that is the ultimate purpose of the discipline. (Zelinsky 1966: 24)

Zelinsky's permissiveness on the question of systematic versus general geography, his call for the search of fragments of laws to explain the geography of the world's population, his joint deployment of the concepts of space (the lure of laws) and place (the ultimate context for truth) and his commitment to exchange with other social sciences, especially demography, all provided trenchant insights into how the discipline would grow.

Because geography and demography intersected most decisively in the USA (and, to a lesser extent, in France) at a moment when the discipline required a new set of approaches that could produce scientific knowledge, the concept of space (and spatial variation) was the key axis through which a quantitative and positivist vision for population and geography emerged. Concepts of environment and place appeared more peripheral to the field, although many geographers interested in population questions continued to deploy humanist and structuralist readings of these concepts. The term 'population' was understood as a bona fide and somewhat self-evident object of inquiry that referred to aggregates that could be statistically represented in such a way as to assess underlying mathematical and biomedical theories of change.

By the late 1960s it was apparent that leading Anglo-American geographers considered the spatial organization of populations and their characteristics worthwhile and sufficient elements of study. Demographers grew increasingly interested in geographic approaches. Donald Bogue, a former Princeton demographer, wrote in the *Annals of the Association of American Geographers,*

> there is a need for a strong injection of some principles of economic and human geography into the study of human populations ... such an approach is particularly necessary in order to describe and explain recent population trends ... This development in the field of social statistics should be of particular interest to geographers, and one in which they should feel impelled to assist. (Bogue 1954: 124, 134)

The kind of approach Bogue had in mind decomposed national trends into their regional and subregional components: it focused on population distribution. By putting population trends in their locational context, clues could be found as to 'the factors involved in a particular type of change'. Like-minded population geographers shared Bogue's vision of how their work could illuminate further research agendas.

The early days of this institutional project were taken up with defining the centre and the periphery of the field; debating what was not part of the field; devising a roadmap for the future and informing research agendas; contributing to local, regional, national and international policy questions. Over time, particular research poles grew, debates crystallized, key individuals became increasingly identified as population geographers and selected geography departments built a reputation for promoting population geography and particular approaches to the field (including Ohio State in the USA and Sheffield in the UK).

Research poles, 1950s–1970s

A number of research poles emerged between the 1950s and 1970s to give shape to the new sub-discipline. While not exhaustive, table 3.3 presents four key poles

Table 3.3 Four research poles 1950s–1970s.

Research pole	Indicative topics	Approaches	Views of population
Describing demographic structures in space	Concentration Segregation Density Flows	Empiricist Positivist	Aggregate
Describing demographic change	Balancing equation Spatial demography	Empiricist Positivist	Aggregate
Explaining demographic change in space and time	Transition theory Diffusion Systems theory	Positivist Structuralist	Aggregate Individual
Ecumene and cultural systems	Migration Culture Environment	Empiricist Humanist	Aggregate Individual

and differentiates them on the basis of their substantive foci, indicative topics, typical approaches and treatment of populations. The first pole investigated how population structures appeared on the landscape and was strongly informed by the visions of Trewartha. The second more demographic agenda described the spatial context of demographic changes and looked at where and why populations grew and declined. Zelinsky's vision also coursed through the third pole that jointly considered how populations changed over space and time simultaneously. Elements of the thinking of Beaujeu-Garnier can be glimpsed in research on ecumene and cultural systems.

Describing demographic structures in space

Descriptions of the arrangement of populations in space moved away from the production of population count maps common in the nineteenth century to consider: measures of and depictions of population concentration and dispersion; the relative size and proximity of urban areas within a population; density and overpopulation; the decomposition of population characteristics, including flows of populations. While this was primarily a descriptive and inferential approach, it often led to research on demographic change over space and time (the third pole discussed below). Researchers made use of statistical data from national and inter-national statistical agencies, regional and local authorities, large-scale social surveys and, to a lesser extent, primary field data. Although Zelinsky complained in 1966 that 'many alarming shortages in ... [population] data and methods are likely to persist for some time' (2), Peters and Larkin (1979) later noted widespread availability of data for making long-term projections and conducting scientific inquiry. Indeed, geographers joined demographers in actively shaping the direction and nature of large-scale data collection exercises.

Geographers developed measures of population concentration and dispersal to conduct inductive analyses at different scales. These measures include the Lorenz curve and the Gini coefficient. Progress was made in summarizing the overall spatial structure of a population. Much of this drew inspiration from social physics. Regarding a measure of the average location of a series of points in a two-dimensional space (a centre of gravity or centroid), Stewart (1947) had recognized that the greater the size of the points the stronger the pull they would exert on the location of the average point; conversely, the more peripheral the points, the less the pull they would exert on the location of the centroid. In the traditional calculation of a population centroid, the size of the peripherality force is assumed to be directly associated with the distance of peripherality.

Such measures of centrality facilitated broad-brush comparisons between population structures. The centroid of the US population is still calculated using measures of size and distance between settlements, and has been memorialized on the landscape: the Monroe County courthouse still displays a plaque commemorating the fact that, in 1910, this Indiana county was located at the centre of gravity of the US population. Currently located in Phelps County, Missouri (see figure 3.2), the centroid's own westward and more recent southward drift is an aggregate testament to the shift in America's population as a result of frontier migration, the Great Black Migration, the growth of the Sunbelt and so on. Moreover, this statistical artefact has something of a cult following, with various websites now devoted to accounts of quests made to visit the exact geographic location of the national and state centroids (one such site active in 2004 was www.geocaching.com).

Measures of centrality also informed facility planning. Stewart recognized that the size of the peripherality force could be adjusted to assess more accurately the advantages of a central, accessible location. By assuming that the influence of a point in space is inversely proportional to distance he derived a measure of population potential. The accessibility of each settlement in the USA was calculated by dividing its size by the distance to the centre of gravity. Maps that plot lines connecting settlements of equal population potential (isopleths) reveal national population potential surfaces. Such a surface can be fine-tuned to repre-

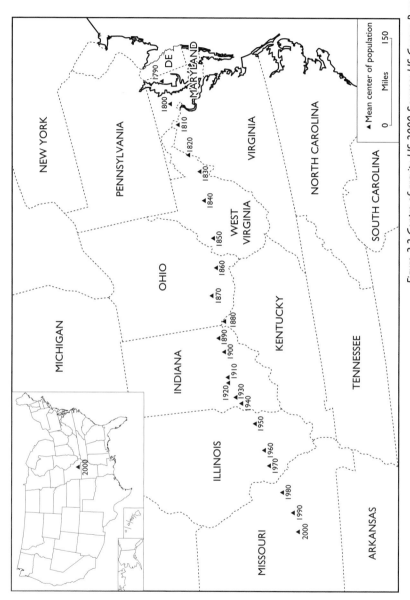

Figure 3.2 Centre of gravity, US 2000. Source: US Census Bureau (2004)

sent particular population characteristics like mean income levels. These maps were used to facilitate marketing and planning decisions and ground analysis of industrial location patterns.

Population geographers developed other measures that summarized the organization of urban places over space. Social physics provided an analogous basis for the rank size rule. While Stewart (1947) groped around for a link between Boltzmann's observation about the distribution of energies among the molecules of gas in thermodynamic equilibrium, and implored readers to be patient while physics offered up a definitive justification (463), many geographers used the notion that a size of a city was equal to the size of the largest city in the system divided by its rank as a kind of norm against which spatial irregularities could be juxtaposed (for example, primacy). In a less well-known empirical relation, Stewart (468–9) proposed that the urban and rural section of population would maintain an equilibrium state over time: for the USA between 1790 and 1940, the total number of urban places (above 2500 people) in any given year could be calculated by multiplying the square of the percentage of the total population living in urban areas by 10,450. Although applications of this relation are hard to find, Stewart's prediction that by the time the USA reached a population size of 260 million the rural population would have all but vanished has proved fairly accurate.

While knowledge about inter-urban population distributions had few practical uses, descriptions of how populations were organized within urban areas were much in demand. In the USA there was widespread interest in the extent to which suburbanization was responsible for altering the balance of political and economic power. Urban population density gradients were used to profile the changes in land use, population size and income levels with increasing distance from the city centre (Edmondston 1975). Analyses of urban unrest drew attention to links between the spatial isolation of ethnic and racial groups and conditions of poverty. Social isolation could be represented statistically using a measure comparing the spatial distribution of one population group against the spatial distribution of a reference population group. The 'index of segregation' became a mainstay for population geography accounts of segregation. In this vein, Harold Rose (1969) examined the ghetto-forming mechanisms in San Francisco and Boston. His account stressed how the demographic phenomenon of the ghetto had changed as it diffused from its cultural hearth (as Louis Wirth had argued earlier, Jewish ghettoes were formed in European cities when Jewish communities were required to live in areas of the city separated by walls or other physical barriers) to the urban context of North America. In the UK context, Pooley (1977) examined how recent immigrants from Ireland were spatially and occupationally segregated in Victorian Liverpool.

More generally, population geographers followed Trewartha's scheme and examined how the physical and socio-economic qualities of population structures varied across space. The most commonly investigated characteristics of population included ageing, race (defined phenotypically, for example Negro (USA), Coloured (South Africa)), ethnicity (defined as largely synonymous with national or regional origin, for example, West Indian) and religion (for example, Irish Roman Catholic). Other elements of Trewartha's attributes were either rarely researched (language, household types), investigated in a more deductive framework (occupational status, unemployment, proportion of working-age population to dependent population) or declared the scope of social geography and anthropogeography and off limits (intelligence, social class, educational status, literacy: Clarke 1965: 101).

How far the results of these descriptive exercises could be taken was a subject of some debate. In her depiction of the distribution of West Indians in Britain, Ceci Peach wrote: 'the geographic variation of a given phenomenon should be a guide to some estimation of its cause. There should be a consistent geographical correlation of supposed case with supposed effect' (1966: 151). However, in 'The changing distribution of the American Negro', John Fraser Hart (1960) warned that 'insofar as possible these patterns are analyzed and interpreted, but they are so complex, both temporally and areally, that no one person could be fully competent to analyze them adequately' (1960: 242). Hart argued that the increased urbanization of the community was driven by three major migration streams: from the south Atlantic states to the urban north-east; from the Delta, Black Belt and the state of Mississippi to urban centres in the Midwest manufacturing belt, including Detroit and Chicago; from the sandy lands of southern Arkansas, northern Louisiana and eastern Texas to Los Angeles, San Francisco and Seattle. While descriptive in tone, this paper's more lasting contribution derives from its implicit recognition of migration channels.

Compton (1976) attempted to link demographic differences between Catholic and Protestant communities in Northern Ireland to sectarian conflict. His analysis keys on religion and asked if differences in population growth rates were linked to an unequal distribution of resources between Roman Catholics and Protestants, and what any differences in population growth rates would mean for the efforts to resolve the conflict. While the Roman Catholic population (as a proportion of the territory) declined from 40.9 per cent to 33.5 per cent between 1861 and 1937, he noted that it has since increased to 36.8 per cent in 1971; overall, and akin to Hart above, he believed that any aggregate spatial trends were masking more complex and informative local pictures.

Another form of disaggregation that sought to describe the spatial arrangement of population focused on flows of populations between two places. Much of this research was inductive and compared actual migration volumes with those predicted on the basis of the gravity model. Stewart's work generated a social physics justification for gravity models that readily provided quantitative bench-mark statements about expected flows of migration (i.e. flow was equal to the product of population sizes divided by their separation). While gravity models provided statistically significant accounts of migration flows (especially when they predicted numbers, not rates), critics again argued that it was difficult to interpret the meaning of 'population size' and 'distance', concepts at the heart of the model (Woods 1982: 152).

In response, considerable efforts were made to extend the classic gravity model. Stouffer (1940) had earlier developed his 'intervening opportunities' hypothesis that stated that migration between two places would be curtailed if an alternative but closer option could be located. This implied that the economic and social properties of distance needed to be considered. Lowry (1966) developed an alternative conception of the drawing power of an area by replacing population size with economic variables. Commenting on the whole agenda, Clayton (1977) questioned the scale at which gravity models should be applied, given the declining significance of distance for many international migrants. In practice, the gravity model framework became co-opted in increasingly sophisticated multivariate analyses of the associations between measures of migration (including net migration (I-E), gross migration (I+E) and migraproduction (I-E/I+E), where immigration = I and out-migration = E). Shaw (1975) and Greenwood (1981) provide helpful summaries of a large volume of accumulated work here.

Research on population distributions over space increasingly sought to connect up pattern with process. These efforts to suggest process often associated population structures in space to variations in absolute site characteristics, that is, environmental correlates. Attempts to capture the relationship between population structure and environment drew on the standard indicators of arithmetic and physiological density and developed new measures, such as the measure of the economic density of population that divided size by a measure of productivity (or latent productivity). The merit of this for comparing populations across production systems was questioned (Clarke 1965). In more urbanized contexts, measures of persons per room, rooms per house and persons per household were thought to reveal more appropriate insights into the underlying concept of overcrowding.

Clarke (1965) provided a general summary of how elements of the physical environment shape the location and potential for growth of human settlements and populations (see table 3.4 below). He stressed that no one factor should be isolated or given causal significance for population outcomes. Clarke believed environmental factors imposed constraints and challenges for development, but not absolute limitations. He argued that the influence of environmental factors would be most likely seen in population distributions, although the presence of certain diseases (for example, the low protein intake condition of kwashiorkor) could increase the incidence of stillborn births in a population, and ecological crises (large-scale famine) could prompt emigration (for example, Irish emigration in the 1840s as a consequence of the potato famine).

While lists of environmental correlates could draw attention to processual links, the 'limits to growth' model attempted to specify how environmental factors like resource depletion impacted upon population growth. This statistical model connected fertility and mortality, agricultural production, industrial production, natural resources and pollution and simulated the behaviour of these variables over time (up to 100 years) and space (world level) (Meadows et al. 1972). The standard run foretold of overshoot and 'predicted' that population decline from increased death rates would follow from increased pollution levels. The model reignited the debate between neo-Malthusians and the *laissez-faire* or boomster

Table 3.4 Environmental attributes and population distribution. Adapted from: Clarke (1965: 16–25)

Continentality
Insularity
Low altitude
Mountain slopes
Valley locations
Piedmont lands (borders between dissimilar environments)
Rivers
Climate
Soil types
Soil erosion
Biotic factors (plant and animal resources)
Endemic disease
Mineral and energy resources

camps. A number of criticisms of the approach emerged: many of the relationships in the model are unknown and untested; social, cultural and political factors are underplayed; relationships are specified at the wrong spatial scale; the language of the model lends it spurious credence.

Analyses of environmental factors turned to the concept of overpopulation to formalize the relationship between environment, resources and population. For many neo-Marxists, rather than a trigger of large-scale famines and problems, uneven population growth was a symptom of structural inequalities in industrial capitalism. Harvey (1974) went on to problematize the ideological and potentially divisive designation of terms like overpopulation by linking its designation to a broader critique of how wealth (i.e. economic power) circulated in society. Marx had argued that it was the nature of historically different production systems (including feudalism, mercantilism, capitalism and socialism) that defined population issues. In capitalist societies, the unequal standing of the working classes was not a consequence of their own making (by being too many), but a necessary feature of the capitalist production system. It was in the ruling classes' interests to oversupply labour in order to keep wage costs down. Population solutions not only missed the mark but, by blaming the victim, further obscured the true nature of society. In this structuralist research, the concept of population is exposed as a label that reflects power relations, and a device through which knowledge could be deployed to control the destiny of (exert power over) others.

Describing demographic change

Addressing the question of why and how populations grew and declined was a key demographic agenda that the new field of population geography informed by describing the spatial context of population change.

Overall population growth

Accounts of the growth in the size of different world regions at different epochs in time suggested that the conventional exponential world population growth curve could be better represented as a series of three growth cycles, i.e. the primary, medieval and modernization cycles. Growth stalled at the end of each cycle as a population reached and exceeded its carrying capacity. It was generally recognized that a more thorough examination of the demographic components of growth – that is fertility, mortality and migration – would not only yield up insights about overall growth trends, but would also prove their importance in their own right. Overall growth was decomposed into that component arising from natural increase (the excess of births over deaths) and that arising from new migration (the balancing equation).

Fertility and mortality

Mapping regional and local variations in fertility patterns revealed differentials based on: age composition; nuptuality (marriage patterns); urban/rural residence; religion; occupational class structure; immigrant composition; and level of economic development. However, as Clarke (1965: 110) noted, different regions with similar risk factors (for example, the same level of development) may exhibit contrasting fertility regimes, suggesting that such regional decomposition was the first of several steps in uncovering cause and effect. Criticisms that reading associations from areal evidence could suffer from the ecological fallacy (relationships that appear at one scale may not appear at other scales) also limited this approach.

Likewise, work on the geography of mortality revealed how, at the regional scale, a series of strong differentials operated. These included: age-sex composition; ethnic composition; urban-rural residence; occupational structure; class; and marriage rates. Of course, this list grows when the range of spatial scales is expanded to include local variations and those seen across developing and developed societies (Jones 1981). In noting that 'there can be no rules about the (urban-rural) differential', Clarke (1965: 118) further disaggregated mortality into its leading causes and examined spatial variations among these causes of death. He is clear that such a focus on cause of death, including the question of disease, involved a more widespread analysis of health and morbidity which, as it was the preserve of medical geography, is an area where 'we must avoid major encroachment' (119). The strength of this sub-disciplinary boundary was also evident in Murray's 'The geography of death in England and Wales'. While regional mapping could 'suggest some possible reasons for the areal differences in mortality' (Murray 1962: 130), such a tactic formed the 'special contribution' for the emerging specialty of medical geography (Murray 1967: 314). Demographers had no such compunctions and did not partition fertility and mortality.

Demographers were no strangers to the idea that breaking down populations into sub-national components, or aggregating national populations into broader macro-regions, could help suggest correlates of population change. Thompson (1929) used the latter tactic to identify clusters of countries with similar experiences of fertility and mortality change during the nineteenth and early twentieth centuries. He described three such macro-regions. Countries of northwestern Europe and those 'settled' by emigrants from this region shared low birth and death rates; countries of south and eastern Europe had low death rates but high, although declining, birth rates; countries in many parts of Africa, Asia and Latin America had high fertility and mortality rates. By grouping like countries he conjectured that mortality and fertility rates decreased in the presence of agricultural improvements, industrialization, urbanization and improved sanitation. Similar work by Landry (1934) and Carr-Saunders (1936) in identifying demographic regions would be instrumental in Notestein's (1945) more formal proposition that population underwent a systematic 'demographic transition': a statement that was to drive much subsequent deductive research in population geography and demography (see below).

Migration

Explorations of migration differentials over space became a significant focus of work. The notion of migration fields was used to represent flows of migrants and investigate selectivity. Unlike gravity frameworks, information fields focused on individuals, and drew on the work of Swedish geographer Torsten Hagerstrand on patterns of diffusion. Using probability theory, a simulated information field was drawn to represent the choices of destinations available to an individual. Each individual's information field was represented by a grid and each cell in the grid contained a probability value that represented how likely the individual was to move to that location. Cell probabilities could be adjusted to reflect different behavioural assumptions (for example, imperfect information, barriers and the feedback effect of recent experience). Individual information fields could be aggregated to form a community or group surface.

Migration information fields were used to explore migration selectivity using 'what if' scenarios. Morrill (1965) designed a conditional forecasting model that wrote the probability of a potential mover settling in any city block as a gravity (distance decay) function, and used the technique to explore the link between marriage and migration in Cleveland, Ohio, Cedar Rapids, Iowa, Seattle, Washington, Asby (Sweden) and Kagawa (Japan). Markov and semi-Markov models also enabled researchers to link together micro- and macro-models of migration.

More commonly, research compared spatial variations in migration with spatial variations in underlying factors. National- and regional-scale research reported that areas with high proportions of the following would, all else being equal, generate more outmigrants: young people; males (if movement was international, females if movement was local); those with educational credentials (especially for regional migration); marital status (single men observed to be the most likely to move internationally); certain occupational types (especially professionals moving regionally within the developed world); and unemployed persons (although Jones (1981: 224) notes that the unemployed themselves may not be moving, but rather professionals and educated workers keen to leave an area experiencing down-turn). Migration selectivity also operated as a result of the differential pull that some locations exerted upon groups. Many elderly migrants sought amenity-rich regions, often coastal; ethnic groups targeted destinations with established ethnic communities. At an intra-urban scale, Pooley (1979) used the diary of one Liverpool resident, David Brindley, to map his moves between 1882 and 1890. Map evidence confirmed that most residential moves were made within areas known well to the migrant.

Age-sex distributions

A population's age and sex characteristics represent a crucial link between recent demographic events and the likely demographic future of the area. Because age-sex structure links the past, present and future so clearly, demographers developed a sophisticated tool kit for interpreting what, at first sight, appears a simple way of describing populations. Graphically, age-sex pyramids provide 'stills' of dynamic populations, and an initial entrée in to understanding how populations work demographically. Pyramids with concave sides and a tapering apex depict rapidly growing populations with high fertility rates and many people under the age of 15. A pyramid with relatively straight sides describes a stationary population with low fertility rates that have not changed for at least two generations. A beehive-shaped pyramid, with a tapering base, depicts a population currently experiencing declines in fertility. Because migration is age selective, pyramids also stand testament to recent in- and out-migration events, especially when con-structed at the regional and local level. For example, Kosiński (1970) overlaid the 1950 pyramids of Polish voivodships on a choropleth map of natural increase (figure 3.3). The result depicted both the link between composition and growth, and the way in which the post-war resettlement of the western and northern territories had already translated into higher in-migration and fertility levels.

At a national scale, the age structure of a country is most strongly determined by its recent fertility past, with countries showing a high proportion of persons above age 65 likely to have experienced a sustained period of low fertility. However, at regional and local levels, migration may play a decisive role in increas-ing births. Figure 3.3 shows this for in-migrants to western Poland, who were young adults starting families. Retirement migration can also increase the share of elderly residents in local areas. Following this logic of selective migration and fertility, rural areas would be expected to have fewer young people and more old people. Given this demographic expectation, Franklin (1958) attributed the more youthful than expected population structure of many New Zealand North Island rural areas to the presence of Maori communities, a population with high fertility levels.

The overall proportion of males to females in a population (sex ratio) and the proportion at any given age is related to three factors. First, biology determines

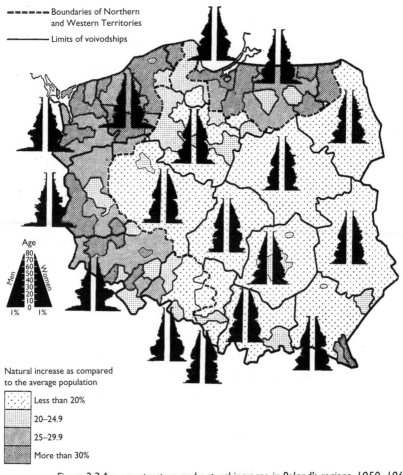

Figure 3.3 Age-sex structure and natural increase in Poland's regions, 1950–1960.
Source: *Kosiński (1970: 49)*

that, for every 100 female foetuses there are 105 male foetuses. Departures from this value of 105 in sex ratios at birth may indicate sex-selective terminations, such as was reported in China during the late 1970s. Countries with a high fertility rate and more youthful population are likely to contain more males than females, all else being equal. However, this is conditioned by the strong influence of sex-selective mortality. While the practice of female infanticide further increases the proportion of males to females in a population, it is generally the case that from young adulthood male mortality exceeds female mortality at every age. This is often linked to the sexual division of labour in society, with men believed to perform tasks more likely to result in poor health and mortality.

Sex ratios are also affected by the sex-selective nature of migration. Oil-rich Gulf states recorded increasing sex ratios during the 1970s as a result of in-migration, while the sex ratio of the Witwatersrand area near Johannesburg of 17 women per 100 men reflected the male-dominated mining migration that was part of the apartheid logic. Most generally, research showed that division of labour, migration and attitudes towards gender all affect the exact age at which the birth-derived preponderance of males switches to an excess of females. Kosiński (1970: 50) estimated that this age of equalization was around 30 years for most European countries.

Spatial demography

It was spatial demography that most clearly articulated the demographic inter-dependencies between fertility, mortality, migration and population composition. In positioning such scholarship at the intersection of demography and population geography, Woods (1984: 44) noted the lack of attention to space and migration by the former, and the 'surprisingly unsophisticated' tools of the latter. Spatial demography was to be a project characterized by the inclusion of space in demographic concepts and models, and the application of geographic probabilistic models and general systems theory to population questions. Practitioners were to provide useful estimates and forecasts of populations where data was either missing or unreliable. Research also developed a series of normative models against which real-world phenomena could be matched and further questions postulated.

Population geographers turned to life tables to supplement population data. These life tables used stable population theory from demography to describe equilibrium characteristics of 'model' population types. For example, life tables suggested that 'stationary populations' with constant fertility rates and equal and constant mortality rates (and zero net migration) would contain a predictable number of people in each age cohort, l_x. Thus, data on composition could be linked to long-term fertility and mortality regimes. More generally, 'stable populations' had constant but unequal fertility and mortality rates (i.e. they were growing or declining) and values of that could be derived from model life tables.

Such life tables were used by Wrigley and Schofield (1981) to derive mortality and fertility indices and population counts back to 1541 from baptism and burial data. Their analyses of the recovered records suggested that the timing of a first marriage was used as a behavioural strategy by couples to improve their long-term income prospects. Elsewhere, Woods (1982: 72–85) and Carvalho (1974) used life tables to investigate regional conditions in India and Brazil respectively, again in the absence of suitable data.

Integrating *migration* into accounts of sub-national (regional) populations emerged as a key challenge for research on multi-regional demographic systems (Rees and Convey 1984). In regional demographic accounting use is made of the full balancing equation by variously obtaining and estimating the values for births, deaths and net migrations of regions within a larger territory. Crucially, the technique also considers the natural increase of the emigrating and immigrating population to obtain a complete picture of demographic events across space and over a fixed time period. In a French example illustrated by Rees and Convey (1984), rows refer to the spatio-demographic starting positions in 1968 and columns refer to spatio-demographic ending positions in 1975 (see figure 3.4). Thus, 365,600 people resident in the Gard in 1968 remained there (alive!) in 1975 (cell 8); a further 69,300 had survived and moved regionally within France (cell 2); and 6,100 had emigrated (cell 4). In addition, 87,000 people alive in 1968 had moved in to the Gard region, but 3,500 of these had died some time between 1968 and 1975. As figure 3.4 shows, while the technique relies on data from vital statistics, emigration statistics and censuses, it is able to generate internal and logically consistent estimates of all the required elements. The uses of this framework again extend to benchmarking reality against expected levels (for example, migrant mortality) and forecasting future regional demographic structures by making assumptions about the continuation of transition probabilities. This was a period of considerable methodological advances. But it was also a period when calls were made for theoretical development, as illustrated by the progress made at the International Institute for Applied Systems Analysis in Austria in research on entropy (Nijkamp 1976).

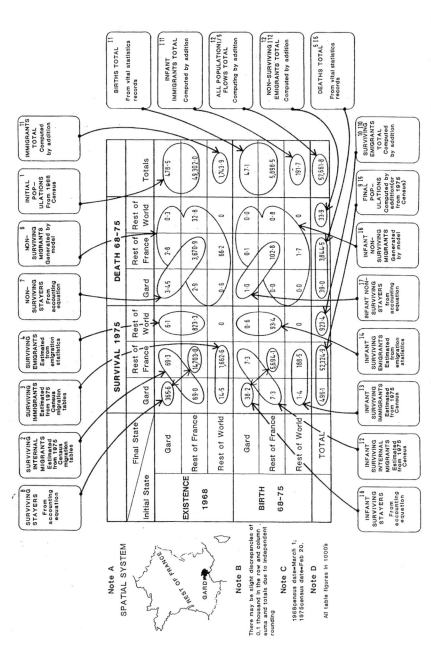

Figure 3.4 Regional demographic accounting matrix. Source: Rees and Convey (1984: 52)

Explaining demographic change in space and time

Demographic transition

Research on the demographic transition best exemplified the field's growing interest in explanation. Princeton demographer Frank Notestein formalized the inductive contributions of Thompson (1929) and Landry (1934) into a series of testable propositions about the general relationship between modernization and population growth. In what became known as the demographic transition model, Notestein observed (1945):

- countries make an orderly transition from a period of high mortality and fertility to a period of high fertility and low mortality to a period of low mortality and fertility;

- the transition from high to low mortality is accompanied by improvements in the material well-being of the population, better food supply, access to improved sanitation and better health that are part of industrialization;

- the transition from high to low fertility follows the mortality transition and is accompanied by increased urbanization and the rise of a more secular and individualistic way of life that encourages the use of rational (non-traditional) means of fertility control.

Population geography contributed to the development of this framework in at least five ways. First, many comparative case studies that described the fertility-mortality conditions of countries and macro-regions at different moments in their history supported the implied idea that over time, populations went from low growth to high growth to conditions of low or no growth. Evidence accrued globally (Trewartha 1969) and for Latin America, Africa and Asia (Stolnitz 1965). Importantly, the universality of this generalization was questioned by Zdenik Pavlík (1964), who proposed three sets of transition: a classic 'English' type identified by Notestein; a 'French' type with near simultaneous declines in fertility and mortality; and a 'Japanese' type, where mortality declines are followed by fertility upturns and, over time, fertility declines. Other case study work to similarly question the sequence of the fertility transition included Carvalho (1974) in Brazil and Hicks (1974) in Mexico. The model's implied patterns of lower fertility in urban areas than rural areas has been widely supported in work on developing countries (Abu-Lughod 1964).

Second, a considerable body of literature examined how fertility transitions unfolded over space. While many demographers constructed explanations based on assumptions of individual rationality found in neoclassical economics (including the rising costs of children in industrial society and the role of relative deprivation, Easterlin 1968), geographic accounts emphasized the importance of: social regulation and marriage; modes of production; culture; and the role of women. Hajnal (1965) reported that west of a line drawn between St Petersburg and Trieste, fertility had declined in agrarian, pre-industrial societies due to late marriage and celibacy. Coale (1969) produced maps of fertility conditions, rates of nuptuality and marital fertility for 700 areas of Europe in 1900 to investigate how marriage was linked to the onset of fertility decline at this time.

Van de Walle's (1978) study of declining French fertility in 1831, 1866 and 1901 used regional disaggregation to investigate why some French *départements* (for example, in Normandy) experienced declining fertility before others (for example, in Brittany). He linked this to variations in the degree of rurality, nuptuality rates and fertility rates inside marriage. By restricting his analysis to rural *départements* and taking account of changes in nuptuality and marital fertility he showed that overall fertility came down first in those areas with low levels of marital fertility. It was only once this rate had declined that nuptuality increased but, crucially, it did not increase to levels high enough to offset the effect of declining marital fertility. Compton (1976) similarly reported that the Roman Catholic community of Northern Ireland experienced a falling fertility rate between 1961 and 1971 because the affect of marital fertility was stronger than that of rising nuptuality. However, analysing fertility changes in the counties and boroughs of the Republic of Ireland between 1926 and 1971, Coward (1978) found that the (negative) contribution to overall fertility levels from declines in marital fertility had been cancelled out by the (positive) contribution from increasing nuptuality, as a result of which fertility increased.

Third, geographers introduced diffusion insights into discussions of fertility change over space and time. The rapidity with which fertility reductions spread from one area to another within a country contrasted in many cases with a much slower pace of modernization and led scholars of the demographic transition to argue that fertility decline should be viewed more of an innovation than an adaptation to changing conditions: 'birth control behaviour is contagious and the fertility behaviour of a population is not the simple aggregate of isolated individual decisions, but the end product of complex social interactions' (Carlson 1966). Diffusion processes were thought to unfold in various ways across space and time (for example, hierarchically, contagiously) and this led to the generation of hypotheses about the role of media, publicity about birth control programmes and the authority and legitimacy given to information through local social networks. Hofstee (1968) linked widespread regional variations in Dutch fertility to distance from the urban source regions of new ideas about family planning. However, Jones (1971) uncovered great uniformity in the decline of marital fertility in 1880s Australia and New Zealand and discounted diffusion processes. Blaikie (1975) argued that caste, literacy rates and family size were more important determinants of fertility reductions in Bihar, India than any neighbourhood affect arising from the diffusion of birth control information.

Scholars of fertility transition in the pre-capitalist societies of sub-Saharan Africa highlighted the roles of culture. John Caldwell (1976) dissented from the proposition that fertility declines followed from the onset of urbanization and modernization. He argued that the concept of modernization stands in for the notion of rationality, which is inherently society-specific. He asked, how does the spread of western-style rationalism – with its normative view of accumulating nuclear families, secularization, mass education, environmental management and control and small family size norms – affect fertility? The cultural and social components of modernization were more precisely articulated by Kirk (1971), who showed that grouping countries on the basis of cultural characteristics (notably, religion) produced a regionalization closer to the patterns of fertility decline than an aggregation based on modernization. The use of this 'cultural region' technique did not satisfy Freedman (1979), who observed that culture, including language and religion, was noticeably absent from theoretical accounts.

Limited work began to explore the specific experiences of groups of the population pertaining to fertility. Commensurate with the economic slant of much demographic theory, research examined how the entrance of women into paid labour led to changing patterns of fertility. Hawthorn's (1978) expansive analysis of fertility differences between India, China and Taiwan includes references to the higher rates of female labour force participation in the latter two countries as a partial explanation for their lower fertility regimes. In a more localized study, Haines (1977) found that the populations in mining towns experienced fertility spikes that coincided with the onset of mine production. He linked the pattern of earlier marriage and higher marital fertility rates to the precariousness of household income, which was related both to the lack of employment opportunities for women in these towns and to the high mortality rates among miners and the consequent need to produce working sons.

Other work adopted a political economy view of fertility change. According to Tilly (1978), the onset of fertility decline in rural eastern Europe that appeared to coincide with later marriages may have been tied more closely to the prominence of rural collectives, and the mode of production more generally. Residents of these large estates held no private land, which reduced the desire to add children to guarantee inheritance. Also investigating the role of mode of production, Grigg (1980) reported Swedish fertility decline prior to the onset of industrialization; however, McGinnis (1977) confirmed that Canadian fertility had fallen after the hypothesized increase in agricultural production. Meillassoux (1972) emphasized the role of the state in affecting production through land ownership and the importance of the tribal/kin/family group as the basic unit of production. In such systems the objective was 'reproduction of life as a pre-condition for production' and society as an 'integrated, economic, social, and demographic system [that ensures] the vital needs of the members – productive and non-productive' (Meillassoux 1972: 100, quoted in Woods 1982: 178). The implications of such a view for fertility were twofold. First, in the short-term, fertility will reach a 'natural' level determined by the sustainability of the group. Second, this level of fertility is likely to increase as and when productive opportunities appear. The fertility spikes observed when mercantile and industrial societies begin to touch agrarian modes of production offers circumstantial evidence of the latter.

A fourth set of contributions to demographic transition theory focused on the involvement of states. Some research flowed from Omran's work on the epidemiological transition which linked mortality declines to the role of state institutions, including the Public Health Department and Water Boards in New York. Tsui and Bogue (1978) examined the family planning provisions of 89 less developed countries to assess the efficacy of family planning programmes for reducing fertility. One generalization to emerge from such case study research was that the influence of this form of state provision was felt most strongly in countries with middle levels of economic development.

Perhaps the most widely circulated contribution to the development of transition theory was Zelinsky's hypothesis of the mobility transition. As this framework impacted migration scholarship more than transition theory, it is discussed below.

Migration

Population geographers constructed their explanations of migration by either treating migrants in the aggregate or by focusing on individual migrant behaviours.

Aggregate approaches included Zelinsky's geographic version of the demographic transition model, systems approaches and cross-sectional econometric modelling. Critiques of these macro-level accounts later fuelled the rapid development of micro-level approaches (cf. Peterson 1958).

For Wilbur Zelinsky: 'the hypothesis of the mobility transition can be expressed most succinctly as follows: there are definite, patterned regularities in the growth of personal mobility through space-time during recent history, and these regularities comprise an essential component of the modernization process' (Zelinsky 1971: 221–2). This statement implied the following relationships:

- mobility involved both spatial and social movement, even though social scientific measures meant the former rather than the latter was the focus of inquiry;

- social mobility may be substituted for spatial mobility;

- modernization accompanies a rise in the levels of (socio-spatial) mobility in society;

- vital transitions (i.e. the mortality and fertility transitions) trigger mobility transitions;

- orderly changes occur in mobility function; frequency; duration; periodicity; distance; routing; categories of migrants; classes of origins and destinations;

- contagious diffusion processes propagate mobility conditions outwards from successful growth points;

- the diffusion process gathers pace over time and is irreversible.

In essence, Zelinsky brought a diffusionist perspective to the treatment of migration (see figure 3.5).

Although he saw his 1971 'reconnaissance voyage' as both deductive and inductive, he was already able to draw upon significant – even if somewhat disparate – research to support his framework. Moreover, his framework stimulated and/or influenced the direction of other research agendas. Thus Zelinsky suggested that a residential transition would be partly driven by the systematic rise of rural to urban migration. However, in the advanced (phase IV) society, high levels of urbanization are now maintained by migration, through a balancing out of increased rates of circulation, high levels of inter-urban migration and low levels of rural-urban

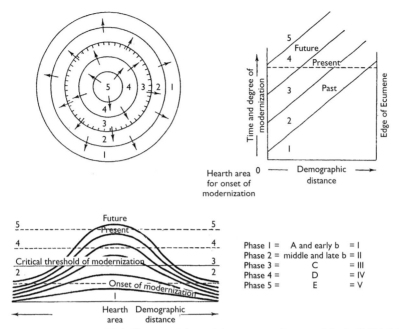

Figure 3.5 *Diffusion and the mobility transition.* Source: *Zelinsky (1971: 228)*

migration. Rowland (1979) tested this hypothesis by analysing the long-term changes in the settlement system in Australia, and concluded that while *gross* rates of residential mobility were high, the settlement pattern maintained itself in a state of dynamic equilibrium because *net* rates of internal migration were modest.

Zelinsky admitted that, as regards the hierarchical diffusion of the mobility condition from colonial cores to the 'advanced outposts' of the colonies and inwards into the colonial holdings, 'the preconditions for the consummation of this process are not at all clear' (243). The principle does resonate, at a global scale, with the hypothesized role of contemporary world cities as nodes of international skilled migration and circulation.

Zelinsky went on to argue that fertility declines in rural areas of the USA followed or accompanied the rise in rural-urban migration between 1880 and 1930. At a later stage in modernization (i.e. 1940–60) any fertility-mobility association diminished. This proposition found support in Friedlander's analysis of France, Sweden and England and Wales. Drawing on Kingsley Davis's aspatial multiphasic demographic response theory, Friedlander (1969) linked fertility and mobility transitions to rural population pressure and found that fertility declined as the number of opportunities for mobility increased.

According to the mobility transition, circulation migration arose during the later stages of modernization and alongside high but stable levels of residential mobility, low fertility, low emigration and rising levels of economically motivated inter-urban migration (243). Neo-Marxist scholars focused on how colonial contact and the penetration of the wage labour norm sparked circular mobility (Meillassoux 1972). This complemented the significant body of ethnographic evidence which already suggested that circulation strategies were cross-cultural phenomena that pre- and post-dated particular phases of economic or political economic organization (Mitchell 1959; Chapman 1978: 563). While Zelinsky's mobility hypothesis reflected the prevailing conception of migration and circulation as distinct mobility strategies, a growing number of authors implied that all socio-spatial mobility had the potential to be circulatory when space and time were conceptualized jointly.

The formal laws of general systems theory provided another means for conceptualizing changes in aggregate patterns of migration. Noting a general dearth of analytical work on rural to urban migration in the part of the world that was experiencing the consequences of this flow most poignantly, under-developed countries, Mabogunje (1970) argued that general systems theory 'has the fundamental advantage of providing a conceptual framework within which a whole range of questions relevant to an understanding of the structure and operation of other systems can be asked' (2). His 'verbal analysis' (see figure 3.6) linked migration in space and time by recognizing positive feedback channels between urban areas and potential migrants. It was also highly suggestive of the kin, village and political institutional contexts through which migration (and of course the current non-migration of potential migrants) was mediated. He concluded (16): 'one of the major attractions of this approach is that it enables a consideration of rural-urban migration as no longer a linear ... cause-effect movement, but as a circular, interdependent, progressively complex, and self-modifying system'. The conceptual legacy of this framework continues to cast a long and strong shadow.

Descriptive and analytical accounts of associations between migration and areal characteristics distinguished between migration at different spatial and temporal scales. International studies addressed migrant workers and the economic impacts of migrants in Europe, migrant workers in the Middle East and mobility practices in Africa, including seasonal and circulation migration, forced migration and return international migration (King 1976). Mitchell (1959) linked circulation migration in south-central Africa to the interplay of centrifugal (the economic pull forces of

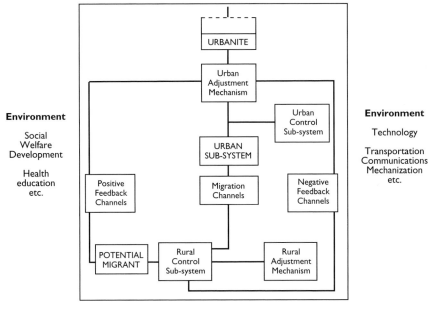

Environment

Economic Conditions – Wages, Prices, Consumer
Preferences, Degress of Commercialization
and Industrial Development

Figure 3.6 Migration system. Source: *Mabogunje (1970: 3)*

urban employment opportunities) and centrepetal (the sociocultural pull forces of residence in rural, small group society) forces.

Research also extended the descriptive insights of gravity models to examine how aggregate migration responded to the characteristics of urban areas and distance. Neoclassical economic theory defined migration as a factor of production that responded to rural pushes and urban pulls and conjectured that migration flows connected low wage areas (including those where mechanization had displaced agricultural workers and created unemployment) and high wage areas. The growing availability of regionally disaggregated statistical measures and popularity of multivariate regression techniques supported a large volume of empirical tests of the framework in industrialized economies (Shaw 1975) and in developing areas. Other economic and non-economic explanatory variables were incorporated, although many were used inductively without strong a priori theoretical justification. For example, Cebula's (1975) analysis of US internal migration broadened to consider race, age and climate measures.

More critical attention began to be paid to differences in the behaviour of migrant groups, as illustrated by the exchange between Greenwood and Ladman (1978) and Rengert (1981). Greenwood and Ladman conducted a standard multi-variate analysis of inter-regional migration in Mexico between 1960 and 1970. While they expected fewer out-migrants to come from high-income states, they found the reverse (and in so doing corroborated prior research in the area). They explained this apparent anomaly as follows: 'Migration flows in Mexico are predominantly from rural to urban areas ... earnings and educational levels of the residents of many parts of rural Mexico may be so low that the persons simply do not possess the skills required for employment in urban areas. Such persons are likely to have little information ...' (23). As Rengert (1981) went on to discuss, this implied that economic logic only applied above a threshold education (income) level, something the rural Mexicans in Greenwood and Ladman's study were yet to attain.

Rengert offered an alternative interpretation: 'Greenwood and Ladman miss asking a significant question: most of the migrants to urban areas in Mexico, as in most other Latin American countries, are female. Because of labor expectations ... few of them will be expecting lifetime paid employment in urban destinations' (1981: 16). Monk (1981) followed this line of thinking and found that male and female migrants on Puerto Rico did indeed move for different reasons and under quite different expectations. Work linking gender and migration would form a key area of growth for population geographers.

While feminist approaches began to explore the role of women in migration, political economy perspectives further elaborated on the role of colonial and dependency relations in creating and perpetuating labour migration. Some applied neo-Marxist concepts of class and labour exploitation to describe the historic and geographic conditions under which migration arose (Amin 1974). Geographers contributed a spatial awareness to accounts otherwise known for their structural determinism. Reviewing the case of labour migration in sub-Saharan Africa, Swindell (1979: 248) noted that it was a 'colonial invention created through the penetration of the domestic modes of production by the external money economies dependent on the metropole.' Riddell (1981) argued that across sub-Saharan Africa there were wide variations in how labour migration practices had evolved under different systems of colonial rule. Colonial practices generally sought to manipulate the size and location of native labour forces through restructuring the space economy and a series of direct coercive measures; West African migration had been more affected by the former, while migration within southern Africa was more obviously the product of coercive measures, including land alienation, legal restrictions and the Chibaro forced labour system. Other advocates of this political economy perspective on labour migration described migrant labour in Europe (Castles and Kosack 1973). Yet despite the growing appreciation of spatial variations in colonial, neocolonial and ultimately dependency relations, there was still a tendency to downplay the sheer diversity of mobility responses.

Gazing back over this period of research, Abu-Lughod (1975: 202) reflected that

> the monolithic category called migrant has had to be broken down into a complex array of subtypes based on the variety of forces operating to stimulate the move, upon the periodicity and degree of permanent commitment related to the move, and upon the location of migrants within the social structures of both sending and recipient units.

However, while decomposition had enabled researchers to 'unhitch' their ideas from blinding alliances to overly structural frameworks (i.e. modernization), it had come at a price possibly too high for more deductively oriented thinkers: 'among the greatest faults of which we are guilty in migration research is being locked in to some kinds of question related to the same concepts of migration that were developed years ago for a particular setting at a particular time' (Goldstein 1976: 428).

Against this sentiment, individual-centred accounts of migration developed rapidly in the 1970s. Neoclassical economic theory had a profound effect on the development of migration theory at the individual and household/family scale. By conceptualizing migration as an investment in human capital (like studying for a college degree: both cost in the short term but should yield offsetting long-term benefits) and employing random utility theory, Larry Sjaastad (1962) expressed the likelihood of an individual moving as a statistical function of theoretically derived explanatory variables together with an error term. The whole framework was extremely flexible and, appearing at about the same time as large-scale individual-level data sets became available, supported a rapidly burgeoning literature. In addition to testing the effects of economically derived variables, including wage levels, educational levels, age and attachment to the labour force upon the probability of migration, the importance of distance for individual migrants could be further explored. Harris and Todaro (1970) extended this logic to focus not on actual economic conditions but upon an individual's expectation of conditions at an unknown destination. Their ground-breaking approach used a simple two-region sub-Saharan African context and stimulated work in a number of spatial contexts. Eicher and Byerlee (1972) extended the two-sector model to better reflect African conditions; their sectors represented rural agricultural sectors; rural non-farm sectors; urban informal sectors; and urban formal sectors.

Further theoretical development of the individual human capital model resulted from Jacob Mincer's (1978) work on family migration. Mincer argued that, among families, migration would occur in the direction of expected total family income. In one-earner families this accorded with Sjaastad's model, but in the increasingly common two-earner family it was the partner with the greatest potential income who effectively determined migration. As men had historically held better paying jobs, Mincer's model implied that many married working wives would be 'tied' movers, and thus not able to accrue the kinds of returns to migration predicted by existing models. Numerous investigations of this 'wife's sacrifice' thesis would follow (see chapter four).

While few researchers questioned the economic basis for much migration, there was a growing sense that crude economic determinism did not apply to all population groups in all places and that among individuals a wide variety of motivations for movement would be discerned. Rossi's pioneering *Why Families Move*, published in 1955, revealed that among Philadelphia residents at least, life-cycle considerations like leaving home, getting married, getting divorced, having children and retiring were frequently cited as motivation for migration. Lansing and Mueller (1967) reported that 24 per cent of those who had moved in the previous five years were motivated by 'family' reasons.

In a radical downscaling manoeuvre, Everett Lee (1966) combined elements of Ravenstein's aggregate laws of migration (for example, the economic motivation of much migration, the tendency of most moves to be short-distance ones) with these more recent findings on life-cycle factors to outline the conditions under which an individual may be minded to move. This decision centred on the migrants' assessment of attracting, repelling and neutral factors at both the current origin and the potential destination, and their assessment of 'intervening opportunities', a set of financial and psychic (disruption) costs associated with making the move. He recognized that the individual personality would explain why, when faced with identical sets of opportunities, two different individuals might react differently.

The same core concept – that places had sets of characteristics (attributes) that would be of different importance to different individuals – lay at the heart of Julian Wolpert's notion of place utility (1965, 1966). This was defined as the difference between the opportunities/resources on offer to the household at the current location and the needs of the households. If the latter exceeded the former, as might occur upon retirement, when proximity to employment becomes less important than proximity to friends and family, the current location would have a low place utility. Households judged their current place utility against that for other known locations (i.e. their action space). What this behavioural sequence suggested to Wolpert was the importance of identifying and understanding the motivation of both movers and stayers. A lasting contribution was this notion of a mover-stayer continuum.

Brown and Moore's (1970) extension to residential mobility focused on two interdependent decisions: a decision to move and a decision about where to move. The authors identified a series of 'stressors' that could trigger a decision to move: 'encroachment and spread of residential and commercial blight in the household's neighbourhood; a change in the racial or ethnic composition of the neighbourhood; relocation of industrial sites; ... change in the accessibility of neighbourhoods as a result of change in transportation technology' (3). At the household scale, stressors included change in occupation, income, class, family size, employment site, marital state and more general advancement in life stage. The subsequent decision of where to relocate was contingent upon information. While Brown and Moore assumed that search intensity was some function of distance decay from the current residence, their view of how searches unfold over time was less sophisticated than, for example, Myers et al. (1967), whose 'axiom of cumulative inertia' clearly linked increased search time to reduced propensity to relocate (i.e. a specific case of what would later be labelled duration dependence).

Ecumene and cultural systems

Drawing on Beaujeu-Garnier's commitment to regional synthesis, a number of rather isolated pieces of scholarship examined how places and regions developed distinctive population geographies. This work was informed by two key concepts: ecumene and cultural systems. Referring to the portion of land that is permanently inhabited, the concept of the ecumene drew attention to the reasons why land was settled and how it was used to support livelihoods. For Trewartha (1969) and others, the ecumene was a crucial concept as it connected together the environmental/ecological and economic/productive contexts of populations, and thus avoided (conceptually) the need to revert to overly deterministic accounts. Research focused on how, within different ecumenes, distinctive population geographies were linked to cultural systems. Notions of cultural systems emphasized the visible artefacts of culture (including religion, language and settlement design) and drew on the idea of cultural regions (Meinig 1965).

John Hunter (1967) combined notions of ecumene and culture to read the distinctive population geography of a small part of the West African savanna zone. Furthermore, he used the concept of overpopulation (which he developed through a measure of population pressure) to relate the experiences of one place (the small state of Nangodi, located in the north-east of Ghana) to a more generic set of places (the savanna zone). What made Nangodi compelling was that, between 1948 and 1960, its population declined by 15 per cent from 16,000 to 13,600. This was all the more remarkable because general improvements in health were continuing to lower the death rate, and the population of Ghana as a whole grew by 63 per cent during the same period.

The key to understanding this dramatic population geography rested on over-population. In Nangodi, livelihood traditionally depended on the cultivation of staple crops (early and late millet, guinea corn and ground nuts) using the home farm system of recultivating the same piece of ground close to the home farm. This intensive system of production was severely pressured when populations grew or when areas of land fell outside the ecumene. Crucially, onchocerciasis (river blindness), endemic in the north of Ghana, was increasingly affecting the eastern lands in Nangodi. As a result, the large-scale abandonment of over a quarter of the state's former ecumene further increased pressure on the remaining home farms. Sheet-wash erosion, gullying, loss of top soil and seasonal caloric intake reductions and body weight loss increasingly characterized the state. A confluence of ecological, population and cultural factors, with the lure of employment in Ghana's southern cities, thus resulted in large-scale and sex-selective emigration from the state. Hunter does raise the possibility that such emigration may in time be linked to patterns of seasonal and semi-permanent migration, which is itself a culturally sanctioned response to challenging conditions. Indeed, Ghana was connected to the wider West African region through circulation and 'turbulence'.

The implicit notion that a culture region is a useful heuristic for constructing an integrated analysis runs through Lawton's (1959) account of the patterns of clustering among Irish communities in nineteenth-century Britain. Lawton sought to connect a particular population geography to the wider system that referenced the interdependencies between Irish-British history and geography that unfolded while the latter's economy was the world's largest. He began by noting dramatic population decline. Ireland's population declined from 8.2 million in 1841 to 5.8 million in 1861 (a loss of just under one-third). An ecological crisis – the 1845–47 potato famine – acted as the event that would 'produce rapid and enduring changes in the population complex ... The study of population is, in many ways, an ecological problem' (35). While Irish workers migrated to Britain before and after the decades of 1841–61, census data giving the numbers of Irish-born persons per county revealed that the 20-year period straddling the potato famine was largely to determine the overall settlement pattern of the Irish immigrants. Important concentrations emerged in the growing industrial centres of Glasgow, Liverpool, London, South Wales and the industrial districts of the north.

By 1861, some 25 per cent of Liverpool's population was Irish-born. In areas where Irish immigrants settled, upwards of 50 per cent of the population was Irish. The pattern of settlement was one of concentration, with the Irish population often crammed into a few extremely overcrowded streets. By 1847, 35,000 people (mainly Irish) lived in the city's cellars, places described as wells of stagnant water: cholera and typhoid epidemics ravaged such areas in the late 1840s. Lawton links this spatial clustering to occupational clustering. Drawing on city-wide samples of individual data records from enumerators' books, Lawton describes how Irish districts exhibited distinctive patterns of employment. Many Irish women entered domestic service in the houses around Abercromby Square. This was an area that attracted second-generation Irish emigrants, many of whom worked in the banking industry. Overwhelmingly, the Irish were concentrated in unskilled and manual work. Many of these workers were awaiting passage to the USA to contribute labour there. By noting the broader social and cultural impacts of this Irish population geography upon Liverpool (the development of a dialect and a large Catholic community) and on Irish–British relations (Orange–Catholic rivalries), Lawton reconnects population matters to the operation of cultural and political systems over time.

Some of the most explicit work to link population geographies with cultural systems within a broad regional and holistic framework draws upon the notion of culture region. Describing the development of the 'Mormon culture region' in the American West, Jackson and Layton (1976) drew on population ideas in two ways.

First, they explored how the process of settlement migration lent a distinctive, unique, but not singular imprint upon the cultural landscape. Second, they evidenced their argument by investigating one aspect of a population (settlement) geography that persists in the contemporary landscape at a local scale of street widths, block sizes and setback distances.

The story of Mormon (that is, members of the Church of Jesus Christ of Latter-day Saints) settlement in the western USA had been generally assumed to illustrate how cultural prerogatives (in this case, related to a strong religious coherence at the heart of communities) could impose a uniform footprint upon a new landscape. Indeed, the founder of the Mormon Church, Joseph Smith, had laid out a City of Zion plan that called for 'uniform blocks of ten acre size divided into twenty blocks of one half acre, uniform streets 132 feet wide, and a central tier of blocks fifteen acres in size divided into thirty lots' (Jackson and Layton 1976: 136). As Mormons moved to the Great Basin after Smith's death in 1844, village settlement organization showed wide variations from the City of Zion plan. Jackson and Layton argue that these variations could be attributed to: a lack of familiarity with Smith's plan; the need for Mormon settlements to function as commercial centres and not, as had been envisioned originally, as villages in an agrarian utopia; the need for settlers to respond quickly to local environmental constraints by formulating plans based on their previous experiences of settlement designs; or lack of appropriate technology.

An examination of settlers' diaries revealed that it was common practice to hold a community meeting upon arrival at a new settlement site, divide the land into a grid of equal-sized lots, orient this grid as close to north–south as could be determined, and hold a lottery to allocate lots to settlers. While such a process did not produce uniformity of settlement design, it did lend particular distinctiveness to Mormon settlements in this region, with Mormon street widths and block sizes larger than non-Mormon settlement averages. While 'set in stone' over 150 years ago, Jackson and Layton note that the visible signs of this population geography still persist in today's rural Mormon villages.

These case studies together evidence a kind of holistic thinking that continued to connect the field to environmental, political economic and cultural systems. These links were accomplished in an explicitly regional and synthetic way. Population provided a window upon an ongoing set of transformations in society, whether viewed at local and disaggregated scales or over time. Such research was the exception and not the rule, and tended to be consigned to the very margins of the new field.

Coming of age

Population geography had come of age as a sub-discipline with a recognizable focus upon the spatial context of demographic phenomena. Spatial demography began to occupy the core spaces of the field. Sheffield geographer Robert Woods opened his *Theoretical Population Geography* by noting that

> at the centre are . . . the distribution and structure of the population; with mortality, fertility, and migration; what causes them to be as they are, why they change through time and through space; and with how and why they themselves affect other economic, social, political, and environmental issues. At the periphery lie . . . urbanisation and social segregation. (Woods 1982: xiii)

The field was moving from inductive to deductive ways of contributing positivist knowledge and had made some brief forays into feminist and political economy literatures. It had contributed both macro-level and, increasingly, micro-level analyses of population behaviours, notably migration. Its most distinctive achievement, however, was convergence around a single vision – Zelinsky's vision.

Where did this leave the Trewartha and Beaujeu-Garnier visions? In some ways, the very capaciousness of their projects proved to be their undoing. Reliant on descriptive and associational methodologies, regional and synthetic work was unable to draw strength from the positivist conceptions of knowledge that permitted models and theories to be admitted as scientific evidence until proven otherwise. For Trewartha and Beaujeu-Garnier, this meant that progress towards the further investigation of population, ecumene and culture would only be made if geographers began the monumental task of rolling out these complex and ultimately local accounts across the world, precisely what they both attempted. In two papers intriguingly co-authored with Zelinsky, and published the year after his now infamous presidential address, Trewartha called for such studies in Tropical Africa and, more specifically, Belgian Africa (Trewartha and Zelinsky 1954). But the absence of reliable data on population geographies – density, distributions, growth and so on – is quickly recognized as a stumbling block to the pursuit of these agendas. We get a giddy sense of expectation and optimism: 'the construction of [population maps] involved something of the excitement and suspense of an exploratory journey, as many previously vague or unknown population regions took shape' (Trewartha and Zelinsky 1954: 136).

The task was hopeless and overtaken by events, not least the growing trend towards 'respectability by specialty' in the sciences and social sciences. True to the cause, Trewartha published the first volume of what would be a trilogic treatment of population across the world in 1969. *A Geography of Population: World Patterns* proved a seminal work, not because it showed how the foregoing agenda could be prosecuted, but because it evidenced the intellectual compromise forced on Trewartha. Even in the preface, it is clear that his thinking had moved beyond the claim that population geography was a kind of 'third way' that bridged the human and physical dualism of the discipline (an idea he attributed to Hooson 1960). Rather, he states that 'population serves as the reference from which all other geographic elements are observed ...' (2). Thus, accounts of geography should reasonably begin with people, an idea that may explain why so many introductions to human geography textbooks open with a chapter on population.

Freed from any obligation to view population as cause and consequence and to connect it to ecumene and culture, Trewartha proposed that descriptions of population numbers, distribution patterns, density and growth should be followed by accounts of the spatial distribution of population characteristics, with regional treatments for the economically less developed world (1979) and the more developed world (1978). This set the model for many of the period's other key texts, including Lester Kosiński's 1970 *The Population of Europe*. Huw Jones's 1981 *A Population Geography* essentially combines Trewartha's three volumes into one book. Other textbooks on the field all showed a commitment to applying positivist approaches to geographic depictions of populations.

Whither place-based accounts of population geography rooted in a classic regional tradition? Tellingly, the development of French geography turned towards systematic research that avoided the conceptual problems associated with place- and region-based studies (not least among them the question, where did regions begin and end?). The *géographie humaine* tradition, once dominant among French geographers, perhaps provided a framework for as few as 5 per cent of the articles to appear in the *Annales de Géographie* between 1962 and 1971; general population studies featured in only 6 per cent of the articles. It seems that the external context, including the strong growth of the Paris region, combined with the desire of geographers to influence planning theory, helped account for the surge of interest in urban geography, which featured in 19 per cent of the articles (Desbarats 1975). By the end of the period, the work of humanists and phenomenologists seemed to provide one sanctuary for those interested in place. Bill Bunge's (1971) illuminating treatment of the Fitzgerald housing project in Detroit weaves social and cultural characteristics of the environment into a personal narrative of the organization of residents into a population which persists through time and space.

In working at a scale unfamiliar to population geographers, in crossing the macro-micro divide, in celebrating subjectivity and in its holistic focus, this was a radical contribution to population geography.

Coming of age had meant theoretical convergence around a positivist search for demographic order in spatial economic landscapes. While notions of environment, place, regions, politics and culture had been largely excluded from this orthodoxy, the field had proved itself as a strongly applied and useful member of geography's fraternity. The future must have looked bright.

chapter 4

THE END OF POPULATION GEOGRAPHY
(AS WE KNEW IT)

This chapter explores how transitions in social and economic contexts during the 1980s and 1990s combined with philosophical developments within the social sciences and geography to drive forward existing population geography research agendas and spark new ones. Critical positions challenged the authority of discipline-demarcated centres of knowledge production. Other research continued to inform public policy by applying spatial analyses to demographic topics. While critical and continuity positions often took up opposing positions within the field, a great deal of intellectual energy was expended in the name of finding a kind of theoretical middle ground: pluralism, mixed methods and tolerance became key terms often overheard at international conferences and in the pages of prominent journals. Like all sub-disciplines in geography, the field was a site of transformation.

In describing the range of research contributions from the 1980s and 1990s, this chapter addresses these questions:

- How did the economic and cultural transitions of globalization – particularly those involving the relationship between states and populations – affect the field's research agendas?

- What did developments in social theory in geography mean for the field?

- What were the possibilities for theoretical *rapprochement* and the location of a middle ground?

Gradually, the field 'as we knew it' (with apologies to several others, including REM) faded. Over the last two decades of the century, population geography thought of itself less as a field with a core agenda and a limited number of established approaches and more as a series of projects that addressed, in quite different ways, intersections between population and geography. As the label 'population geography' weakened, greater attention was paid to what was meant by population and geography and, perhaps paradoxically, the intellectual possibilities for individual population geographers grew.

Transitions

While some population 'big issues' of the 1980s and 1990s had been on the international radar screen for some time, others appeared quite unexpectedly. Linking economic development with population growth continued to attract significant international attention. The successive meetings of the International Conference on Population and Development in 1974 (Bucharest), 1984 (Mexico City) and 1994 (Cairo) cast population growth as anything from the key determinant of economic development to a relatively unimportant factor. The policy recommendations for national governments shifted from family planning interventions (supported by countries of the North in 1974 and generally opposed by those of the South, who argued that development was the best contraceptive), to *laissez-faire* market-driven solutions (espoused by the North in 1984, but opposed by the South, who favoured family planning), to the promotion of reproductive rights (supported by many countries in the South in 1994, but opposed by some religious groups). These shifting positions were somewhat reflective of the dominance of free-market, conservative governments in the USA, the UK and Australia during the 1980s and 1990s, which worked towards free trade and neo-liberalism. The 'doomster' positions derived from Malthusian precepts were countered with 'boomster' evidence that pointed to continuing (global) increases in per capita food production, rising standards of living and, after the 1970s, a reduction in the global rate of population growth.

As Domesday-like concerns over population growth temporarily receded, public attention shifted to the role of the 'forgotten' demographic component of migration. Of course, international migration had played a decisive economic role in the development of many countries, including the USA between the 1860s and 1910s, and had been more recently and selectively tolerated in those post-war economies that faced labour shortages, through programmes like the Bracero Accord and guest worker agreements. Despite shifting routinized production offshore, many northern countries faced continuing labour shortages and immigration policies were significantly liberalized in the 1960s and 1970s. By the 1980s, with more than 20 years of experience of international migration, it was apparent that countries of immigration had to confront urgently social, economic and ultimately political questions. Some questions were not new – Chinese groups had experienced discrimination, racist exclusion and hate crimes in California in the 1890s. Other issues, including the increased impoverishment of recent immigrants, were confounded by the timing of much migration, which exposed arriving groups to labour markets undergoing recession. This meant fewer job opportunities for immigrants. It also fanned the fires of racial hatred by allowing far-right groups to make a connection between rising levels of unemployment, deprivation and the arrival of immigrant groups.

Other issues associated with migration were new. By the close of the century, more people than at any point in history were on the move: to appropriate the title of an influential inventory of international migration, 'worlds were in motion' (Massey et al. 1999). The United Nations estimated that just under 120 million people were living outside their country of birth at the start of the 1990s, representing about 2.3 per cent of the world population total and implying that at least 1 in 40 people worldwide had moved internationally. Portrayed as 'the new untouchables' (Harris 1995), immigrants flooded the North, where they besieged its labour markets, overran its housing markets, drained its social services and, most profoundly, undermined the cultural project of the nation state. Immigrants were often depicted as a numeric and cultural threat to security. Discriminatory ideas about outsiders, their terms of entry and the benefits to which they were entitled became key components of political discussions about NAFTA, the migration policy of the EC and citizenship rights. Discriminatory practices were also extended to supposed insiders, like Europe's Romany communities. In the Czech city of Ústí nad Labem, the local authority started constructing a 2.65 m wall to 'restrict' its Romany population to one part of the city before a national and international outcry stopped the project in 1999.

The political significance of refugees and asylum seekers greatly increased. States devised new and increasingly restrictive ways of approaching refugee populations, in response to reduced state budgets; the difficulty of disentangling supposedly legitimate political motivations from illegitimate economic motivations to mobility; the sharp rise in the volume of asylum seekers worldwide; and increasing concerns about cultural homogeneity and security. These policies included active deterrence (border patrols), passive deterrence (talking tough) and strategic embrace (the differential treatment of Haitian and Cuban groups by the USA). In some cases, as with the Kosovan refugee crisis, the production of a refugee flow became a specific tactic of warfare. In other ways, the embrace of refugees helped define national identity, as in the case of Canada's commitment to multiculturalism (Richmond 1994).

The context of below replacement population growth in Europe, sustained low fertility in North America and recent rapid reductions in fertility in countries like China raised the profile of rapid demographic ageing. Like discussions of migration, debates on ageing have been framed in economic and cultural ways that point to transformations in the ways that states understand and manage populations. Debates often assumed that ageing will increasingly impact the global economy in negative ways. This is because of shortages in the supply of younger workers, reduced savings rates and the need for greater state expenditures upon infra-structure like housing and health care, social support and pensions. Accompanying these debates, cultural attitudes about 'what it means' to be young/old or working/retired shifted. Ageing affected gender roles, as more men assumed care roles, and household structures, as more pluralistic household types emerged and new norms about nest-leaving and returning took hold. Ageing became tied to transformations in the roles of individuals and groups in society, and presented new challenges to the relationship between states and populations. The fact that these challenges are occurring in concert with neo-liberal regimes that stress state frugality leads many to cast demographic ageing as a significant crisis waiting to happen.

While migration and ageing were two concerns anticipated on the basis of trends in population structure and globalization, the re-emergence of infectious and parasitic diseases as global killers was not widely touted. The coincidence between rates of prevalence of HIV-AIDS, structural poverty and knowledge of how HIV-1 is transmitted suggests that this uneven geography is being affected and perpetuated by political factors in the same way that many famines result from political mismanagement and repression (Farmer 1999).

While the latter two decades of the twentieth century raised foreseen and unforeseen population issues, society was confronted with a sense that familiar concepts – east/west, north/south, good/evil, political/non-political, past/present – were no longer as fixed and authoritative as they had appeared to be. This included the concept of the nation state. The re-emergence of killer diseases, the failure of the international community to do anything other than pick its nose while 800,000 Rwandans were slaughtered in 1994, two space shuttle disasters, Chernobyl and Bhopal and the earlier demolition of an icon of state-led technological progress (the Pruitt-Igoe housing complex that stood from 1954–72) all eroded confidence in the ability of states to deliver a future that was better than the present.

New beliefs and loyalties emerged. Some communities – including funda-
mentalist Islamic groups – referenced pre-Enlightenment belief systems. Groups
long disenfranchised from the nation-state grid pushed for independence by
appealing to constructed ethno-nationalisms. Other communities, often with
overt intervention from states, constructed diasporic identities. States themselves
explored new tactics for encouraging belonging and membership. In South Africa,
the Truth and Reconciliation Commission offered guidance on how the new
national community would remember its past. European states responded to the
new economic and cultural context of globalization by supporting its articulation
of a pan-European identity with new supranational institutions that delivered
human rights, such as the International Court of Justice in The Hague. Elsewhere,
disadvantaged groups formed horizontal alliances through the global information
networks of capitalism to fight for social justice (including the Zapatistas' cyber-
resistance to NAFTA's neo-liberal agenda in the Mexican state of Chiapas).

Population issues became increasingly linked to the more generic project of
globalization. As the Sex Pistols' *God Save the Queen* played in bars from the Kings
Road to Christopher Street, events like the geopolitical reconfiguration of
relations between East and West, North and South and Islam and non-Islamic
worlds, the 'return' of global pandemics like HIV-AIDS and the growing crisis of
secularism all shook a number of core beliefs that, one way or another, had underpinned the Enlightenment project. This would have at least three sets of implications for the field. First, social and cultural factors claimed equal importance to
the more traditional foci on economic and political factors. Second, globalization
heightened awareness of geographic interdependencies. Third, globalization meant
that population matters were political matters that extended beyond the confines
of state governments to encompass members of population groups themselves.
States had moved from being part of the solution to being part of the analysis.

Power, knowledge and context

Population geography was affected by profound changes in beliefs about knowledge.
As global interdependencies and uncertainties buffeted society, long-standing
Enlightenment beliefs were opened up by a number of social theorists, including
Derrida, Bourdieu, Foucault and Lefebvre. They asked, was it possible to imagine
new ways of thinking about space, about time, about progress and about politics?
Acknowledging interdependence, Derrida overturned the Cartesian logic that order
and disorder were separate and absolutes and suggested that order and disorder

made each other in relational ways: one could not exist without the other. The idea that knowledge could be relational was revolutionary and added a new dimension to the approaches that social scientists used to understand the world around them.

Relational views of knowledge had particular salience for a geography project long committed to a Kantian search for meaning in proximity and context. As order and disorder could make each other, space (and time) lost ontological primacy and were no longer 'out there, then' but 'here, and now'. Contingency and context mattered. Proximity was still relevant, but only as one of a number of properties of space that helped make society. Across the social sciences and humanities, theorizations of space became part of discussions of how knowledge was produced in a way rarely seen since Kant's earlier treatises. Geographers like Ed Soja, David Harvey, Derek Gregory and Doreen Massey were deeply committed to these discussions and helped infuse geography with social theory and social theory with geography.

The significant waves of theoretical development in human geography that have been associated with feminism, the cultural turn and the new regional geography debated this relational view of knowledge. They further considered the implications for thinking about context, and for thinking about the links between power and creating knowledge. At the risk of over-simplification, and following Gregory (1996), the approaches to geography in the 1980s and 1990s can be compared along three axes. The first two axes refer to how each approach treats context and power (i.e. the same distinctions made for the approaches of the 1950s and 1960s). A third 'post-Enlightenment' axis differentiates approaches based on their view of knowledge as absolute or relational.

Within population geography, relational thinking flowed through a limited number of approaches, including geographical materialism, social constructivism, poststructuralism, postcolonialism and structurationism. To be sure, human geography was busy exploring several other readings, including critical realism and postmodern (textual) landscape analyses, but the five identified above were the main ones that infused – to varying degrees – relational thinking within the field. Figure 4.1 'locates' each approach and can be compared with table 3.1 to illustrate how population geography enlarged its view of the world after the 1970s. In introducing how such relational approaches connect together population with the concepts of space, environment and place, my twin goals are to establish the intellectual context for the research agendas that did emerge during the 1980s and 1990s, and to beg a series of questions about research agendas that did not appear but *could have* appeared.

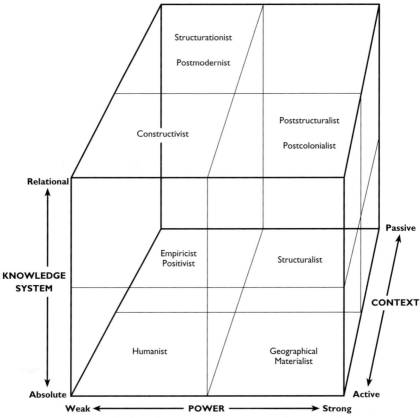

Figure 4.1 Approaches in population geography, 1980s–1990s

David Harvey's continuing development of a geographical materialist approach to the nature of urbanization under capitalism (Harvey 1982, 1985, 1996) serves as a strong example of how context informed some structuralist approaches and how population geography remained on the fringes of social theory. While Soviet population geographers had established interests in the territorial and urban organization of nodes of population in relation to production processes, western population geography restricted its attention to describing how rural-to-urban migration prompted Third World urbanization, and how migration was implicated in counterurbanization trends in many developed country settings. In *The Urbanization of Capital*, Harvey (1985) had taken similar empirical insights and argued that uneven development at a regional scale triggered fixed investments in urban infrastructure. Over time, as capital located more profitable spatial and sectoral opportunities, much of this infrastructure became obsolescent, which led to crises for the state (unproductive land uses) and population groups (unemployment). Inherent contradictions within capitalism were internalized in the form and functioning of the city and its population. In hitching space and time to capitalist and class restructuring, Harvey had begun to incorporate contingency into his corpus.

In the subsequent *Justice, Nature, and the Geography of Difference* he extended this commitment to the contexts of political action and class consciousness to 'define a set of workable foundational concepts for understanding space-time, place, *and environment (nature)*' (2, italics added). Just as spaces and places transmitted material, representational and symbolic contingencies to social life, so too did nature/environment:

> discussion of the discourses of nature has much to reveal, if only about how the discourses themselves conceal a concrete political agenda in the midst of a highly abstract, universalizing, and frequently intensely moral argumentation ... dominant systems of power can advance and protect a hegemonic discourse of efficient and rational environmental management and resource allocation for capital accumulation ... they can also strive ... to manage the heterogeneity of discourses to their own advantage. (174)

While attentive to context, the account did not specify in any detail how populations (what is referred to as community solidarity) affect social change.

Criticisms that Harvey's geographic materialism was foundationalist and masculinist opened the door to approaches with more explicit relational thinking. Much anti-foundationalist thinking in population geography has been informed by feminist arguments that object to the invisibility and passivity of women in research. Social constructivist perspectives underpinned work in the new cultural geography that addressed how group (population) identities were constructed by individual actors. Constructivists reject an essentialist position that groups and individuals hold an identity that is based on any unique, naturalized attributes. Drawing on theorists like Stuart Hall and Judith Butler, geographers have examined how identity is performed in space and place (Valentine 1995). In this work, the label 'social' is important because identity performances are linked both to individual self-concepts and enactment, and also to relationships between individuals and communal representation. Constructions thus emerge in a relational sense (individuals within groups and settings), and destabilize fixed notions of gender, race, sexuality and age that had been based on biological or anthropological precepts (Rose 1993). Furthermore, constructivism implies a focus not upon the maintenance of stable categories, but upon a continuing process of assuming multiple identities. Space plays a contextual role and places represent life worlds where self, other and community come together and drift apart (Anderson 1991). Less clear is how these fluid, always in progress, acts of becoming translate into coalition building and political action.

Poststructural approaches also address themselves to the relation between individuals, groups and their social settings, but do so more explicitly through the lens of discourse production and circulation. Meaning, experience, ambition and the possibilities for coalition and change arise from and through discourse, and are not simply reflected in it. Discourses transmit and reproduce unequal power relations, but can also be sites of political action and intervention. Feminist poststructural approaches focus on gender systems, rather than the category male (or female), and link gender systems to the flow of power in society. Geographic research explored how gender systems arise in particular places at particular times, how they are maintained and what this means for social life (Rose 1993). Concerning race, White and Jackson (1995: 117) called for 'trac[ing] specific processes of racialisation rather than mapping and measuring the categories that are handed down to us in successive censuses'. As poststructural approaches investigate how difference (inequality) arises through the production and circulation of discourse in society, the question of how population groups arise in particular spaces at particular times takes on considerable significance.

Postcolonial approaches in geography have extended the work of post-structuralists in several directions. While Foucault sketched the ways in which discourses of knowledge production unfolded as (western) society passed through feudalism, mercantilism and capitalism, he further suggested that this 'progression' in time was 'placed' in key ways in space. That is, Enlightenment views of knowledge were shown to be contingent on the relations between the colonial West and the colonized non-West. This implied that knowledge about, and knowledge from, the colonial other was not just important for 'off-shore' projects, but also an integral if invisible part of how power circulated 'onshore', that is across all social systems. In *Orientalism*, Edward Said (1978) links the 'dispossession' of colonies to their depictions in the West as 'distant exotic others'. This depiction occurred through systems of naming and spatial (architectural and cartographic) incursions that imposed new and alien notions of order.

Feminist scholars have recognized that dispossession also occurs through gender and sexuality systems. Mohanty (1991: 10) writes:

> Black, white, and other third world women have very different histories with respect to the inheritance of post-fifteenth century Euro-American hegemony: the inheritance of slavery, enforced migration, plantation and indentured labor, colonialism, imperial conquest and genocide. Thus, third world feminists have argued for the rewriting of history based on the *specific* locations and histories of struggle of peoples of color and postcolonial peoples, and on the day to day strategies of survival utilized by such peoples.

Postcolonial approaches can circumvent the positioning of women as dependants. As Mohanty elaborates:

> it is not the descriptive potential of gender difference but the privileged positioning and explanatory potential of gender difference as the *origin* of oppression that I question . . . the problem is that [this strategy] assumes men and women are already constituted as sexual-political subjects prior to their entry into the arena of social relations. (1991: 59, italics in original)

Taken together, poststructural and postcolonial approaches have inspired population geography to consider how differences between population groups are produced and circulated through acts (like marriage), performances (like parenting) and institutions (like family). This has the potential to contribute to a deeper understanding of how population makes the political and is made by the political.

The structurationist approach of Anthony Giddens foregrounds the relationships between knowledgeable individuals and their agency, and institutions, structures and their constraining and enabling features. Social life is described as purposeful and meaningful, and both constitutes and is made by aggregate social systems. However, while this (re)constitution happens in space and place, the result has been criticized for ignoring 'the concrete specificities of space, place, and landscape' (Gregory 1996: 123). That is, space and place appear through the notion of *time-space distanciation*, which describes how, as modernism proceeds, social life has become less anchored through any particular connections with specific locales and more integrated with translocal spheres. Notwithstanding, population geography has completed some productive forays into this terrain with investigations of migration (Goss and Lindquist 1995).

Positions

While post-positivist thinking swept across much of human geography, its immediate influences on population geography were more subtle. At the risk of oversimplifying multiple positions, I characterize three commonly expressed views about the field, its nature, and its future directions. First, there was a desire for continuity in focus and approach: to many, the field wasn't broken and didn't need fixing. Second, an increasingly confident group of scholars saw the field as supporting pluralistic approaches to familiar topics: the rise of mixed-method approaches symbolizes this stance. Third, a smaller contingent of scholars has been critical of an inattentiveness to issues of representation.

With the growth of membership in its specialty (research) groups, participation in international conferences, joint research projects and an increasing number of specialized publication outlets (including journals, newsletters, list-serves and so on), the field's practitioners had an array of opportunities to think about and position themselves *vis-à-vis* transformations in society's reading of population issues and social theory. Such introspection had, for some time, been shared through the specially commissioned 'progress report' review articles that appeared in the widely circulated journal, *Progress in Human Geography*. However, the launch of the *International Journal of Population Geography* in 1995, and the relaunch of international population geography conferences, brought into sharp focus the divergent projects within the field.

Just as many population geographers were deeply concerned to define what was (and was not) part of their field in the formative days of the 1950s and early 1960s, issues of definition resurfaced throughout this period. Discussions of boundaries between the field and medical geography, spatial ecology, demography and population studies appeared as border disputes rather than forward-looking attempts to develop theory. Findlay and Graham (1991) noted that the strengthening of the field's demographic identity in the 1980s was:

> far from the traditional research territories of population geographers. Symptomatic of the need to educate UK population geographers about research developments in demography ... reviewers in journals such as *Progress in Human Geography* started to report under the heading 'population studies' rather than 'population geography'. Indeed, by 1988 only 11% of the references in the population studies review section were written by geographers. (154)

By the early 1990s the field stood at a crossroads. Those who favoured more, not fewer, exchanges with demography, and the extension of demographic thinking into the field, made a persuasive case for continuity of the identity acquired by the field in the 1970s and 1980s. Other scholars, including Findlay, were keen to return to broader questions, about populations, famine and fertility, for example, but also to retain the recent developments that had been made in quantitative and qualitative approaches. In characterizing Noin's (1991) feelings about the discussions of 18 population geographers from around the world about the orientation of their subject, White and Jackson (1995) noted that:

> the majority of respondents made no connection between population geography and wider social contexts, preferring to define the sub-discipline in terms of the elucidation of empirical data, the development of GIS and geodemographics, providing a commentary on major world 'problems', and the discussion of population-environment relations. (114)

Zelinsky, for one, called for further attention to geodemographic factors in the future of the global ecosystem.

The vision of a pluralistic, real-world population geography underpinned by, first, continued use of the label population, and second, the use of both quantitative and qualitative methods, rose to prominence during the 1990s. It involved a re-examination of the use of quantitative methods to avoid 'methodological mono-culture of qualitative research', and to acknowledge that:

- quantitative skills are needed to use large data sets and produce applied products like population projections;

- quantitative data help contextualize the specifities of local cases against global processes;

- statistics are an effective tool for monitoring the activities of politicians and key decision-makers;

- quantitative data are an integral part of mixed-methods approaches adopted by many working from structurationist, realist and feminist positions;

- policy work needs arguments that can be generalized statistically, such as those produced by economists and demographers with numerical data;

- new data sources have provided new opportunities for creative research.

By the early 2000s pluralism meant balance, and a commitment to 'tackle the population issues at the heart of social theory', like the size of youthful age cohorts in Islamic states (Findlay 2004: 182, after Philo 2001).

In locating a 'middle ground' where the field could 'have its cake and eat it', pluralism stood open to criticism from those who felt it paid insufficient attention to the wider critiques of relational thinking in the discipline. Again, according to Findlay: 'the security of position allocated to population experts within the academy ... does not of course remove the moral responsibility of thinking critically about how that position is used, but it certainly demands an ability to engage in a powerfully analytical fashion with large, usually numerical government datasets' (183). While many pluralist approaches concurred that population was a politically useful term and a productive position from which to engage with 'real worldly' issues, those working from a relational frame generally resisted this deployment and argued that politics was an ontological matter.

Scholars with diverse backgrounds – including Michael Brown, Keith Halfacree, Peter Jackson, Jennifer Hyndman, Susan Craddock, Chris Philo and Yvonne Underhill-Sem – argued that post-positivist critiques of knowledge obliged the field to rethink its concepts, approaches and research questions, and to re-imagine its role within the academy and society. They explored the implications of questions about essentialism, reductionism, positionality and politics for the field. Essentialism refers to the assumption that there are inalienable properties of things and categories that have merit in scientific inquiry. Essentialist approaches to populations as groups not only infer group meaning from component character-istics, but regard these components as fixed, naturalized and stable elements. Historically, population groups have been defined on the basis of now discredited biological frames of reference (i.e. racial categories based on skin colour, facial features and other aspects of physiognomy), and increasingly troublesome cultural frames of reference (for example, ethnic categories based on language, religion, ancestry, membership in a national community and so on). Essentialism is also criticized for implying that population groups could only possess one 'true' identity and that this identity was fixed by space and time. At the level of the individual person, the idea that a fixed gender identity could be ascribed on the basis of the biological category of 'sex' is questioned by those who believe gender (sexuality, race and so on) is performed, not handed down (Butler 1990).

A second criticism referred to the field's use of reductionist strategies. These seek knowledge by breaking down objects of inquiry into component parts, seeking explanations for these parts and then rebuilding a synthetic whole. Many 'core' ideas in the field, including the demographic transition concept and the notion of migration systems, had been researched using reductionist assumptions. Reductionism is implied by the space-as-codex epistemology, and may also lurk in more agent-centred accounts of taken-for-granted everyday landscapes, including Pierre Bourdieu's (1977) concept of *habitus*.

A third criticism surrounded the degree to which the positionality of population geography researchers was seen to be unproblematic:

> all research has a political context and is itself a political activity, involving choices and priorities ... much census based geodemographic work serves the interests of capital through the targeting of markets and products; but it has important consequences for more vulnerable groups in society through the redlining of under-class areas and similar processes of social exclusion. (White and Jackson 1995: 119)

While the field is recognized as dominated by white, able-bodied, middle-class, heterosexual males, its positioning as a Euro-American endeavour has more recently been illuminated and problematized. Skeldon's (1995) case for 'greater awareness' noted that 'there is reluctance on the part of some British-based population geographers ... to look out, either to the developing world or to the work of colleagues elsewhere ... Many of those working in the developed world appear to be oblivious to the research of those working within the developing world' (93–4). For Underhill-Sem (2004): 'various reasons have been posited for why Pacific population geography, and by implication geographies from other out-of-the-way places, has been rendered invisible on the intellectual canvass of both geography and population studies, but some arguments point to the marginalizing effect of the politics of knowledge' (55).

Fourth, relational ontologies acknowledge the inherently political nature of knowledge production and circulation, and oblige researchers to think through and practise what it means to collaborate (give and take) with the researched and, indeed, with the wider world. Feminist contributions to 'situated knowledge' explored how communities in particular settings negotiated their own under-standings of and resistance towards supposedly universalizing ideas like patriarchy and class relations. Lefebvre argued that social life under capitalism has been trans-formed through the production of new contexts in space (1991). However, the full force of the re-entrance of space into contemporary philosophy recognizes that context is inseparable from the individual, from reflection and from action. As context constitutes thought and action, and is constituted by thought and action (recursivity), the separation of research and activism is undermined. The impli-cations of this critique are further developed in chapter five, becoming more prominent as the field involved itself with research on HIV-AIDS (Brown 1997), for example.

Research poles of the 1980s and 1990s

The remainder of this chapter explores how research activities reflected the three positions of continuity, pluralism and critical engagement. While by no means exhaustive, the following review attempts to capture something of the balance of contemporary scholarship in the field. It identifies four poles of research activity. The first of these concerns 'movement' and focuses on descriptions and explanations of human mobility. The increasingly diverse and complex array of mobility at all scales attracted both public and research interest during this period. The second research pole describes geographic work on natural increase and decrease, focusing on fertility and mortality and morbidity. Also strongly influenced by stable population theory, work on the third research pole explores geographies of population compositions. The final research pole concerns 'non-demographic' consequences and evidences a shift from livelihood-focused studies to more general research on the social, cultural and economic dimensions of population change. For each research pole, representative studies illustrate how those adopting continuity, pluralist and critical positions contributed substantive knowledge. The chapter concludes by considering how reconcilable these positions might be.

Movement

Discussions of movement, broadly defined, dominated the field's research output during the 1980s and 1990s. When the *Geography in America* collection appeared,

Table 4.1 Continuity, pluralist and critical positions 1980s–1990s.

Pole	Continuity	Pluralist	Critical
MOVEMENT	Migration differentials Migration systems Regional migration Random utility theory	Skilled international migration Gendered migration Family migration Life course	Geopolitics of mobility Migrancy and sedentarism Racialization and sexualization of migration
NATURAL INCREASE & DECREASE	Second demographic transition Health inequalities	Social capital Environmental justice	Politics of reproduction
COMPOSITION	Replacement migration	Social context of age	Politics of ageing
LIVELIHOOD & WELL-BEING	Remittances Population and environment	Family migration Immigrant labour markets	Gendering and racialization of migration

five of the six themes in the commissioned chapter on population geography featured movement (Gaile and Willmot 1989). Globalization was accompanied by an increasing diversity of streams of migration and by a set of new challenges for states, and the field explored both. Refugee crises, the growing politicization of immigration law and policies on asylum seekers and chronic shortages in local housing markets all motivated research on migration and its geographic structure. Dominated by positivist and micro-economic approaches, this work typically distinguished between the causes of migration (for example, wage differentials between rural and urban areas) and its consequences (for example, urban over-crowding and assimilation). While this section focuses on the causes of migration, the growing importance of pluralist and critical perspectives on movement under-mined this strict distinction between cause and consequence. By the close of the 1990s, many practitioners had enlarged their thinking about the role of the state by stressing economic, cultural and political expedients of movement.

Much research reduced the diversity of migration events into a manageable number of analytical categories by adopting a classification based on: the distance of a move; its intended permanence or temporariness; and its motivation (voluntary or non-voluntary). The demographic definition of movement as an event that occurs in the life of an individual continued to dominate the field's approach to the study of human mobility. Positivist research took data on migration events and associated them with ecological and individual variables to account for spatial variations in origins, destinations, flows and the probabilities that individuals and families would move. Thus, Bill Clark's widely consulted intro-ductory module, *Human Migration* (1986), discussed: residential mobility (typically, housing moves where employment remains fixed); regional migration (often undertaken for employment reasons); and international migration (divided into immigration/emigration, undocumented migration and refugee flows). Similarly, surveys of extant research on movement differentiated studies based on: residential mobility; urban housing and households; counterurbanization; internal migration; international migration; population and development (Gaile and Willmott 1989).

Immediately prior to 9/11, human migration was thought to pose the single most important security threat for the coming century. The increased complexity of refugee issues contributed to global insecurity and attracted the field's attention. Cold war proxy conflicts in Afghanistan, Central America, southern Africa and South-east Asia, the disintegration of the Soviet bloc, including Yugoslavia, and decolonization were among the key geopolitical triggers that resulted in between

10 and 20 million refugees seeking protection in any given year in the 1990s. While the term 'refugee' was originally defined as a European-specific and ideologically specific concept by the UN in its 1951 convention, Black and Robinson (1993) were among those to demonstrate the geographic complexity of refugee flows and link this to the undermining of the international refugee regime.

In the case of the approximately 1 million Salvadoreans, who fled civil war and low-intensity conflict in the 1980s to the neighbouring countries of Honduras, Guatemala, Mexico and, increasingly, the USA and Canada, Jones (1989) argued that political violence prompted displacement and flight from a number of the country's more conflictual zones, including Morazan. However, for many *desplazados*, movement to western Honduras was as much a continuation of long-existing and culturally defined livelihood strategies (circulation) as a kinetic reaction to political repression.

Further place-based accounts of the conditions surrounding flight revealed the complex interactions between the direct and indirect actions of political regimes, and various other economic, ecological and cultural factors. Accounts of the Africanization of newly independent countries like Uganda, the building of dams, ecological crises, industrial accidents and the rise in organized networks of people-trafficking led the field to a broader consideration of refugee issues using the notion of 'forced migration'. More generally, the role of individual states and international alliances in mediating forced migration was linked to the set of political and cultural insecurities that states faced (Loescher 1993). A case in point concerned the way that states chose to respond to one significant loop-hole in the international refugee regime that exempted internally displaced persons from UNHCR protection. Sudan had a growing population of internally displaced persons which numbered as many as a million, but were ineligible for UNHCR protection owing to the fact they had not crossed a national border (Deng 1993).

Research focusing on 'voluntary' international migration pointed to a growing diversification of migration streams (Castles and Miller 1993). Surveys of migration trends in Europe, the Caribbean, Asia and North America all revealed a growing number of origins and destinations (Massey et al. 1999). Age and socio-economic profiles departed from the stereotypes of international migration as a process that involved young adults, who were mostly single and had average or above-average educational credentials (Koser and Lutz 1998). The feminization of international migration was widely recognized and played a key role in energizing theoretical debates about the causes of these diverse flows (Buijs 1993).

The changing relationship between states and immigrants infused individual-level, microeconomic accounts of international migration. The assumption that spatial differences in migration rates could be reduced to push-and-pull factors and some measure of the distance between an origin and a destination did not stack up with evidence about the role of labour markets, regions, governments and households in migration. Four global regions received more immigrants than would be expected if only economic differences and distance (gravity model hypotheses) were motivating migrants. Three of these include the classic nations of immigration, the USA, Canada and Australia, societies where immigration was closely connected in the popular imagination with the growth of social and political institutions. Within the fourth region, the Middle East used aggressive government policy and special labour provisions to attract workers. Sub-Saharan Africa also witnessed more immigration than would be expected, reflecting embedded circulation livelihood strategies and the colonial superimposition of boundaries on cultural regions. Japan, China and, until its dissolution, the Soviet Union, received less international migration than gravity hypotheses, for reasons related to ethnic homogeneity and strict border controls. Commentators identified a number of deficiencies with the prevailing macro- and micro-accounts of international mobility that included: the operation of chain migration and networks; the way rapid shifts in former empires and regimes have precipitated regional migration patterns; the role of colonial and imperial contact; the political context of migration; and the cultural context of migration.

This desire to better understand migration under conditions of globalization lent greater prominence to structuralist accounts, many of which drew on world systems theory and global cities literatures (Sassen 1991). The thesis that global cities have bifurcated labour markets that need to attract both highly skilled and unskilled workers was informed in a number of ways by research on skilled international migration and domestic worker migration (Koser and Salt 1997). International recognition of qualifications varies by sector and makes some mobility (including that of engineers) easier than other (including lawyers: Iredale 2001). Reflecting its pluralism, this research explored how both the economic/institutional and cultural/gender contexts of skilled migration shaped the sex and occupational selectivity of intra-firm transfers (Iredale 2001). National governments played a variety of roles in shaping incoming entrepreneurial migration and in promoting international out-migration as a development strategy. This last strategy involved both the highly skilled and the unskilled. In the case of the former, many countries, including China, looked to reverse the effects of brain drain by encouraging the return of skilled workers (brain gain). However, in the case of Chinese overseas students, only one-third of the nearly 300,000 who left to study abroad after 1980 had returned by 1997, despite political and some cultural pressures, including the Confucian belief of *Ye lo hui gen*, that falling leaves return to their roots (Broaded 1993). China, in common with an increasing number of other states, also began to encourage the out-migration of unskilled workers. This involved a great many women, who moved independently to work in informal sector (unregulated) settings and remit money to kin and community.

Research on gendered migration enlarged understandings of links between states, population institutions and migration. Kofman (1999) was critical of the lack of serious attention that gender received in research on unskilled and skilled worker streams. She maintained that previous research had either rendered women invisible or, if present, treated them as dependent migrants who lacked agency. Corrective accounts emphasized how gender operated through institutions – including the state and the family – and became a feature of gendered migration research in the field. Structural accounts of domestic workers positioned gendered migration within the global restructuring of production under globalization – or, in the words of Chang and Ling (2000), the 'regime of labour intimacy'. Jim Tyner, in a series of studies of the Filipina maid industry (1994), emphasized the explicitly gendered nature of government policy that has helped produce the maid trade. Similar points were made in the context of Singapore by Huang and Yeoh (1996).

Doreen Mattingly's consideration of domestic workers living in San Diego extended gendered migration theory by looking at an international division of labour of *reproduction* rather than the international division of labour of production. Mattingly noted that 'no production system operates without a reproduction system, and it should not be surprising that the globalisation of production is accompanied by its intimate "other", i.e. reproduction' (2001: 372). Reproduction connoted both human reproduction, the reconstruction of structures that undergirded relations of production, like ideology, and the work of caring for and sustaining humans (the economy of caring). As production begets a gendered form of reproduction (i.e. women are over-represented in caring economies) and that reproduction is mediated by state, family and economy in different ways in different places (i.e. middle-class women in the USA are relatively cash-rich and time-poor, while lower-class women in Mexico are cash- and time-poor), the 'migration' of domestics can be seen as both a response to the production–reproduction dialectic and a heavily classed (and racialized) process. As Audrey Macklin remarked: 'the grim truth is that some women's access to the high paying, high status professions is being facilitated through the revival of semi-indentured servitude. Put another way, one woman is exercising class and citizenship privilege to buy her way out of sex oppression' (1994: 34). While middle-class San Diegans sourced domestic work locally, their employees were financially unable to meet their own care needs through subcontracting arrangements and instead wove complex international networks of caring that often meant prolonged periods of separation between them and their children/extended family, and increased backwards and forwards mobility across the border (see also Hondagneu-Sotelo 1994).

Gendered migration research also addressed the family (household) context of international migration. For Goss and Lindquist (1995), the household, together with migration networks, was one of the two key conceptual locations where 'top-down' and 'bottom-up' forces of globalization intersect to prompt migration. Families and their kin networks were long believed to nominate male target migrants to initiate mobility streams, with women following later in a dependent role as partner or partner-to-be. Families are also institutions where social norms about out-of-wedlock children, divorce, inheritance structures and return migration may prompt female out(or re)-migration. Pulsipher (1993) showed how some women in the West Indies made a conscious decision not to move internationally, but to remain and seek empowerment from familiar local networks of support.

Gendered migration research investigated how the intersection of class, ethnicity, race and gender systems underpinned mobility. Hondegneu-Sotelo (1994) found that moving/delaying/staying strategies varied by class and gender, with middle-class Mexican households 'more egalitarian' in terms of the gendered sequencing of moves. Focusing on skilled workers, Hardill and MacDonald (1998) found normative gender roles to be significant constraints on how partners in dual-career families negotiated decisions about international relocation. Reflecting the plurality of approaches, further work extended the 'new household economics' hypothesis that households use mobility strategies to minimize economic risk. Long-distance migration was a strategy for those surviving children in families where adults have been killed by HIV-AIDS in southern Africa.

In addition to households, migration networks mediate relationships between states and migration. Qualitative accounts of the migration networks of South–North (labour) migration continued to attract sustained interest and to draw attention to the importance of context. The idea of place contingencies described circular and cumulative causation that telegraphed individual decisions up to community norms which, in time, affected migration behaviour (Massey 1990). The rise of institutionalized migration networks and systems both reinvigorated systems approaches to migration and stimulated more culturally oriented frameworks. The recognition that contract migrants, skilled migrants and entrepreneurial migrants participate in global labour markets spurred the emergence of a systems approach which bears more than a passing resemblance to Mabogunje's earlier work. Motivated by a desire to spark policy-relevant work on the implications of migration between countries in Asia and the Pacific in the 1990s, Skeldon (1992) argued that migration systems (not events) should be studied. For Asia and the Pacific, he drew attention to settler migration; contract labour migration; skilled migration; student migration; and asylum-seeker migration.

Extending the social and economic focus of much of this work, a number of scholars of migrant-trafficking turned to more culturally based explanations. For Biemann, the 'remotely sensed' female body became the new cargo in international trade (2002). Investigating the trade in sex workers, other authors explored how the commodification of bodies and performances was place-based. Emplaced discourses of sexuality also affected the possibilities for the return and reintegration of former sex workers who are often ostracized and excluded by culturally conservative regimes (Kempadoo and Doezima 1998).

Research on the global sex trade illustrates the strengths and weaknesses of locating analyses of contemporary global migration at either household or network sites. According to the UN, women and children enter the global sex trade either as a result of an approach from a sex establishment, as a result of being 'bonded' (that is, given to the trade) by family or by being deceived and/or coerced into the trade. The internationalization of crime networks like the Italian Camorra, the Chinese Triads, the Russian Mafia and the Japanese Yakusa, who often deal in drugs as well as human cargo, offers the means and sometimes the coercion for the trade (Raymond 2002). However, much trafficking is underwritten by geographic and gendered variations in poverty, i.e. the structural inequities in global society (Kojima 2001). Some workers see trade in their bodies as a viable economic strategy, rather than something forced upon them by unscrupulous traffickers.

The broader question of integrating 'agency' with the 'structural' components of international migration also runs through discussions of the growing internationalization of the 'marriage' market for brides (the so-called mail-order bride industry: Kojima 2001). For many in population geography, discussions of the relative importance of structure or agency seemed like reruns of debates between those favouring macro-approaches to migration and those favouring micro-approaches. The rise of relational thinking – and particularly structurationist approaches – seemed to avoid the dead-end of this either/or debate.

Structurationists saw that accounts that studied structures or agents separately, and as opposites, were guilty of perpetuating a 'phoney war' between the two. According to Richmond, this view avoided the policy-limiting dichotomy between 'worthy' refugees and 'burdensome' economic migrants: while exclusively political factors underlie the 'traditional' UNHCR definition of refugee, reactive migrants are here motivated by a combination of political, economic, ecological, social and biopsychological factors. His typology recognized that individuals, groups and communities played some role in mediating structural imperatives, including opportunities for (or the potential for) economic development and the selection of when to leave and where to go. In their case study, Goss and Lindquist (1995) used structurationist thinking to analyse the activities of individuals and institutions involved in the contract labour system that connected Filipinos with global employment opportunities.

Weaving together structure, agency and context with the shifting role of states were key concerns of poststructural and postcolonial accounts of movement. The focus on the production and circulation of a discursive context meant that migration was not an isolated event with a discrete set of causes and consequences, but embodied and emplaced. Ideas and norms about movement contributed to the development of social life and its spatial (contextual) expression; context was both made by migration and could serve to renegotiate and reconstruct the power relations in society. Illustrative of a postcolonialist feminist perspective, Mohanty (1991) argued that the ways in which states produced citizens and races was one of five discourses that linked migration to patterns of inequality in society. Her complete list included the discursive contexts of: colonialism, class and gender; state, citizenship and racial formation; multinational production and social agency; constructions of Third World women as 'native'; and consciousness, identity and writing.

Noyes (2000) develops a relational approach in his analysis of how the colonial German state managed ideas about nomadism and sedentarism in south-west Africa at the close of the nineteenth century. He argued that early and generalized colonial discourses that constructed nomadism as a trait located *both* in Africa (i.e. pastoralism) *and* Germany (i.e. a cultural propensity to wander) created colonial anxiety by not sufficiently 'differencing' the colonial state from its colony 'other'. Lawson (2000) explored the intersections of colonialism, modernization and multinational production, and gender/class constructions in the livelihood strategies of rural-to-urban migrants in Ecuador. Elsewhere, Halfacree linked trends in counterurbanization to the construction of a discourse of idealized rurality in post-industrial England (1994), and Cresswell explored the discursive construction of mobility and gender systems among female tramps and hobos (1999).

A key feature of poststructural and postcolonial accounts of movement is that they either cut across geographic scale or attempt to retheorize it. Thus, while some accounts of movement blurred the lines between what was international and what was national and regional, and questioned the implied organizational framework, the vast majority of research continued to study migration at one discrete scale. While accounts of international migration diversified theoretically, research on regional (internal) migration continued to be strongly influenced by traditional positivist frameworks.

Thus it was that research on urban(or rural)-directed migration destinations tended to adopt scale-specific frameworks. The continuation of rural-to-urban migration in the global South, and the growth of urban-to-rural and semi-rural migration streams in many post-industrial societies (Hugo 1994) were approached using economic-centred and positivist-leaning theories. Zelinsky's now classic 'Hypothesis of the mobility transition' played an important role in organizing a good deal of work on internal migration, particularly those efforts to link changing patterns of net migration to aspects of modernization. In one case – the elderly mobility transition proposed by Andrei Rogers (1992) – research directly extended the framework. Work on repetitive (circular/pendular) mobility that characterized the livelihood regimes of many Melanesian and African communities countered Zelinsky's generalization by placing movement in much broader economic, cultural and political ecological terms (Prothero and Chapman 1985).

Aggregate flows of regional migration were approached in three broad ways. Gravity (spatial interaction) models investigated how the volume and direction of migration was related to the distance between an origin and a destination, spatial structure effects stemming from the concept of competing destinations and push-pull proxy measures. More generalized frameworks, which typically used multivariate regression estimates and treated distance as a variable rather than a structural component of a model, also assumed that meaningful process insights could be derived from aggregated data. While generally supporting the idea that net migration flows reflected amenity differentials (Cebula 1975) and suggesting that internal migration may be linked to (prompted by) international in-migration (Frey 1996), many of these analyses failed to find positive associations between migration and wage differentials predicted by human capital theory. This was one reason why the relationship between scale of aggregation, zonal scheme and pattern of causality prompted methodological research on the so-called Modifiable Areal Unit Problem (MAUP). This research sensitized researchers to the need to better account for local effects. Emilio Casetti's geographically weighted regression approach and multilevel modelling were two such frameworks that could investigate how 'universal' effects (like distance decay) actually varied spatially, but neither was extensively used in the field. Some practitioners were less concerned with process insights and more focused on making accurate predictions of flow sizes. Considerable work was done to improve the estimation of regional migration in national accounting models (Rogers and Willekens 1986).

Broader issues of urban unrest and the implications of state withdrawal from social provision motivated research on why some groups were more likely to be mobile than others. This stimulated the convergence of individual and household-based accounts of migration and migration decision-making with the work being done on more aggregate models. While the behavioural tradition had already made a number of key contributions, particularly on intra-urban mobility, new approaches to individual preferences, the structure of decision-making and, more generally, the role of information and uncertainty meant that those interested in the *local* context of internal migration could begin to draw strength from both behavioural and microeconomic insights. Clark and Whiteman (1983) drew on job search theory to argue why it was in the rational interests of a worker in a fictional 'Poortown' to discount the higher potential wages in 'Richtown' and, contrary to human capital, reject moving. For the authors: 'rather than concluding that urban poverty and inequality is the result of poor individual motivations or some sub-optimal social attachment to a particular community, our model suggests that *place* characteristics are very important in determining the behavioral responses of individuals' (101–2, italics in original).

Random utility theory further deepened the appreciation of place context in models of migration. This framework had developed in transport economics as a way of providing reliable estimates of aggregate events (like traffic jams) while acknowledging that the individuals whose idiosyncratic decisions to contribute to the jam by being at that location at that particular time could and should be conceptualized as behaviourally different, albeit *within reason*. While human capital models of migration allowed for some group differences in behaviour, random utility theory allowed for individual variations in migration propensities – which behavioural research had evidenced – to be much more fully considered. These variations not only referred to differences in aspirations, motivations and attributes, but also to changes in these qualities and structural factors (like unemployment levels) over time. Did individuals become more risk-averse the longer they searched unsuccessfully for a job and adjust their expectations downwards? Did those who had moved before respond to adversity more quickly than migrant virgins?

This was an important development that required exacting data on the timing of key events (migration, job change, life-cycle events, recession etc.). Little such longitudinal data was available from traditional census sources. Being sourced from expensive panel studies, geographic representativeness was somewhat compromised. While these data yielded better information on the timing of population events, this often meant a trade-off in terms of geographic specificity. Results suggested that decisions about migration depended on individual characteristics, place characteristics and how these two sets of factors changed over time and with prolonged residence.

The growing desire to 'place' migration coincided with feminist critiques of accounts of internal migration. In conjoining these discussions, family migration theory represents a good example of how one specific research agenda became increasingly pluralistic. As with research on international migration, the household was seen as an important site where trade-offs about migration decisions were made. In the classic family migration model, Jacob Mincer had argued these trade-offs were ungendered in the sense that they only took account of who could earn what in a perfect market: if, as was still the case in most families in the 1980s, husbands earned more than their wives, it was in the family's interest to move in the direction of the male wage, even if that meant under- or unemployment for the 'tied' or trailing spouse. Quantitative research confirmed that, in many cases, migrant wives did appear to be acting as trailing spouses (Cooke 2001). Qualitative research helped show how family migration was gendered with migration seen as 'women's work' (McCollum 1990) for some. These women and their families planned accordingly, perhaps by choosing occupations like education and health services where employment opportunities were more likely to be available in a wide range of locales. Other women resisted moves or lobbied for moves that could help them meet their gendered (caring) responsibilities, increasingly to their elder parents.

Much internal migration research explored the implications of changes in the social structure of society for movement. Key socio-demographic trends included the increased diversity of household forms, changing patterns of cohabitation and out-of-wedlock births, delayed nest-leaving by young adults, the rise of blended families, level but historically high divorce rates, baby bust and boom cycles, demographic ageing and the increased participation of women in the labour force. Plane and Rogerson (1991) and Plane (1992) showed how the boom-bust structure of the US population had a strong impact upon migration rates. Other research explored the changing context of leaving home, marriage and migration, childbirth and migration, divorce and migration, and widowhood (Boyle et al 1999). The rise of dual-earner/dual-career households held important implications for the locational trade-offs required of married partners. In many cases, members of these households substituted long-distance commuting for regional migration to balance home-work tasks.

The rise of demographic ageing focused attention on the migration decisions of the elderly. One set of approaches to 'retirement migration' linked amenity theories of migration with the life-cycle event of retirement to generate hypotheses about the timing and direction of elderly mobility over the later stages of an individual's life. Accounts cast retirement migration as a life-cycle event whose operation in national spaces could be linked to modernization (Rogers 1992). Retirement patterns in Japan, Italy and the UK evidenced the three stages of the Elderly Mobility Transition (EMT), respectively. Work in the USA confirmed that retirement migration patterns shadowed overall population redistribution to the Sunbelt, and was amenity-led. More specifically, the link between retirement migration and rural housing markets emerged as a key feature of the internationalization of this stream. Indeed, the choice of rural destinations among many British retirees in France led Buller and Hoggart (1994) to characterize this flow as 'international counterurbanisation'. Ackers and Dwyer (2001) extended the focus on amenity and housing markets to consider the impact of personal savings and wealth, and the differential access to local services offered to retirees within Europe. Noting the growth of temporary (seasonal) migration, the growth in use of Recreational Vehicles (RVs) and the growth in the market for second homes in the USA, McHugh and Mings (1996) focused on the meaning of home among seasonal elderly migrants. In identifying 'three strikingly different lifecourse trajectories' among seasonal migrants (circular migrants still rooted in home, pendular migrants attached to two homes and linear, footloose migrants), the authors suggested that place attachments can play an important role in affecting mobility strategy.

The amenity, EMT and place-based frameworks all contributed to the further development of the life-cycle model of elderly migration. This hypothesized that while many initial elderly mobility events are related to labour market transitions and a search for amenity, and many elderly people make their last move in late old age for institutional reasons related to disabling health, the elderly also make a series of intermediate 'second moves' that are related to chronic health events and conditions that make it difficult to perform daily household tasks. While apparently freed from the locational requirements of paid work, retirees continue to face different structural constraints that make place context important in new ways. Ties to family and community – ties that elders both offer support through and receive support back from – are mediated by household structures, housing markets and changing patterns of government support. In turn, the sudden onset of dramatic life-changing conditions (often but not exclusively related to personal mobility, morbidity, death of a partner) means that the premium on proximity to networks of support both varies from individual to individual, according to their level of risk aversion, and over time for the same individual, as their expectations of themselves and their lives shift. The field has contributed to this thinking by examining co-residence, the separation between adult children and their elder parents (Rogerson et al. 1997) and, more generally, by considering elder location decisions within extended family life.

While life-cycle views had enabled some progress to be made in theorizing how social transformations were affecting migration, the growing interdependence between generations and the changing role of state provisions stimulated the development of a life-course approach to population matters, including mobility. This sought to integrate demographic life-cycle concepts with underlying social and political/economic transformations. The life-course approach sees individuals as social agents who are connected to society through linked, interdependent lives that are structured by three readings of time: biographical time (the role of events at one time in an individual's life that may enable and constrain options later); historical time (the roles of economic restructuring, globalization, geopolitical change, demographic ageing, civil rights frameworks etc.), and social time (the role of age-graded norms, expectations and institutions: Elder 1994).

To move this agenda forward, the Netherlands Organization for Scientific Research funded a decade-long research initiative; prosecuted by members of the NIDI, and involving collaboration with international colleagues; this initiative added to the work already underway in the USA (Van Wissen and Dykstra 1999). The framework has a number of specific advantages for studies of migration (Dykstra and Van Wissen 1999: 7–14):

- The search for order in the microbiographical details of individuals' lives conforms to epistemological assumptions common in demographic accounts.

- The tripartite reading of time draws on interdisciplinary understandings of structure–agency links (including the work of demographers, social psychologists, sociologists, anthropologists and historians).

- The emphasis on linked lives that are interdependent means that mobility events at one scale (residential mobility) can be seen as triggered by earlier events (job loss of a partner), but constrained/enabled by current circumstances (savings, presence of friends and family networks etc.). In short, places matter as sites of resources and constraints.

- The emphasis on biographical time encourages a more sophisticated understanding of how prior choices trigger, constrain and/or enable current mobility strategies. This includes a consideration of distant events and an exploration of how two different individuals, growing up in different places (with different experiences of historical time), may respond differently to two similar triggers.

- The interplay of biographical and social time means that an individual's factual biography (an actual sequence of activities and commitments) and virtual biography (how these activities and commitments are remembered and constructed) diverge in relational ways. That is, individuals not only remember and assess migration according to their own values and judgements, but in relation to prevailing norms about such behaviour, which unfold over social time. Again, place matters as a site where both biographical and social times come into focus.

- The focus on social and historical context also draws attention to the diverse institutional structures (firms, families, nations etc.) within which migration systems unfold.

To date, this kind of thinking has sponsored quantitative accounts of residential relocations, marriage and migration, transitions to independent living and the development of micro-simulation approaches to modelling interactions between individuals and their social context (Boyle et al 1998).

While life-course approaches were found in an increasing number of studies of local-level migration, amenities approaches to residential mobility continued.

Amenities – particularly proximity to central-city nightlife, museums, water-fronts, parks and the like – were invoked as partial explanations for rising levels of gentrification noted in many post-industrial cities in the 1980s and 1990s. Accounts of suburbanization ranged from those that implied that urban-to-suburban mobility was underpinned by a broad slate of quality-of-life considerations to those that saw the more general process in the context of structural inequalities in society. The aggregate phenomenon of counterurbanization, observed in many post-industrial societies in the 1970s and 1980s, suggested that migrants were leaving metropolitan areas for rural and semi-rural locations. Explanations focused on the role of employment opportunities, deep economic restructuring and amenity factors (Fielding 1986). For Gordon (1991), such counterurbanization required the insertion into the traditional mobility 'scale-process' hierarchy ('regional-labour', 'local-housing') of a third type of migration, 'intermediate-environmental'. In the US context, Gundars Rudzitis (1993) linked rural in-migration in the West to federal designations of wilderness lands.

Accompanying and supporting the theoretical diversification of accounts of movement was the growth of innovative methodologies. These included developments in: biographical approaches, ethnographic techniques, mixed methods, longitudinal modelling, simulation and three-dimensional life tables. Likewise, pluralistic sourcing of data saw innovative treatments of narratives (Chambers 1994) and literature, with King et al.'s (1995) *Writing Across Worlds* demonstrating, for one reviewer, 'the extent to which creative literature can enrich our understandings of the migration process' (Ogden 1998: 105).

Natural increase and decrease

Although rates of global population growth slowed after the 1970s, local rates of population increase and decrease showed increased variation. National and regional governments continued to demand demographic knowledge about how fertility, mortality and migration contributed to these differentials. The field produced further research on the demographic context of natural increase and decrease by developing spatial demographic methodologies and stressing the importance of demographic interdependencies. While some explanations for the patterns of uneven growth returned to transition theory and its modernization hypothesis, mixed-method approaches evidenced a diversity of experiences that demanded explanations more sensitive to the linked cultural and economic transitions of globalization. Critical positions began to address broader questions about the politics of reproduction and health.

Geographies of population growth and decline

With the underlying rate of population growth slowing, interest shifted onto the differential growth rates of populations across space. Governments were increasingly concerned about an immediate manifestation of these differential growth rates, counterurbanization. First described in the USA in the mid-1970s, census-based accounts suggested that the growth of non-metropolitan (often rural) areas occurred alongside patterns of population decline in metropolitan areas (Champion 1989). As some countries like the USA and the Netherlands witnessed an apparent reversal of the trend of non-metropolitan growth in the 1970s to show signs of urban revival and metropolitan growth during the 1980s, Geyer and Kontuly (1993) proposed a more generalized model of differential urbanism which, borrowing strength from the mobility transition of Zelinsky, argued that countries moved through stages of urbanization as modernization and economic restructuring proceeded.

Accounts of the regional diversity in growth patterns were often framed using the demographic transition. Van de Kaa (1987) proposed a second demographic transition for a European population, much of which had been declining for over 50 years. Kuijsten (1996) argued that the pluralization of lifestyles and the increased diversity of household structures characterized population change in this new setting. Rees (1997) focused more explicitly on ageing and its role in affecting population decline. Working outside Europe, Graham (1995) linked the future of demographic transition in Singapore to the role of education within this autocratic setting. Across South-east Asia more generally, land availability underpinned population growth; the implied 'frontier hypothesis' was further tested in a historical study of population growth on the Neolithic frontier in northern Europe (Bogucki 1988).

Paradoxically, while many accounts of population growth from within geography sought to explore its variability and associate this to non-geographical factors (including education, marriage and environment), demographers continued to hold that processes of geographical diffusion were important contributors to uneven patterns of population growth (Kirk 1996). However, despite continuing calls for further demographic transition theory development, demographers – and geographers, too – increasingly specified separate fertility and mortality transitions.

Fertility

Empirically driven research on fertility explored the spatial contexts of unequal fertility transitions. Two strong examples refer to the USA (Morrill 1990) and Ghana (Agyei-Mansah and Aase 1998). Local fertility variations characterized the border region of the former East and West Germanys (Lechner 2001). As China released more population data in an effort to better understand the implications of its own population and economic development projects, within-provincial fertility variations were reported for Guandong province.

Such empirical work extended transition theory in several ways. First, urban-rural fertility differentials persisted. China's fertility transition showed different experiences in rural and urban areas. Following the 1982 National Fertility Sample Survey, Coale and Chen (1987) disaggregated provincial fertility levels by urban and rural sectors and found higher fertility in rural areas. The existence of such differentials stimulated research on the following questions: how is population policy mediated by particular local places in rural and urban areas?; what role does temporary migration play?; what role does socio-economic development play, including agricultural reform policies?

Second, research questioned the universality of the demographic convergence thesis. Lechner argued that the fertility regimes of the communist and non-communist territories of Germany were converging over time. Sobotka (2002) countered that, in common with other transition economies where housing opportunities are in particularly short supply, fertility in what was East Germany may fall still lower than the 2000 (TFR) level of 1.3. Invoking notions of demographic momentum, Coleman (2002) maintained that divergence should be expected given that recent economic, political and cultural transformations have played out in different ways in different parts of the world.

Third, the field contributed to frameworks that sophisticated the links between modernization and fertility change. These included work on diffusion, micro-economic, secularization, gender and regulationist perspectives (Kirk 1996; Bongaarts 2002). Noin (1991) discussed if and how fertility transitions pass from one country to another. The diffusionist approach has its detractors (Greenhalgh 1995). Karen Oppenheim Mason (1997) noted a 'leader and follower' dynamic among national populations in Europe, with 'leaders' experiencing a set of economic, cultural and political triggers that reduce fertility, and followers adopting the example set by the leader, even if they themselves do not experience the same set of process controls (449). Empirical evidence was mixed, with district level work on fertility decline in India (Bocquet-Appel et al. 2002) undermining elements of the framework.

While the progress of fertility transitions was of continuing concern to international agencies and national governments, the period marked growing interest in the fertility experiences of groups sometimes considered to be at the edges of society. This attention was fuelled both by the higher profile that feminist scholarship had given to reproductive rights, and the budgetary concerns of organizations like the World Bank, who wanted to design efficient fertility interventions (including 'safe motherhood': Smyth 1994). Population geographers began to describe the experiences of teenagers, minority groups and those located in the non-metropolitan periphery. Population programmes and campaigns used powerful representations of bodies and sexuality to draw population performances into the public domain. Figure 4.2 shows a recent campaign image from the USA. By looking at the cultural constructions of fertility and reproduction, critical positions linked population acts like intercourse and abortion and population performances like pregnancy and parenting to changing social norms and state population agendas.

Research on teenage pregnancy illustrates the field's enlarged approach. Rates of teen pregnancy showed significant variation over space. The relatively higher age-specific fertility rate of women aged between 15 and 19 in the USA was tied to the differential between white and black teens (Caldas 1993) and access to social support. These factors had a much less clear role when geographic variations in teenage pregnancy were examined within countries such as England, Wales and Scotland. Here, conception rates for 15–17-year-olds varied from 75 (per 1000 women, 15–17 years old) in the north-eastern industrial port of Hull to 16 (per 1000 women, 15–17 years old) in Tanbridge, a leafy-laned dormitory town close to London. While poverty and levels of deprivation account for some of these variations, not all conceptions result in live births. The geography of teen conceptions intersects with another complex geography of abortions.

Geographies of termination suggested that girls growing up in the more affluent areas of southern England had rates twice those of girls growing up in deprived areas of the north. In the late 1990s, the per cent of conceptions in Hull and Tanbridge leading to abortion were 31 per cent and 59 per cent respectively. Still other areas have high conception and high abortion rates, and low conception and low abortion rates. Religion is one factor that may undergird this spatial complexity. In the USA, Gober (1994) found that the size of a state's Jewish and Catholic population was related to variations in abortion rates because of the

diapers at home.

I want to be out with my friends. Instead, I'm changing

DIRTY

sex has consequences | www.teenpregnancy.org

Figure 4.2 Constructing teen pregnancy.
Source: *www.teenpregnancy.org/media/psa/ads/ad.asp?imgName=dirty (accessed July 2004).*

ways that state governments translated the Supreme Court *Roe* versus *Wade* decision into legislation. Such complexity suggests the usefulness of further research on the local dimensions of, for example: attitudes towards abortion and how these vary by social class and ethnicity; marriage (nuptuality) patterns; attitudes towards out-of-wedlock conceptions. Historical reconstructions of fertility and nuptuality behaviour uncovered local variations in norms about premarital sex and carrying illegitimate children to term (Woods 2000).

Work in economic sociology deepened understandings of the links between minority status, teen pregnancy and place. Patricia Fernandez-Kelly (1994) drew on ideas about social networks to explore the meaning of childbirth to teens growing up in a deprived neighbourhood of West Baltimore. We meet 12-year-old Towanda, a 'gorgeous woman-child with a grainy inflection and eyes full of dare', and quickly appreciate how the gendered and raced rites of passage for this teen moving into adulthood do not involve the middle-class norms of education, with its implied returns and promise of participation in a market economy. This is because Towanda and her friends have place-centred social networks that do not reference the trappings of success, but illuminate signs of the African–American community as an 'underclass' problem to be resolved (the presence of social services, police patrols): 'Towanda Forrest is neither shunning mainstream values nor comporting herself a pliant victim. At every step of her disfigured life, she has deployed knowledge and made decisions to control the resources available in her environment, one of which is the ability to procreate' (108). At 17, Towanda had abandoned school, was expecting her second child and noted 'some things are just meant to be'.

Just as Fernandez-Kelly's reading of teen pregnancy went beyond demography, MacLeod and Durrheim's (2002) examination of how South African medical literature depicted black teen pregnancy as deviant underscores the cultural and political significance of population acts and performances. The authors describe how racialization ('a representational process whereby social significance is attached to certain biological – usually phenotypical – human features') in South Africa recently morphed from an apartheid-era view of whites as superior to a post-apartheid depiction of black Africans as inferior. The deviancy of black teen pregnancy emerges as a key part of this representation of inferiority. The authors show how biomedical discourse 'explains' the increasing levels of black teen pregnancy as a response to the collapse of traditional social structures and to 'contact with western culture . . . that had shattering effects on the traditional life of blacks' (790). The problem and deviancy of teen pregnancy is traced back to the inability of traditional (African) culture to adapt. Medical discourse legitimizes state policies targeted at black groups to reduce teen pregnancy. The article also suggests how state-funded knowledge systems can co-opt population acts and performances for political ends, in this case, the repositioning of blacks in the newly emerging spaces of the nation state.

Yvonne Underhill-Sem's work contributes to the development of such a 'politics of reproduction'. She examined how communities in the Wanigela region of Papua New Guinea represented and took meaning from pregnancy, childbirth and maternal mortality. Her 2001 study is informative at multiple levels. First, it suggests that discourses about population acts constitute relations between

139

individuals, and thus communities and places. Second, it suggests that these discourses call on place-specific and embodied notions of time and space. By referencing the transition from 'staying' to being in a state of 'activity' (i.e. pregnancy) in terms of the moon phase, women were embodying a construction of space-time that both cut them a degree of flexibility (control) over the 'due date', and was linked to the rhythms of their means of livelihood, subsistence gardening. In a sense, how they talked about being pregnant served to reproduce the links between gender systems, space-time and place. Underhill-Sem further supports this point by noting that an absence of discussion about the circumstances surrounding conception, pregnancy and childbirth was not related to any sense of prudishness, but out of the respect that community members had for each other's silences about the experiences of a dangerous moment. Absence was as much part of the social field and interactions as presence. Third, while the author makes no apology for exploring a discursive approach to the broader question of 'bodies that bleed – too often – to death', she makes no attempt to hide the very real difficulties of merging this politics with a more positivist and seemingly policy-relevant approach. As she concludes: 'an ethnographic context does not tell us everything either. As I have shown about talking and not-talking about child-bearing in Wanigela, the unsaid is not the unknown, but the differently known' (209). Such poststructural accounts can offer 'different but valid' insights to the field.

Mortality and morbidity

Research on the links between mortality, morbidity and population structures turned from a demographic focus on patterns of death and disease, inequalities and the ecological analyses of these spatial variations, to embrace broader views of how space, place and environment linked to health and wellness (Gattrell 2002). It benefited from the tearing down of institutional divisions between the field and medical geography, medical anthropology, health geography, epidemiology and political ecology (Rosenberg 1998).

As with the approach to fertility and migration, descriptions of the spatial variations in demographic events (deaths) and the incidence of those events in taken-for-granted populations formed the springboard from which exploratory analyses of cause and effect were launched. While overall levels of economic output increased over the period, global differences in mortality rates showed a persisting gap between the North and South (Cliff and Haggett 1988). Indicators of morbidity (poor health) confirmed that the global burden of disease was shouldered by the majority world of the South. The Disability Adjusted Life Years

(DALY) indicator sums the years of life lost due to premature mortality and severely disabling conditions; in 2000, the sum of DALYs from countries of the South accounted for over 90 per cent of the global disease burden. The impact of dramatic political economic restructuring was revealed by studies of within-European variations in mortality over the 1980s and 1990s. While national life expectancies increased (as they did in Japan and the USA), the rate of change varied spatially and socially: Eastern Europe, affected by the dislocations of the fall of the Soviet orbit, witnessed slowly improving life expectancies for women, but dramatically declining rates for men (Noin and Woods 1993). In Hungary, male mortality rates increased over 50 per cent during the 1990s. In western Europe, sex-specific life expectancies also diverged, with French women expecting an additional eight years of life compared with men (while the Greek gender gap was just half this: Meslé and Vallin 1998).

Spatial variations in mortality and morbidity between the regions of nations revealed further differentials. In the UK, the government-sponsored Black Report (DHSS 1980) flagged such inequalities and sparked an ongoing research agenda that links north-south variations to social class, lifestyle, diet and poverty factors, among others (Dorling 1995). In the USA the differential life expectancies among whites, African Americans and Native Americans focused attention on how race and ethnicity differentials might intersect with regional (Deep South, Appalachia) and urban (inner-city) variations. Just as the Black Report had suggested persistence in many patterns of mortality in the UK, research in the USA has pointed to the coincidence of spatial and temporal structures in mortality (Morrill 1990). Cossman et al. (2004) counted how many times each county of the USA had been ranked as one of the most 'unhealthy' in the USA for six five-year periods between 1968 and 1997. The map of figure 4.3 suggested six spatial 'clusters' of temporal persistence: the Piedmont belt of the south-east; the Mississippi Delta; central Appalachia; Michigan's Upper Peninsula; western South Dakota; and northern Nevada. While many of these locations played signal roles in the Civil Rights movements of the 1960s, their continual reappearance throughout the 1970s, 1980s and 1990s as places where one fundamental human right – that of health – is threatened suggests much still needs to be done.

Some of the most exciting local work to appear drew on historical reconstruction. Dobson (1997) presented a detailed picture of infant mortality rates of the local parishes on the isolated, low-lying, reclaimed expanses of the Romney Marsh in south-east England. This area's formerly harsh mortality regime is still very much in evidence today, with deserted churches lying miles from the nearest

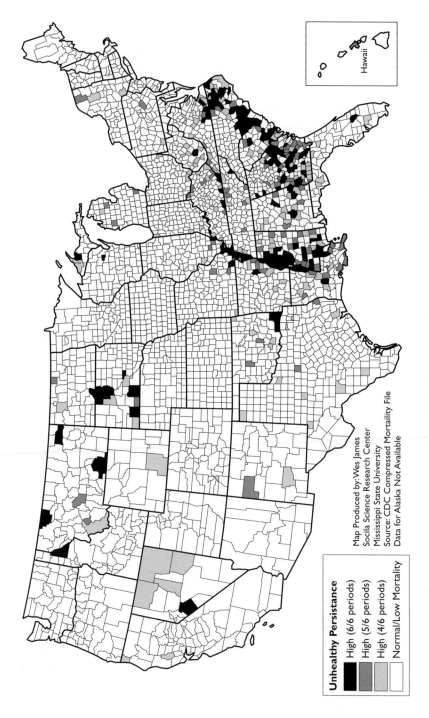

Figure 4.3 Persistently unhealthy places to live, US 1968–1997. Source: Cossman et al. (2004: 90)

settlement. However, causality is hard to infer. Environmental factors, including dampness and often stagnant water in the extensive network of drainage ditches, intersect with political economic factors, including the extreme impoverishment of the region and its reliance on trafficking for income supplements, to paint a complex picture.

Where data have been available, ecological modelling of spatial variations in mortality and morbidity broadly suggest associations with: genetic programming and population mixing, lifestyle factors, social norms and social capital, working conditions, health services and provisions, deprivation and poverty and environment. Prior migration patterns have also been shown to exert a significant effect upon the aggregate patterns of morbidity and mortality. Research on disease clusters used new methods of visualization and analysis (Openshaw et al. 1988; Anselin 1992).

These empirical contributions in turn fed into at least five research agendas. Three of these – concerning the role of diffusion, the epidemiological transition and the roles of the environment – were well established and deepened understandings of the ways that state policies affected the mortality and morbidity of groups in different ways. Scholars also looked at how the political and cultural context of globalization affected health by using constructivist approaches to study identity and poststructural approaches to view health as embodied and emplaced. Together with the renewed interest in work on the environment, the latter agendas responded to epistemological concerns about the reliability of the categories used in the earlier work of health differentials (including age, sex, race and disability).

Research on the spread of infectious diseases as a diffusion process had a well-established pedigree in the field. The near singular opportunity to work with particularly detailed local historical records in the nearly closed (and ethnically homogeneous) system that is Iceland led to a series of publications on the changing nature of influenza epidemics (Cliff et al. 1981). This diffusion approach was also applied to understand the spread of HIV-AIDS and to point to areas of future risk.

Population geography contributed to the development of epidemiological transition theory (Omran 1983). Clarke et al. (1989) argued that 'natural disasters', like earthquakes and river-bank flooding, should be considered alongside public health interventions. Avinoam Meir (1986) argued that one little investigated element of modernization in nomadic societies, sedentarization, was sometimes associated with elevated mortality rates. He found that sedentarizers 'made up' for higher mortality with higher fertility regimes. This kept rates of natural increase sufficiently high to support the introduction of new production regimes. Likewise concerned with economic transitions, albeit in a different context, Demko et al. (1999) reported that the marketization of formerly centrally controlled economies undermined social supports and public health provision and reversed the epidemiological transition in the former Soviet Union. McLafferty and Tempalski (1995) tied the uneven geography of low birth weights in New York City to changes in health-care regimes across the city.

While the environment had long featured in the field's accounts of mortality and morbidity, a growing recognition of the global scale of many 'ecological' processes, like ozone depletion and climate change, and the attendant links to globalization, prompted re-examination of the links between ecological, economic and social change. Efforts to theorize the environmental contributions to mortality and morbidity cut across disciplines and epistemological approaches. Epidemiological analyses investigated how specific environmental properties may be related to health outcomes. Work addressed the linkages between air quality and health (including specific studies of the Bhopal disaster: Kayastha and Nag 1989) and water quality and health (including research on specific diseases, like cholera and schistosomiasis, and the presence of pollutants in water supplies: Hunter 1997).

Some population geographers worked with a disease ecology framework (Learmonth 1988) to formalize the often local roles of the environment. Global climate change is often associated with the increasing frequency of so-called 'extreme' events. To take the recent case of 2003, a record number of tornadoes were recorded in the US Midwest; record temperature levels 'caused' the death of over 11,000, mostly elderly, people in France, 1000 people in India and 700 people in the USA; Asia experienced severe floods (as had central Europe the summer before); and bush fires threatened land in Australia, Canada and the USA. Analyses of how global climate change might have triggered these mortality spikes reveals that new land-use practices, themselves the product of agribusiness production regimes, played contributory roles.

While some accounts of global change connected mortality and the emergence and spread of contemporary diseases to the way in which political economic factors have produced unstable environmental contexts, others focused on the specific arenas and systems through which environments affect health. To take the example of food production, research continued to develop variants of Malthus's hypothesis. During the 1980s, global food production increased at a rate faster than that of global population growth. However, the consumption of food actually declined in sub-Saharan Africa and parts of Asia. The World Health Organization estimated that around 340 million people worldwide (but mostly in the global South) consumed less than 80 per cent of their benchmark 'adequate intake' at this time. For Grigg (1995), the changing nature of world food markets, driven by western consumption patterns, also contributed to the morbidity effects of famine by rewarding farmers for producing non-staple crops for export. While war, political dysfunction, fuel shortages and generalized lawlessness are all cited as contributors to famine, Jowett (1987) argued that poverty relations within societies were underlying causes, not neo-Malthusian population-resource balances involving environments. Most generally, structuralist commentators argued that famine and the production of 'natural disasters' were often endemic features of colonial and imperial systems of control, which had devastating consequences for local health.

While neo-Marxist approaches to theorizing environment–health linkages provided a counterweight to neo-Malthusian theories based on scarcity, the increasingly social and populist connotations of what constituted the environment led to the development of research that sought to better integrate the 'social' into the equation. The Rio Earth Summit and the difficulties surrounding the Kyoto Protocol substantiated the position that national governments were unlikely to be the only actors who could 'manage' the environment. Other global agreements – about reproductive rights for example – had been reached, suggesting that mult-scalar alliances between non-governmental organizations, local governments, businesses and so on could be effective. For Harvey (1996: 377–83), the development of what he termed the 'ecological modernization' perspective was further enabled by the sense of living in a 'risk society': floods, famines, pandemics and other extreme environmental catastrophes could touch any of us, anytime.

Accordingly, some geographers called for greater attention to the health implications of natural hazards, and for pluralistic approaches to intervention (Kates 1987). Others – noting the growing body of health inequalities research – suggested that the idea that the environment acted in such a way as to put us all equally at risk of poor health was, in fact, flawed. A growing focus of work linked patterns of health inequality to the politics of environmental justice. Environmental justice scholarship maintained the political position that because social groups (especially those based on poverty, race, ethnicity) exhibited health inequalities that are associated with the distribution of environmental hazards, it is these inequalities that should be the focus of environmental research and activism, not the environment itself (Cutter 1995).

Population matters informed research on environmental justice in at least four ways. First, empirical studies looked for evidence of any disproportionate burden being placed on certain groups in local places. The United Church of Christ (1987) and Bullard (1994) argued that impoverished and minority communities were more likely to be exposed to pollution because of where they were living. Geographic analyses of environmental justice demonstrated disproportionate burdens for children and minorities (Bailey et al. 1994). Second, the act of migration (and its absence, immobility) presented a disproportionate exposure to harmful environments. Low-income groups may be forced to live on marginal land where rents are cheaper but where hazards are greater and regulations and controls are weaker. In a market economy, these residences often have low resale value, and low-income groups remain trapped in such areas.

Third, the gendering of population performances like mothering implied that low-income women may be more exposed to local harmful environments than those with wider quotidian assignments. Fourth, discrimination has often been targeted at specific population groups. Rafiq's (1991) analysis of female child mortality rates across Bangladesh suggested sex-specific forms of discrimination. Furthermore, discrimination was shown to operate through the production and circulation of discourses of difference. The positioning of differenced and marginal populations on marginal land produced discourses of symbolic violence against these communities, further undermining health (and, with racist and hate attacks, leading to mortality).

Like environmental justice scholarship, work on the links between social constructions of identity and health focused on how systematic health inequalities arose in particular places. Feminist readings of the unequal health burdens carried by women formed a stimulus for the field. In turn, some of these approaches had been partly influenced by the direction of international support for social programmes under an increasingly neo-liberal context. During the 1980s, the World Bank had begun linking its development interventions to specific social targets, which included the reduction of maternal mortality rates. Smyth (1994) described one of the bespoke 'safe motherhood' initiatives introduced in Indonesia, which reorganised the delivery of primary health care and birth control provision in an attempt to prevent unwanted pregnancies and improve women's basic health status. However, ideology prevented the programme from reaching unmarried pregnant women. Cultural norms meant these women often sought traditional or unregulated terminations, which generally increased their chances of morbidity and mortality.

Feminist critiques to such top-down and essentializing interventions drew attention to their mis-specification of the important role of identity constructions and social norms in affecting behaviour (Correa 1995). The 1994 International Conference on Population and Development in Cairo took the WHO view that health was not so much an absence of disease but a 'resource for living', and as a basic human right was best protected by ensuring groups had the resources for living they needed. For mothers, this meant having access not only to procedures of 'safe motherhood', but also to educational, economic and political resources in their societies. The growth of this 'reproductive rights' agenda (Grimes 1999) played an important role in putting the social construction of identity – including the identification of restrictive and empowering norms and expectations – centre stage in investigations about women's health.

In *Geographies of Women's Health*, Dyck et al. (2001a) present a collection of essays that discuss how gender systems, often intersecting with other identity systems, affect: reproductive health; health outcomes amongst immigrant women; differential access to health care, often as a result of gendered quotidian assignments like commuting and childcare constraints; health in the sex industry and in other workplaces; health across the life course; and how law impacts the health of women. In a similar vein, Susan Craddock (2001) deepened the analysis of HIV-AIDS in East Africa by considering women not just as sex workers, but also as actors who are more generally constrained and enabled by place-based identity systems. Ezekiel Kalipeni et al.'s (2004) *HIV and AIDS in Africa: Beyond Epidemiology* further explored how intersecting identity systems of gender, sexuality and race affect HIV-AIDS transmission and treatment.

An emerging tranche of research looked to 'understand the healthy or ill body outside medical discourse ... picking up on general questions concerning gender, place, body, and subjectivity' (Dyck et al. 2001b: 12). Poststructural and postcolonial interpretations provide ways of reading how 'health' is inscribed on bodies (for example, wheelchair users), performances (for example, childbearing) and population groups (for example, refugees hailing from countries with high HIV prevalence) in ways that are not only place-contextualized, but place-constituting. Gesler (1993) argued that places could function as therapeutic (health-enhancing) landscapes. Others have considered discourses of chronic illness (Moss and Dyck 1996). The self-reflexive discussion of their research on 'the geography of/ geographies of' home death by Brown and Colton (2001) echoed Underhill-Sem's concern that poststructural and positivist approaches to knowledge may not be 'reconcilable' in any kind of pluralist way, but could offer different and equally valid insights.

Geographies of population composition

Through their work on population composition, geographers confronted two increasingly important global population issues: demographic ageing and race/ ethnicity. A good deal of this work continued to describe demographic inter-dependencies between age, sex and social structures and fertility, mortality and migration over different spatial scales. It was appended by pluralist and critical investigation of how population groups like children, the elderly and minorities were placed by and in society. As the field's concerns enlarged, particular attention was given to how the economic and cultural transitions of globalization changed the relationships between population groups, space/place and states.

Males to females

The field's scholarship on sex ratios demonstrated variations over space and explored how local, place context lay behind these uneven distributions. In a widely read piece, Sen (1990) argued that as many as 100 million girl babies had 'gone missing' globally, due to sex-specific differentials in fetal and infant mortality. Decomposing this aggregate picture facilitated the comparison of sex ratios across urban areas and regions and pointed to sex-selective migration and cultural norms surrounding son preference. As the use of qualitative methodologies grew, universal declarations that societies practised female infanticide were replaced with more nuanced debates about the cultural factors surrounding fertility, accessibility to ultrasound technology, educational levels of women and repro-ductive rights (Tien 1984).

Examination of male-female ratios in rural China demonstrated how demo-graphic explanations could be supplemented usefully with accounts that took state interventions in population matters seriously. Two bequests of China's one-child policy were an unbalanced sex ratio (more males than females) and demographic ageing. The presence of fewer siblings alongside the continuation of gendered norms about elder caregiving meant that many rural women will face an increased burden of care for elder family members. Furthermore, many rural women will face increased pressure to earn income outside the home, but, if moving to seek work in cities, reduced means to do so, owing to a policy of restrictive housing access in some Chinese cities. Finding time for relationships and family life is likely to reduce rates of nuptuality and could further suppress fertility. Thus, the demographic system connection between sex composition and fertility is complicated by the interaction between migration, gender roles, household structures, work and past and ongoing state policies.

Age

The field's research on age composition encapsulated its overall shifts in focus over the 1980s and 1990s. Spatial demographic approaches focused on the growth of populations in census-defined age groups and fed into debates about economic productivity, pension provision and social services. Pluralist and critical approaches argued that age was a social construct that took meaning from and contributed to the experience of place and space.

Demographic ageing began to be presented in the media as an economic and cultural crisis of global proportions akin to the fall of the Roman Empire. A special issue of the journal *Population and Environment* (2001) illustrated the range of perspectives surrounding ageing, economic growth and immigration. Using the dependency ratio as a summary statistic of the balance of the 'productive' population (aged 15–64) to the 'dependent' population (aged under 15 and over 65), forecasting models suggested demographic restructuring was indeed imminent. In the USA, the ratio of the working-age to elderly-age population was projected to move from 5.3 in 2000 to 2.8 in 2050, while in Italy the comparable statistics were 3.7 and 1.5, and in Japan, 4.0 and 1.7. In each case, a hypothetical worker would be asked to support around twice the number of elderly residents in little more than a generation.

Contributors argued that the levels of immigration that would be needed to get countries back to some former value of the ratio of working-age to elderly-age would be so high as to generate significant cultural dislocation. Such scenarios have prompted the United Nations Population Division to debate the strategy of increasing immigration to meet labour shortages ('replacement migration'). Arguments against any strategy that increases population growth note that continuing low fertility levels would be in the global ecological interest (for example, the USA could reach its Kyoto targets sooner with fewer consumers, assuming continuing per capita emissions rates). Other perspectives criticize the UN's decision to focus only on migration destination countries and not consider the simultaneous impact of replacement migration upon countries of origin, many of which depend on economic remittances (Conway and Cohen 1998). The ability of ageing countries and regions to compete under free trade conditions has also been questioned. Such debates highlight the value of continuing methodological developments in forecasting (Woods and Rees 1986).

Research on the geographies of elderly populations expanded from its traditional concern with the size, composition and dynamics of elderly communities. At the start of the period, Warnes (1982) called for new geographic research on the global geographies of ageing, the local circumstances of the lives of elders and analyses of the temporal changes in interactions between geographic environments and elderly people. Rowles (1986) called for more attention to be paid to social integration of the elderly in society (including the roles assigned to the elderly and their social and spatial distance from other members of society), dependency between elders and family members and other groups, environmental setting and issues related to physical mobility and elderly migration behaviour.

Reflective of a continuing concern with areal differentiation, many accounts of the elderly thus proceeded from maps of the distribution of the population aged 65 years or over (with data available from national censuses). International (North–South) variations in the relative share of elderly populations were traced to the recency and speed of fertility declines, that is, to fertility transition theory. While these trends were apparent in comparing northern and southern Europe, the growth of International Retirement Migration (IRM) was shown by the population profiles of southern France and the Algarve (King et al. 1998).

Sub-national patterns of ageing revealed sharp regional differentials in the growth of elderly populations (for example, in states like Florida and Arizona in the 1980s and Idaho and Montana in the 1990s). These patterns were 'complicated' by the extent to which elderly population concentration led, or followed, more general trends of population deconcentration. In an indicative approach, Warnes and Ford (1995) considered the different housing needs of the young old (65–75 years of age, or early late age) and the old old (75 years of age and above, or late late age) in Britain and found that even among the old old, a trend to urban deconcentration had been underway in the 1980s. Other quantitative research explored the diversity of the elderly using such continuums as health status, personal mobility status and the need for care/assistance.

Commensurate with its readings of space, the field sought to explain the characteristics/nature of elderly populations with reference to patterns of elderly migration and access to care. A significant body of work has applied the main theories of elderly migration outlined above to explain observed spatial variations in elderly locations and settlement concentrations (for example, Newbold 1996). While work on international retirement migration stresses the role played by positive amenities in attracting retirees to southern European locations, longitudinal work and case studies both demonstrate the diversity of migration strategies and the importance of ties to family and friends in certain places in affecting how long elderly groups remain *in situ*. Many of these ties have developed over considerable periods of time, and the duration of these linkages and their strength can offset the role of health events in prompting or postponing migration. Qualitative work is also suggesting cross-national differences in adult–child and elder parent proximity relations, and in how caring arrangements are organized along class and gender lines within families (Smith 1998).

Research increasingly questioned the use of the age concept to define elderly. Patricia Sachs' (1993) evocative description of the ex-coal-mining community of Deckers Creek, West Virginia, started from the position that ageing is 'a social process that can be analysed in terms of how people have actively constructed their lives, and how earlier life experiences and wider world events have shaped the condition in which they live' (157–8). For Sachs, social relations within Deckers Creek were based on the values of those remaining residents who had experienced the town during its mining days, and the values and experiences of those who had moved to the community more recently. While the first group was 'older', age *per se* was only one dimension along which groups were separated: the others being the lack of kin connection between the groups and their different (gendered) work histories. Thus 'it was the older generation who effectively defined the unspoken rules of the community ... these rules were based upon how one should properly neighbour, operate a household, keep one's yard, define the boundaries between houses, sweep the sidewalk and care for one's garden' (157).

This constructivist view illustrated how experiences of being elderly varied from place to place and across space, and how the construction of old age was tied to the production (and reproduction) of social relations and place. Critical perspectives explored discourses associated with ageing. Pain et al. (2000) traced ways in which leisure spaces used by elderly people were constructed along gender, ability and class lines. The production of difference around ideas of age and aged performances in space both enabled and constrained elderly people's projects, and helped reproduce notions of leisure spaces.

Problematizing the age concept expanded the field's research on other population groups, including children. In truth, children had been something of a novelty to the field in the early 1990s. Thought of as demographic and political dependants, children were not perceived to be active agents in their social or cultural settings, despite making significant economic contributions to family livelihoods in many societies. Economic and social trends, including growing levels of consumption, patterns of youth delinquency, supposedly deviant behaviours (including teen pregnancy as discussed above), and the sex trade involving children, helped to change this. A new journal – *Children's Geographies* – aimed to 'discuss issues that impact upon the geographical worlds of children and young people under the age of 25 and of their families'. Coinciding as this did with the field's interest in how identity was socially constructed in particular places, a number of practitioners wrote 'geographies of children' and 'geographies of childhood' (Matthews et al. 1998 and Holloway and Valentine 2000).

In their edited volume on the topic, Holloway and Valentine (2000) asked how space helps children to be purposive social actors who actively construct childhood. The volume shows how three performances – playing, living and learning – not only shaped childhood, but also constituted the family that children are part of and variable notions of home. Among street children who lacked a single place of residence, the idea of home was found to be an imagined place imbued with notions of protection and sanctuary. The theme of children as active cultural producers also runs through Chatterton and Hollands' (2001) depiction of how teens and young adults produce distinctive nightscapes. This research is important because children, and youth, come to be defined by their economic and cultural performances in place, not on the basis of calendar years (Valentine 2001). Furthermore, in this process of becoming, they reproduce local (cyber)places and help reconstitute population groups like families. Ruddick (2003) argued that new discourses of youth and childhood are accompanying the restructuring of capitalism in place-specific ways. States are key players in this. Concerns with the shrinking supply of workers underwrote lifelong learning agendas in the EU. Discourses surrounding education constructed childhood in relation to wider neo-liberal strategies.

Households and families

Households and families were traditionally studied as demographic structures that affected fertility (through nuptiality), mortality and migration. The pluralization of household formations across societies sparked new research on how context affected the rise of household forms, the roles of households in society and how home–work balances varied across urban and rural places. This cross-cut with debates on identity in social geography, and patterns of work, consumption and leisure in economic geography.

Noting European trends towards a lower mean household size, Hall (1993) pointed to the decline in the number of very large families, and the rapid increase in the number of single-person households. While multigenerational households were increasingly rare, complex patterns of blended households and one-parent households were emerging. Kuijsten (1996) contributed an influential depiction of this growing diversity of family organization, which he interpreted both in terms of the pluralization of lifestyles and the onset of the second demographic transition. Reher (1998) likewise emphasized the divergent experiences of southern and northern Europe and traced these back to long-standing historical differences between these regions. Research also suggested local and regional variations in, for example, the concentration of one-person households, dual-career households and same-sex households (Valentine 1995; Green 1997). Immigration policies, marriage markets, residential patterns and cultural preferences were all seen to play a role in increasing the incidence of mixed marriages, ethnically/racially blended households and mixed-race partnering.

Spatial divergence in these household geographies was linked to variations in nuptuality (including age at marriage, cohabitation and remarriage), parenting, separation and divorce, and how these are impacted by employment, housing, consumption and policy contexts. One way in which the field contributed to understanding these linkages was by investigating the circular relations between migration and household structures over space. International skilled migrants who move as family units often concentrate in particular neighbourhoods of large cities (White 1998). At a regional level, Jarvis (1999) showed that the mobility prospects of households were contingent upon their employment structures. In addition to patterns of work, household geographies were also responsive to the relative locations of adult children and elderly parents (Liaw et al. 2002). Many of these studies used life-course approaches to integrate the home–work concerns of families with more contextual considerations of employment and housing markets and changing government policies. Duncan and Smith (2002) suggested that local gender constructions of partnering and parenting may be beneath observed geographic variations in household forms in England and Wales.

Ethnicity and race

Throughout the 1980s and 1990s, ideas about race and ethnicity occupied central positions in public discussions about the meaning of cultural identity under globalization, and why it was that some population groups continued to be more impoverished than others. However, a 1984 collection of the field's scholarship devoted less than a page to a discussion of race and ethnicity (Clarke 1984). Progress in developing the field's contributions on race and ethnicity mirrors the shift from demographic to social and cultural perspectives seen above. Over the period, readings of how population acts and institutions produce discourses about ethnic and racial communities helped it enlarge its view.

The dominant treatment of race and ethnicity explored how these census-derived markers of identity varied regionally and locally. This included descriptions of how the five major race/ethnic groups were distributed in the USA (African Americans, Asian and Pacific Americans, Hispanics, Native Americans and whites: Allen and Turner 1996), the distribution of Asians in Canada (Kobayashi 1988) and how new immigrant groups were located across Europe (Peach and Glebe 1995). Other studies of the geographic organization of ethnic groups that did not involve the use of census data included Kaplan's (1994) analysis of Francophone and Anglophone linguistic groups in Canada, and a growing tranche of research on diasporic and transnational communities (Cohen 1997; Van Hear 1998).

Concentration and segregation emerged as key empirical motifs that described the spatial experiences of ethnic minority communities, and the field set about accounting for these patterns using a demographic systems lens (White 1993). This drew attention to how international and forced migration was mediated by government policies on admissions (including family reunification programmes) and settlement. Minority communities were also affected by the propensity to return migration among groups including West Indians in Britain and guest worker populations in Europe (Waldorf 1994).

Concentration and segregation were further impacted by migration through the tendency of many minority communities to adjust their initial settlement geographies to cluster in particular cities and regions (for example, Hmong groups in Minneapolis-St Paul). Some formerly clustered communities – including Cubans in Miami – began exhibiting regional patterns of dispersal and deconcentration. More generally, the link between international and internal migration was explored in the US context by Frey (1996) and Wright et al. (1997). Frey argued that patterns of 'demographic balkanisation' resulted from the displacement of low-income whites from immigrant gateway locations like Los Angeles.

Clark (1998) explored how the local geographies of ethnic and racial communities were affected by housing and labour markets. His analysis of California suggested that 'many immigrants from diverse backgrounds – Canada, Europe, China, Korea, and the Philippines – have become (home) owners . . . and are well on their way to economic incorporation and acculturation . . . substantially poorer immigrants of Mexican origin have greater difficulty in becoming owners' (136). Large populations of Mexican and Latino migrants arrived in California at a time when house prices were increasing and housing supply was tight. Reduced access to housing opportunities had also had a negative impact upon the educational portfolios of these communities, with implications for their ability to break out of a 'cycle of inadequate education and low-paying jobs' (137). This can be compared to the experience of many Puerto Ricans in New York City in the 1970s.

Research also suggested that the future growth of ethnic and racial communities was being shaped by how migration and settlement affected age-sex structures. In the Netherlands, the government immigration policy of family reunification had the effect of elevating fertility rates of Turkish and Moroccan immigrants to levels somewhere between those of the origin areas and those of the native Dutch. The relatively youthful profiles of these 'recent' minority communities contrasted with the ageing profiles of longer-established groups, many of whom migrated as family groups, like Italians in France. For White (1993), the future dynamics of immigrant communities is best understood through the interplay between migration streams, state policy and settlement strategy.

While such research did illuminate important patterns (including the persistence of segregation and likely demographic futures), assumptions about the data it used were exposed and criticized (Bonnett 1996). For example, was the use of census definitions of ethnicity responsible for the invisibility of Irish communities in work on the geography of the British population? In the UK, the public recognition by the Committee for Racial Equality that people of Irish origin had been subject to racial discrimination demonstrates the limits of majority-minority frameworks that had drawn attention away from invisible minorities like the Irish (Walter 1998). Did the absolutist and phenotypical basis of race classifications set a majority white group up as a normalized population, against which the behaviour of others should be compared? In the USA, the emergence of Hispanics as the largest minority population undermined the use of the traditional black-white binary used to understand race relations. Were Europe's largest minority community, the Rom, better described in racial or ethnic terms, or were limits in both constructs partially responsible for the singular lack of attention given to this population? How was identity to be recorded by the children of mixed-race parents?

The field responded to these critiques in several ways. Some called for new census categories (Bonnett 1996) or adjustments to existing classifications (Allen and Turner 2001). Many acknowledged that ethnicity and race (like sex, age and households) were social constructs. Social constructivist approaches suggested that these labels were made/negotiated/contested in specific places around specific cultural ideas. This 'particularity' encouraged ethnographic and qualitative approaches that demonstrated the diversity of experiences. More critical readings suggested that race and ethnicity, along with other poles of difference, helped create and maintain societies' power structures through the production of place-based discourses. These discourses involved the acts, performances and institutions of populations (including migration, partnering, childbirth, parenthood, households, caring: Anderson 2002). Discourses surrounding migration and ethnicity enabled South Africa's post-apartheid regime to construct a new space for its national identity (Croucher 1998). By articulating illegal immigrants as threats to the (new) national interest (bringing as they did disease, competition for jobs and demands on scarce social services), the state could mobilize a population act for its political ends. Households were also identified as key sites where new identity discourses emerged. For Wright et al. (2003: 470) the household formation 'collectively constructs, contests, and performs paradoxical racialised identities'. Twine (1996) and Pratt (1997) focused on how emplaced population acts such as dating recreated the race hierarchies experienced by college 'brown skinned white girls'.

Livelihood and well-being

Population geographers examined the implications of various population acts, performances and institutions for individuals and societies. As these agendas expanded their hitherto empirical and largely economic foci on individual livelihoods and national development profiles to consider more fully links between population, economic and cultural transitions and states, approaches which emphasized the active and constitutive role of population attained more prominence. Accounts of livelihood and well-being turned to relational ways of reading and writing social change.

Trewartha's general schema for population geography incorporated descriptions of characteristics like educational levels and employment experiences (1953). Its shadow continued to fall across the field in the 1990s, as is evidenced by the subjects of Noin and Wood's (1993) chapters on population livelihood: spatial variations in education, total employment, unemployment and female employment across Europe. Livelihood was measured using economic and aggregate markers of labour market performance. Spatial variations were linked descriptively to economic context, national sociological context (for example, the strength of the Catholic Church and the roles of women) and demographic change (migration and age structure).

Across the social sciences, research on how population growth/decline impacted national economic fortunes moved away from a concern with overall population change to more detailed analyses of the components of that growth. Commensurate with broader political concerns, this meant more research on how demographic ageing and migration would impact development. Reflective of the political and academic shift in onus, Menken (1994) reported that few studies of the relationship between overall population growth and economic development proved an outright causal link, either positively or negatively. New crises – particularly ageing – demanded attention. For the Commission on Global Aging, the worsening demographic situation after 2010 posed a significant threat to the world economy.

Within population geography, Skeldon (1997) argued that the relationship between development and migration was mediated by a series of demographic interdependencies that demanded a demographic systems approach. Elsewhere, work shifted from its dependency theory-led consideration of brain drain to examine: how immigration affects host economies (Massey et al. 1999); how and why states encourage out-migration as a development strategy; and how remittances affect the economic development of source countries. While debates about the net impacts of immigrants on destination economies featured the work of prominent social scientists (Harris 1995), the field's own contributions come in the form of case studies (Coleman and Salt 1992).

The geographies of remittances have received the field's attention as an example of a demographic and economic transaction that exploits the needs that many states in the global South and their populations have for cash, and that many states in the global North have for cheap and expendable labour supply systems. Remittances have become, quite literally, big business (see figure 4.4). They grew from an estimated global volume of $71 billion in 1990 to over $100 billion in a decade. First- and second-generation immigrants typically remit between 6 and 16 per cent of their household income, which, in Latin America, contributed to between 8 and 15 per cent of the GDP of source countries. By contributing qualitative and ethnographic case studies, population geographers deepened the debate about how these financial flows impact source countries and regions (Connell 1992). Remittances helped many families avoid poverty and were spent on essentials like food and clothes. Remittances can also generate multiplier effects and new business opportunities, including specialized courier companies that service the increased cross-border trade. They improve a country's balance of payments and access to foreign currency. The pervasiveness of remittances in El Salvador was one reason that led that country to 'dollarize' its economy in 2002 and start phasing out the use of its national currency, the colon.

Figure 4.4 Constructing remittances. Source: *www.bracbank.com/remittance.asp (accessed July 2004).*

Case studies also suggested that remittances created dependency. This fuelled further out-migration and made foreign investors less likely to invest in local employment schemes. For many governments, remittances are hard to track, tax and otherwise divert into national economic planning strategies. Remittance income is dependent on economic, political (in terms of work permits and immigration controls) and geopolitical events (war, such as the invasion of Kuwait in 1991). These are often outside the control of source governments and thus variable and difficult to incorporate into macroeconomic planning. Meanwhile, the growing prominence of the notion that international migration might be regulated in a way that recognizes the interdependencies of demographic systems makes continued case-study work timely (Ghosh 2000).

While the growth of remittances signalled new ways in which state policies enabled and constrained population behaviour, debates about how and if states should manage the relationship between migration and regional economic development had occupied the field's attention in the 1980s. Human capital accounts of internal labour migration had shown that those with higher levels of education were more mobile and thus more likely to be entering (and leaving) regional labour markets. Political wisdom of the 1980s argued that those who could, generally did (migrate), and that the government's role in promoting economic growth should be to reduce the constraints on factor (including labour) mobility. A British cabinet minister of the day famously remarked that unemployed workers should 'get on their bike': by reducing individual constraints on mobility, the public social good could be enhanced. In his thoughtful critique of this orthodoxy, Gordon Clark (1983) adopted a social justice perspective that advocated using a community integrity justification for bringing jobs to the workers, rather than the free-market logic of bringing workers to the jobs.

The growth of return migration in diverse contexts (including the US South, Caribbean and southern Europe) sparked work on how social norms and local cultural expectations affected regional economic fortunes. King's (1986) contributors recognized that returning international migrants could bring with them capital, skills, networks and access to government grants that would all promote growth. The evidence also suggested that many returnees had retirement in mind and were sometimes resented by locals, because they had been absent from the community and they might have received preferential access to grants upon return. Noting that some returnees had been away for several decades, local cultural and economic practices had often shifted quite dramatically in this period, and some returnees found it hard to readjust.

In addition to analysing the role of migration upon economic change, researchers also examined the contribution of age and household structures. Plane and Rogerson (1991) noted that the regional location of the US baby-boom cohort would play a key role in shaping that country's internal migration flows and influencing the changing size of regional labour markets. Added to this, declining fertility and changing nuptuality patterns had diversified the organization of households across space. This had increased the demand for single-person households in areas experiencing in-migration. Thus, population geography contributed to what Myers (1990) called an emerging concern with 'housing demography' when it recognized the geographic dimensions of demand for physical and social infrastructure.

Assessments of the direct impacts of migration upon the economic standing of individuals rather than regions or nations drew on the human capital approach that saw migration as an act expected to generate microeconomic returns that could be measured through wage growth, labour force participation rates, career progression and so on. The field argued that an awareness to place context enhanced this framework (Brown 1994). Clark (1998) reported that immigrant employment experiences in California were strongly segmented by gender and ethnic origin.

Dual labour market theory hypothesized that immigrants were increasingly likely to be segmented into the secondary sector where low-paying and unskilled jobs gave them few opportunities for advancement. Demographic and socio-economic shifts – including the rising levels of women in the workforce and the unwillingness of many native-born workers to staff secondary jobs like cleaning and transportation – contributed to this increased polarization of fortunes.

Rather than emphasize external forces, adherents of social capital approaches to segmentation argued that the internal resources and information networks of immigrants often led to niche and occupational concentration. While considerable work looked at ethnic enterprises, Ellis and Wright (1999) explored how social capital reduced risks for both employers and employees and promoted segmentation. Examining the experiences of those often thought to occupy the primary labour market, the field also concerned itself with how the internal labour markets of firms, as well as opportunities for promotion and career enhancement, underpinned the geographic organization of, and outcomes to, highly skilled migration (Koser and Salt 1997).

Gender differentials in returns to international migration were widely reported among refugees, undocumented workers and formal immigrants. In common with work on ethnic segmentation, gendered analyses record diverse outcomes over space, such as those described among Chilean political exiles in northern California (Eastmond 1993). While human capital approaches pointed to differences in factor endowments (typically, education), feminist scholarship explored how interactions between gender systems and contextual factors lay behind differential returns. In Malaysia, Eden (1989) linked international migrant women's economic situation both to macroeconomic change and the (cultural) labour market practice of letting women go first when recession or a downturn in orders approached. Indeed, often members of the secondary labour market, many immigrant women had been hired on part-time contracts.

Subject to structural discrimination and the pressures of meeting cultural obligations in dual locations, the employment and locational strategies of many Puerto Rican women in the USA were framed in economic and cultural ways. Puerto Ricans had circulated between island and East Coast mainland since the 1960s. Research suggested that individual economic standing in what remains one of the most impoverished groups in the USA was related to human capital variables, like education and age, and to time of arrival and availability of entry-level employment, particularly in textiles. Overt racial discrimination and more subtle employer perceptions about female circulators demonstrating an appropriate lack of commitment to work also contributed to lower employment rates. Ethnographies further revealed that many women used circulation to deliver productive and reproductive responsibilities on the mainland and on the island, and had developed gendered migration strategies over their life course that incorporated (in an active way) flexible/partial attachments to the labour market (Ellis et al. 1996). Thus, just as structure and agency debates infused work on the 'causes' of migration, so, too, did it characterize discussions of returns to immigration. Indeed, skilled migrants who were women, and partnered, illustrated ambivalence about the nature and meaning of their apparently unequal returns on prior human capital investments, compared to their husbands.

While empirical work suggested that migration led to a variety of livelihood experiences, critical perspectives argued that gender and ethnicity were not so much categories to be compared or variables to be modelled, but integral parts of broader discourses on immigration, work and space. One example of research which read the work experiences of immigrants in more critical terms was Evans and Bowlby's (2000) investigation of the work practices of first-generation Pakistani-born Muslim women in the south-east England town of Reading. What was considered 'appropriate' work became linked to the intersection of gender, class, diaspora, characteristics of the local labour market and the life-cycle stage of women. Patterns of work, in turn, changed how women represented themselves and how they were represented. The authors reported that some respondents opted for a preferred lifestyle of caring for children and home-based roles rather than a formal work career.

Patterns of diversity in the economic returns to internal 'family migration' also began to be acknowledged. The genderless expectations of human capital theory became successively complicated by research that suggested race, household structure, return migration to a previous place of residence, the structure of the local labour and housing market and life-course events made a difference to how negative (or, in some cases, positive) the economic impact of a migration event proved for married women (Boyle and Halfacree 1999). Gender-role theory and structurationist approaches began to organize these and ethnographic findings around expanded views of gender and race.

While theoretically and methodologically pluralistic, much of the family migration agenda focused on the experiences of women in the developed world (see also Boyle and Halfacree's 1999 edited volume on *Migration and Gender in the Developed World*). Regional-scale family migration work kept its distance from addressing international migration, and from the more local hypothesis of the spatial mismatch. This examined the returns to commuting and immobility for women and men. While family migration acknowledged demographic inter-dependencies and became more interested in context, it paid less attention to scale, neo-liberalism, cultural change and household pluralization. For Halfacree (2004: 409): 'we must expose the intimate associations shown between everyday understandings of terms such as migration, career and commitment, with the priorities of the capitalist globalization project.'

While family migration agendas rarely ventured into the global South, generalized accounts of how migration affected livelihoods in developing countries continued to attract considerable interest. Some of this research built on dependency theory to explore the gender dimensions of how migration perpetuated continued structural underdevelopment and focused on how urban destinations fuelled the continuing cycle of underdevelopment and labour migration (Mukherji 1997). The Habitat Agenda, arising from the Second UN Conference on Human Settlements in Istanbul (1996), drew attention to how (over)-urbanization affected livelihood through the operation of demographic (migration and health) and geographic (networks of production) interdependencies. Wasserman (1999) noted that the feminization of migration in Latin America had bequeathed the feminization of urban poverty in the region's cities. However, with changes in international division of labour, and particularly the growth of the *maquila* (cross-border assembly plant) sector, many women had moved to work zones where infrastructure provision, health care, work practices and environmental regulations raised serious concerns about their health and the region's ecology, and thus the ability of many women to sustain themselves economically.

Links between the ecological outcomes to population growth and livelihood were also explored by Bilsborrow (1998). Fincher (1991) stressed the inter-dependence between economic, population and environmental transitions and argued that, in Australia, environmental degradation was more likely to be triggered by local patterns of consumption, local population redistribution and the export-driven economy, than by patterns of immigration or refugee settlement. Gilbert (1998) believed that global patterns of governance and political inter-dependencies affect the role of environmental contingencies.

In acknowledging the growing import of global interdependencies, accounts of population livelihood increasingly sought to theorize the changing roles of states under globalization. Charged with maintaining borders, the visible signs of capital and labour hypermobility across and through these increasingly porous zones suggested weakness. Yet, borders also offered a discursive opportunity for the state to re-establish political and cultural legitimacy. Research focused on how state discourses constructed documented immigrants, undocumented immigrants, asylum seekers, refugees and other migrants, and how these constructions affected the livelihoods of these groups (Ong 1995; Van Ewijk 1998).

The ways that individuals and their communities constructed new identities also deepened understandings of how new communities and populations were merging under globalization. Gendered migration literature showed how gendered identity norms could, in some places and times, be contested following migration. Chilean refugee women recast their roles within the exile community in California as they became the main wage earners in households (Eastmond 1993). For Morokvasic (1991), however, such shifts were likely to be façades only, with the reality of (immigrant) women having to engage in paid employment to support the family and continue to perform their reproductive and caring duties, contributing to poor health. Many of the contributors to Buijs's (1993) *Migrant Women* found that migration, partnering, mothering and caring served to reinstate unequal power relations between women and men, and between women and their immediate and extended families. Context emerged as a key element in shaping differential outcomes:

> the conditions available to refugees and migrants in the host countries shaped and mediated adaptation and facilitated in some cases the ability of women to take control over their own lives ... for those strong enough to resist ... imposed identities and who managed in the face of odds to accommodate new lifestyles, the boundaries which they crossed provided hope and inspiration for the future. (18)

Over the period, the field came to view terms formerly taken for granted, like sex and gender, in a different light. In joining the fecund discussion of census and international data standards and methodologies (Dale et al. 2000), Ellen Percy Kraly (1997: 225) argued that:

> gender should not be considered a descriptive characteristic of migration but a universal dimension of social relations, culture, power, and economy and thus a crucial structural dimension of the causes and consequences of migration, refugee movements and population displacement. Accordingly, age and gender must be incorporated in fundamental concepts of international migration not merely to reveal differences among men, women and children, but to reveal the relationships among gender, migration, and development.

Any sort of final solution?

Change more than continuity characterized the field over the past two decades of the century. Research poles addressed issues that were increasingly presented (and understood) as having complex and intersecting demographic, economic, social and cultural dimensions. The field acknowledged and responded to new contexts of interdependency. Addressing how demographic interdependencies affected population issues had long been a defining trope of the field. Theorizing processes that were simultaneously demographic and economic and social and cultural prompted explorations of methodological and epistemological pluralism. While pluralist positions seemed equipped to soldier through various 'phoney wars', for example, between qualitative and quantitative methods, structure and agency and economic and non-economic factors, critical positions introduced an edge to discussions of geographic interdependence. Rather than reduce 'geography' to passive context, critical thinking urged scholars to explore how space, place and environment 'answered back' and shaped the kinds of knowledge that were produced as researchers encountered the researched. Relational views of the world challenged what was meant by geography, what was meant by population and, by extension, how the field understood itself.

The field's treatments of the interdependencies of globalization have several bearings on its further directions. The use of the term population has enlarged beyond its traditional demographic deployment. Population continues to function as an adjective that signals a narrowing of focus, as with the phrases 'population determinants' and 'population acts'. While this usage formerly sponsored research on, for example, the economic consequences of demographic events, the field is increasingly concerned with the social and cultural nature of population acts and performances, and how these affect lives, communities and places. Population also functions as a noun when it refers to social groups like 'national populations', 'prison populations', 'gay populations' and so on. How the noun takes on its multiple attributes becomes the subject of work on constructions and discourses. Table 4.2 summarizes some of the ways in which the concept of population has been enlarged.

Second, future directions would seem to depend on what the treatment of interdependence implies for theoretical rapprochement. While theoretical convergence has been called for between medical and health geography, and detected for political geography (Mayer and Meade 1994; Agnew 2002), it seems less likely in population geography. In some regards, the contemporary phase shared an

Table 4.2 Progress in expanding the population concept.

Demographic events and concepts	Indicative population acts, performances and institutions	Discourses
Migration	Residence, home	Migrancy
Fertility	Pregnancy, parenting	Sedentarism Nomadism
Mortality and morbidity	Disease	Nationalism and transnationalism
Age grades	Childhood, youth, adolescence, adulthood, old age, retired	Ageism Ableism Familism Healthy bodied
Marriage, divorce	Dating, partnering, widowhood	Sexualization Individualism
Group membership	Gender, class, sexuality, race, ethnicity, nationality, religion, family	Secularization Racialization Modernism Colonialism

eclecticism and fragmentation with pre-1950s population geography. There are significant differences, however. The division between contemporary scholars identifying with the term 'population geographer' and those desisting often reflects ontological rather than ideological disagreements. In reflecting upon their juxta-position of a foundationalist, positivist analysis of spatial variations in home deaths in Washington, with a poststructural critique, Brown and Colton (2001: 817) concluded: 'the nature of the debate is more extensive than being merely disputes over method or topical purview, but reflects a more profound dispute over the nature of truth and our relation to it as scholars ... we underscored the import-ance of recognizing the impossibility of ever reconciling these radically different perspectives'. For the authors, there was 'no final solution' – no rapprochement – in sight.

Most generally, what kind of field is population geography becoming? Compared to the dominant view at the start of the period of a field with a definable core (demography in its spatial context) and clear boundaries (Woods 1982), there is now sufficient uncertainty over what are the core concepts, and, more signifi-cantly, there is enough distrust of the very notion of a 'core' concept in any field of inquiry, that the field, as we knew it, has ended. That said, rubbing the terms population and geography together continues to generate intellectual heat.

What seems to be emerging is a field that lacks a single core, a clear hierarchy, an agreed-upon set of methods, or theories, or ontology, but which nevertheless seeks knowledge that informs society about the intersections between population and geography. In this regard the field has elements of the Motown about it: variously a record label, a set of recognizable musical outputs and a more generalized cultural aesthetic negotiated by fans, the music industry, the state, media and so on. That is, its institutional 'label' is still alive and, for many practitioners, an important source of professional identity. It continues to contribute to certain theoretical agendas and debates, and thus has recognizable outputs (including research on migration and ageing). But it is increasingly appearing as an aesthetic, 'made' by those interested in producing and acquiring knowledge (scholars, states, communities, activists), made by its past reputation and space-environment-place 'sound', made by its representation in the media and civic society and made by its relation to the ongoing institutionalization of geography within academia.

As a more 'networked' project, the field draws strength from its past contributions and its relations to society, geography and academia. Collaborations across specialisms, teams and nations, and alliances with diverse groups in society can both address (in a reactive but contributory sense) and call into being (in a proactive and agenda-setting sense) population matters. Some of these emerging agendas are introduced in the final chapter.

ALTERNATIVE FUTURES

This chapter examines how population geography continues to be made. While the intertwined geopolitical, cultural and theoretical dislocations of the turning of the millennium have profoundly shifted society's questions, knowledge and politics, the valency of 'population' and 'geography' persists. While there is disagreement over which versions of 'population' and 'geography' to use, the growing disparity between the world's rich and poor and the worsening state of the environment suggests there is work to be done in formulating alternative visions of society. Contemporary population geography believes that the intersection between population and geography offers a productive means of contributing alternative visions.

I discuss how three research agendas inform alternative visions. These agendas refer to transnational geographies, the geopolitics of population and activism. My purpose is not to suggest these will become the defining tropes of the field over the next decade: not only is this somewhat disingenuous, as these themes are already quite well established in many corners of the literature, but it is also inconsistent with the idea that any particular research theme would dominate and exclude other perspectives. What these themes do enable me to discuss is how the field continues to remake itself with reference to the opening theme, the changing role of the state under globalization.

Population, security and neo-liberalism

Freed from the strictures of paradigmatic thinking and having to uphold disciplinary boundaries, the field's practitioners seek new knowledge alliances across subjects and with non-academic partners. However, with fewer sources of funding for research and trimmed state budgets, it seems likely that capaciousness may be directed to a few strategically funded and multidisciplinary research agendas that address the topical priorities of society. For contemporary states, population matters are being framed increasingly by the twin concerns and demands of security and neo-liberalism.

Events of 11 September 2001, as well as those in Bali, Madrid and elsewhere, have made debates about security key political sites of engagement. This has led to the creation of new political structures (the Department of Homeland Security) and the up-resourcing of others (the intelligence services in the UK received a significant budget increase in 2004). Population groups (Muslims) and global regions (George Bush's 'Axis of Evil') are demonized in political and popular rhetoric. As the space-shrinking technologies of globalization enabled capital to go on a global 'walkabout', states became increasingly concerned about the conditions of access to their territories and their populations.

Underlying heightened security concerns is a growing ambivalence about the role of technology in public life. Diverse technologies – including the application of science to the production of food and the regulation of free trade – offered to bring progress to society by following the precepts of a global neo-liberal agenda. However, the development of Genetically Modified (GM) crops has been slowed in some cases (notably wheat) by fears of consumer backlashes, motivated by a heightened sense of risk and loss of food security. Mad cow disease, foot and mouth disease and outbreaks of bird flu further illustrate global (food) security concerns about the practices of modern farming and the effectiveness of states in regulating these practices.

In political, ecological and economic ways, security matters represent an urgent challenge to the role of the state under globalization. Similarly, arguments that question the extent to which neo-liberalism is promoting global development through free trade, open markets and reduced state welfare provision further call into question exactly what sort of role states should be playing to deliver social progress.

Population issues intersect with these security and neo-liberal agendas. For Zygmat Bauman (1998), differential movement under globalization has been a key element in the transformation of welfare states, the rise of neo-liberalism and in affecting the access different groups have to opportunities and resources. The diversity and complexity of global migration has stretched to breaking point (and beyond) those political institutions (national belonging, assimilation, cultural pluralism, multiculturalism) that had promised to deliver social progress to all (Castles and Miller 1993). Growing levels of migration have been interpreted as threats to national identity and, more recently, national security. Other population matters are also seen as threats to security and neo-liberal strategies. Ageing threatens economic security; internal migration threatens the security and integrity of local infrastructure; and global pandemics remind us all of our mortality.

With its enduring interest in states and its enlarged perspective on populations and space, the field of population geography has begun to contribute some productive ideas and approaches to contemporary discussions. The balance of the chapter introduces three agendas. First, transnational geographies connect people, products and ideas in ways that both transcend and, ironically, reinvent, the state. Some states reassert themselves by using population-based strategies of enablement and constraint. Second, the geopolitics of population considers how diverse tactics and technologies are used by states and their agents to reassert the state's political, economic and cultural agendas. This geopolitics of population infuses bodies, borders, communities and societies. Third, activism and action-oriented research inform population geography. Taken together, these research poles begin to outline some of the roles population geographers play in working towards alternative visions of social justice.

Transnational geographies

Members of transnational societies lead daily lives that reference and transcend national boundaries and that support multiple ways of belonging. In some cases, particularly among the international business elite, new ways of belonging are facilitated by frequent and near-immediate communication across borders, where hypermobility appears the norm and connectivity is everything. In other cases, including sex workers and domestic workers, constraints on identity and belonging accompany the illusion that borders are equally porous to all. Indeed, in population geography, and across the social sciences, such 'transmigrants' are often cast as harbingers of a new, transnational social order. Such an individual is perhaps in possession of multiple passports and maintains dual (or more) home bases and a commitment to daily life in each of these homes. As such, the transmigrant is distinguished from a settler, who would have progressively fewer connections to an origin, and an exile, who would maintain only a partial commitment to their temporary refuge.

Evidence of the growth of transnationalism comes from the strength and enduring nature of commitments to dual home bases marked by the dramatic rise in global remittances (see chapter four). While many of these will be sourced by contract labourers working fixed-term contracts, there is evidence to suggest that such workers rarely return permanently, but instead seek new contracts and thus an ongoing commitment to a way of belonging that both references and transcends national borders. The size of remittance flows, and the impact they could make to local economic development is not lost on many national governments. States increasingly accept transmigration and attempt to manage it through the granting of dual identity (see below). By the mid-1990s, individuals in seven of the ten largest immigrant streams to the USA were eligible for dual citizenship.

While it is tempting to reduce the essence of transnationalism to a population act (transmigration), an emerging tranche of research in the field argues that studying the tensions of living daily life 'between here and there' provides a more profound insight into a social form moulded by the contradictions of neo-liberalism and maintaining security. In searching for non-demographic accounts, practitioners have been attentive to at least three debates outside geography. First, US-based cultural anthropologists and political scientists focused on trans-national social fields that interposed the cultural experiences of two places (supporting new forms of identity and belonging) and refashioned the relationship between migrants and nation states. Nation states became 'de-territorialized' in the sense that national (political and cultural) discourses and projects were not anchored by specifically demarcated state boundaries.

The fact that 'national' projects and discourses remained as an important reference within transnational social fields distinguished this heritage from a second orientation, more akin to cultural studies. Appadurai (1996) explored how elements of cultural change under globalization untethered identity and belonging from 'national' discourses and examined how identity and belonging emerged under more abstract and hybrid situations, noting that the state was 'on its last legs' (6). The possibility that, for example, new social groupings could emerge in a transnational space that was beyond the nation state, either 'above' (concomitant with the rise of post-national rights) or 'below', sparked lively discussions about borders as sites of resistance (Anzaldua 1987) and, most widely, the construction of diasporic identities (Huang et al. 2000).

While both these streams of thought acknowledged coincidence and connection between transnationalism and globalization, a third set of inspirations drew from economic sociology, world systems theory and consumption theory to more explicitly integrate accounts of transnationalism with the global circulation of products and cultures and the transformation of global governance (Portes

1996; Smith and Guarnizo 1998). While various commentaries on the 'state of play' of transnationalism can be regarded as attempts to nudge what has become a quintessentially multidisciplinary agenda towards one or other of these edges (Bailey 2001; Crang et al. 2003), much extant work, such as that discussed below, sought to combine these insights.

Population geography has engaged with this literature through a nuanced discussion of how population contributes to and arises from transnational geographies. I give five examples here. First, the repeated population acts of movement between here and there and over national boundaries forms one way in which transnationalism is constituted. Second, other population acts, including parenting and the construction of inter-generational relations, unfold in distinctive ways under transnationalism. Third, the circulation of commodity cultures and the economic contours of globalization underpin how daily life links to belonging. Fourth, belonging is renegotiated as identity systems – gender, ethnicity, race, affinity etc. – are remade by the tensions of living between two places, that is, of living relational lives. Finally, transnationalism has implications for how we theorize space, and therefore how power to effect social change is vested with the state and other groups.

Transnationalism and population acts

How do population acts contribute to transnationalism? This was a key question in Mountz and Wright's (1996) study of the ways that daily life in a small Mexican community had become 'stretched' over space and time. Like many Mexicans living in the USA, those hailing from San Agustín, Oaxaca, had built up a chain migration stream to one specific destination, in this case, the deindustrializing Hudson Valley city of Poughkeepsie, New York. The first *Agustino* began working in a restaurant in the city in the mid-1980s, and within a couple of years was joined by relatives, and later by other friends and so on.

What Mountz and Wright add to this established networked view of migration, with its inbuilt idea of demographic and cumulative causation and consequence, is a more sophisticated, structurationist reading of movement, social space, networks and community. Their study focuses on the daily events in the social field that is the transnational migrant community connecting Oaxaca and Poughkeepsie (OP): events like migration between the two places of residence; the transfer of material resources; and the circulation of gossip, innuendo, favours, obligations, corpses, medicines, videos and affection. With over one quarter of the 'village population' working in Poughkeepsie in the mid-1990s, and most of these males, the functioning of OP plays an integral role in the life of the Mexican community and, in different ways, in communities north of the border. For example, the study revealed a general lack of desire to settle in the USA, partly fuelled by experiences of exclusion, and suggestive that belonging was being defined with respect to OP rather than either of the specific locations of residence. Indeed, the experience of OP was so pervasive that a new semiotics had begun to develop.

The authors examined how migration promoted and shaped OP. OP had developed strict gender assignments over space as a result of migration strategies. Poughkeepsie was 'normed' as a male employment space and San Agustín as a female space of reproduction (a kind of transnational nursery). This system was predicated on the flow of remittances, which in turn made visible a new 'conspicuous consumption class'. Their activities, expectations and projects (in space, such as construction, and in community time, such as fiestas) helped transmit new consumption, migration and gender norms. While other work has also read 'transnational' gender systems as extensions of traditional practices (Mahler 1999), Mountz and Wright go on to discuss how the transnationalism of OP is resisted by individuals and groups through population acts (see table 5.1).

The role of a population act like migration in fostering and shaping trans-nationalism is clearly complex and goes beyond demographic notions of migration

Table 5.1 Population acts and transnational dissent. Source: *Mountz and Wright (1996: 421–4)*

Group	Nature of dissent
Los irresponsables	Break conventions of OP by not remitting, failing to stay in touch, and participating in deviant activities like drug use.
Female migrants	By leaving San Agustin, women migrants not only enter male production space but also turn their backs on reproduction activities: many also risk marriage possibilities as their virginity reputation is undermined.
Seventh Day Adventists	Numerically subordinate to the village's Catholics, Adventists remit to family rather than community, and are unsupportive of public projects including festivals.
Practical questioners	Oppose the development of a public culture in OP and target remittances into investments in their children's futures through education.
Wife robbers	Men – and assenting women – who desist from the practice of investing in a week-long marriage ceremony elope to Poughkeepsie and call home to report.

as 'adding people' or 'changing the selectivity of the population' to encourage a deeper reading of how social systems are functioning over space and time.

Work on the links between transnational belonging, migration and caring deepened understandings of population performances in contemporary society. Of the immigrant Latina mothers in Hondagneu-Sotelo and Avila's (1997) sample of Californian domestic workers, 40 per cent had one or more of their children living in Mexico or Central America. For many contemporary immigrant women, transnational motherhood, a reality of daily life, is anchored by the concerns of 'milk, shoes, and schooling' (562): that is, managing sustenance, protection and preparation activities over space and through complex kin and community networks.

Motherhood was transformed under transnationalism in several ways. Latinas had to negotiate new meanings for and practices of motherhood that borrowed elements from both their own cultural heritage growing up in Latin America, and from the (middle-)classed and (white, Euro-American-)raced women many worked for as domestics. Attitudes toward motherhood were both enabled and constrained by the overwhelming desire 'to do what is best for one's kids', against a backdrop of material deprivation. When they could afford to do so, many women brought their children to the USA. This practice ran against the grain of the poorest and the richest strata needing to/choosing to subcontract out mothering tasks. Notwithstanding these generalizations, variability in the supply of local opportunities for income, strength of network connections, time away and commitments to the extended family led to a diverse range of motherhood strategies being deployed. In turn, both transnational belonging and migration were transformed by these motherhood practices.

Over time, Hondagneu-Sotelo and Avila observed less frequent migration but higher levels of remittance flows and instances of other forms of regular communication. This substituting of migration for 'virtuality' was also a feature of the changing practices of transnational grannies, who transacted caring between the Caribbean and England (Plaza 2000). Distant grandparents and godparents formed important resources for mothers and stretched transnational geographies socially. In a study of Salvadoreans, some US-based women extended their residence in the USA to better perform their roles as transnational mothers who could provide financial support for the education of their children based in El Salvador. Preparing their children for the future by earning enough to fund their education ironically implied bringing children to the USA at a later date. Despite sending back remittances, messages, affection and other resources to their children, anxieties over the daily lives of their distant children, which included fears of neglect and even abuse, increased tensions between kin. Transnational space became freighted with information, surveillance, gossip and other forms of knowledge circulation. In some cases, persistent misunderstandings split families (Miyares et al. 2003).

In other contexts, discourses about parenting and childhood support different transnational geographies. Systems of caring and the circulation of affection have been examined through discourses about childhood. Orellana et al. (2001) suggest that the strategy among some South Korean families to send 'parachute kids' to the Los Angeles suburbs to access education is one case where children 'lead' transnationalism. While the international locational position of children is carefully managed by (current or intending) immigrant parents and tends to reinforce child–parent power relations, the authors also point to the ways in which the norms surrounding childhood are transformed as a consequence of 'childhoods' being constructed as central to transnational belonging. Transnationalism, migration and caring are redefining the meaning of population in contemporary immigrant communities and, in so doing, affecting how we understand the making of current and future population groups.

Transnational society

Research on transnationalism deepens our appreciation of how population groups arise in a networked society. For Portes (1996), transnational societies exemplify globalization from below. Just as finance capital and commodity cultures have adopted new and lucrative forms of global organization and hypermobility, so, too, has labour. Just as these multinationals adopted global strategies that exploited differences in national level opportunities (wage levels) and constraints (environmental legislation), so, too, could workers and their communities reorganize themselves into transnational communities – like OP, the overseas Chinese, non-resident Indians and so on – that exploited globalization by transcending the nation. National interests have long extended to the management of both economic production and social reproduction, and rather than displace these national interests, what some suggest is that globalization from below has rewritten national projects (Harris 1995). The management of transnational populations has become a key component of rewriting nationalisms. Nowhere is this more obvious than among the largest transnational community, the post-1978 new migrants from China.

Pál Nyíri's (2001) exegesis of how the Chinese government actively produces a discourse with idealized transnational behaviours, meanings and commitments opens up a series of important questions about how contemporary populations are being produced. Citing official publications he notes that:

> the state brokers of migration are thinking of the migrants as people who remain part of the Chinese economy and polity, strengthen the ties of the overseas Chinese to China and, as highly skilled professionals and successful business people, improve the standing of Chinese in their host societies ... new migrants, unlike the old diaspora, are bound to China not only by ties of blood and culture but also by sharing the modernizing goal of the state. (638)

This transnational discourse is facilitated through the increasing reach of media (world wide web, satellites, cable) and the appearance of new migrant media that are based locally (for example, *Ouzhou Daobao* is one of around eight Chinese newspapers or periodicals based in Hungary) or designed to reach more widely (*Tianxia Huaren* – Worldwide Chinese – has a global circulation and is produced in London). In their depictions of daily life, Nyíri notes that these media present a standardized discourse that 'continually reproduces the Chinese/foreign dichotomy and re-"others" the foreign' (640). This discourse also distances itself from traditionalist, rural southern tropes of Chineseness that are deemed insufficiently 'modern, global, or mobile' (644). We are left with an irony: while mobility threatens the idea of fixed 'national' populations, ideas about mobility enter a new patriotic and decidedly nationalistic discourse as one of the tropes of contemporary transnational society (Samers 1997).

Mitchell (1997) and Willis and Yeoh (2000) explore the broader relationships between identity systems, diaspora, transnationalism and population groups. With an eye on context, this work challenges 'the reductionism of universalizing women's experiences in diaspora' (Huang et al. 2000: 392; Dwyer 2000). The use of postcolonial and feminist perspectives examines how transnational meanings of origins (there) and destinations (here) suggest more than (the absence of) proximity. In an analysis of discursive constructions of nannies, Pratt (1999) intimates that the here and there of transnational society are relational concepts that reinforce historical and geographical asymmetries. Identity – be it class, gender, ethnic, national, sexual – intersects with the differences and unevenness of transnational society through the relations between here and there. In his postcolonial manifesto, Kumar calls for a shift away from 'an eclectic celebration of difference' and on 'to a premonition of difference as tearing despair' (2000: 225) that can begin to expose the 'narrative of the tussle in between'.

One of the most penetrating readings of just this tussle emerges from Monisha Das Gupta's (1997) work with Indian women living in New York City. Over a million 'Asian Indians' (the census category) make their home in the USA, and are part of a worldwide diaspora (see figure 5.1). Many non-resident Indians (NRIs) have preferential access to investment schemes in India and maintain ongoing links with India. First-generation Indians arrived in New York after 1965 and constructed identities that drew on glorified images of there (India) that was understood as 'not-here' (i.e. which helped them distance their community from the 'degenerate' USA: 1997: 578). Their construction of India referenced nationalist readings of British imperial constructions, which had in turn emanated from middle-class Victorian British society. Das Gupta notes that, over time, and as first-generation Indians paid return visits to India and witnessed an increasingly modern/western society, their own constructed sense of Indianness in New York became even more traditionalist: they became, for Das Gupta, more Indian than Indians in India. For daughters of the '1.5 generation' (those born in India but who had grown up in the USA) and the second generation, conforming to this trans-national norm meant restrictive educational opportunities, limited to attending nearby schools, regulated sexuality and arranged marriages. For their parents, as Johanna Lessinger (1995) notes, the simultaneous desire to maintain a cultural distance from US norms, maintain Indian class divisions and circumvent US racial discourses by being absent from political activism and seeking 'honorary white-ness' all promoted a kind of insular transnationalism that ill-prepared community members for overt racist attacks against them, such as occurred in Jersey City between 1986 and 1987.

Like their parents, many second-generation Indians continue to maintain strong links with India (Lessinger 1995). Unlike the former generation, the desire to return to India permanently is less strong. The second generation appears less likely to see India and the USA as binary opposites, preferring instead to work towards combinatorial if sometimes contradictory and shifting identities. Some second-generation women discussed how these tensions surfaced as they made choices about home–work balances, choices, broadly speaking, about their roles as carers and their roles as providers. Rather than the ABCD typecast (American Born Confused *Desis* – natives), Das Gupta draws on Anzaldua's descriptions of the borderlands identities of 'new mestizas' to explore how identity systems are reordering hierarchies of difference under this Indian transnationalism. While the first generation struggled with the betweenness and tussles of here-there, and constructed a virulent traditionalist and somewhat insular Indian identity, the

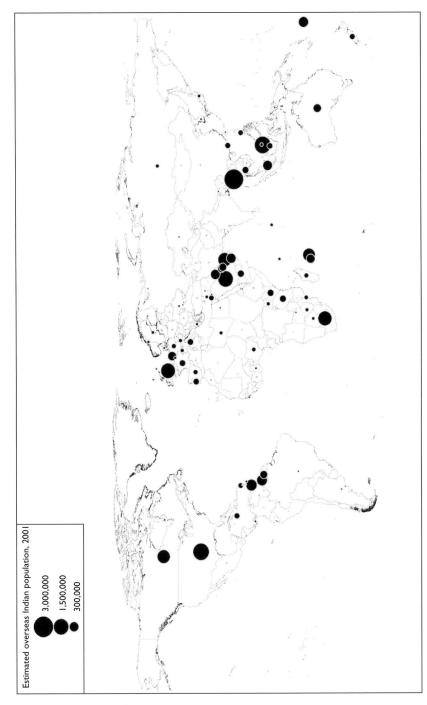

Figure 5.1 *Global Indian diaspora, circa 2000. Based on: Ministry of External Affairs, Report of the High Level Committee on the Indian Diaspora (2001)*

Estimated overseas Indian population, 2001

3,000,000
1,500,000
300,000

second generation additionally struggled with the tussles of their own and their parents' (sometimes unsuccessful) experiences of transnationalism. Identity, then, and through it belonging, is doubly relational.

This same point is made in the recent work of Rachel Silvey (2000), who foregrounds the roles of origin-destination here-there relations and inter-ethnic place-based interactions between migrant workers in South Sulawesi, Indonesia. We are left with the suggestion that discourses of ethnicity that do not acknowledge their immediate settings may not provide resilient modes of belonging for communities (which, of course, has broader implications for the translation of cultural pluralism into a meaningful politics). A still broader question concerns how difference gets produced (through identity systems, the state etc.), both across space (between here and there) and within place, as intra-group (generational) and inter-group interactions unfold. Society's answers inform the set of rights available to groups, and the nature of exclusion and participation in civil society.

Precisely these questions about cultural and political systems lay behind the broader agenda of theorizing the nature of space and place under a neo-liberal and security-conscious context. Accounts of transnationalism, including those reviewed above, undermine any binary approach to space as abstract and 'out there', and place as intimate and 'in here'. From OP to NRI, space and place appear as mutually constitutive of each other. Furthermore, notions of a de-territorialized world of unmoored cultures and uncertain politics do not jive with transnational materiality or the circulation of new discourses of nationalism (Mitchell 1997).

Relational and material-based accounts of transnational society developed by population geographers add to a much broader debate in geography and the social sciences about the nature of space under globalization. Political and economic geographers argue that globalization has led to a relativization and nesting of spaces and scales, and even suggest that the production of geographic scale is tied up in the reproduction of capitalism. While much of this work has accented the political economic imperatives of such rescaling projects, population geographers have contributed to this view by stressing how emotional and familial needs and obligations, often related to social reproduction, cede leverage to state constructions about access to residence. These state discourses construct particular forms of space-time that discipline the population acts and performances of individuals and groups. In turn, this impacts upon material experiences and can perpetuate structural inequality (Bailey et al. 2002). Marston's (2000) call to insert theories of social reproduction into views of the geographic production of scale is substantiated by the empirical evidence on how population events like migration and acts like caring constitute transnational spaces.

Elsewhere in geography, Thrift (1999) has espoused a relational view of actors and networks that constitute space. Similarly, rather than view space or scale in an absolutist way (e.g. local, regional, national, international), Amin (2002) has argued that space, place and time make each other through the material practices of daily life. While space has a physical presence, its nature both encourages and constrains action. Therefore, space is transformed by action even if such action is delayed or unrealized: space is made by networks through action (presence) and not-quites (absence: Thrift, in Amin 2002: 390). Herein lies another connection with the field's view that transnationalism is a negotiation of becoming across and through spaces of presences and absences.

Geopolitics of population

Studies concerned with the 'geopolitics of population' examine how states and their agents deploy geographical strategies on population groups to reassert power. In the context of security concerns and neo-liberal practices, states look to exert control over aspects of their political credibility, economic integrity and cultural legitimacy. Drawing on theorists like Foucault and Spivak, the field's research explores how strategies focus on various population formations, or sites, including sexualized bodies, healthy bodies, refugees in flight and streams of undocumented migrants. Much of the state's power draws its strength from violating and punishing individuals who are charged with crossing geographic or social borders and lines: individuals who are somehow out of place. Norms about geography and population become central in the exercise of power. Much of the work I review below calls on the experiences of refugees and other mobile groups who lack access to protection.

Acts of genocide against unprotected groups and communities show how state violence is designed to do more than eliminate military targets. Selective 'community' cleansing uses a geographic demonstration effect to send a message to a broader population about state power and control. The now disappeared community of El Mozote in El Salvador is one such example. During the late 1970s, 40,000 people were killed in a civil war in El Salvador that was regarded as a cold war proxy battle. The economic, political and ecological disruptions of the war displaced over 1 million people (out of a total population of 5 million). Many Salvadoreans travelled north into Mexico, and eventually the USA, where, by 2000, the population had grown to over 1 million.

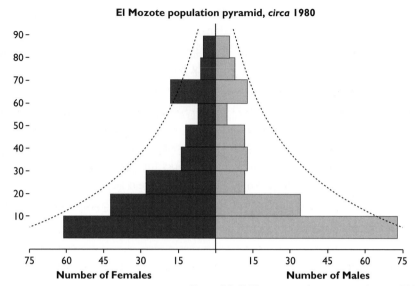

El Mozote population pyramid, *circa* **1980**

Figure 5.2 El Mozote population pyramid, circa 1980

The population pyramid of figure 5.2 shows El Mozote in about 1980. Read in demographic terms, it suggests that population growth is generally expansive (for example, there are more children than young adults). However, by comparing the age-sex profile of this population with the ideal type for an expanding population (shown as a dashed line in the figure), more distinctive properties of our population come into focus. Where, for example, are the missing parents? Why are there relatively fewer young men aged 20–29 than women of the same age? We may hypothesize that young men had left the village to join armed forces and that those who could had fled to safer locations, leaving behind the children and the elderly. In such an unstable cultural and environmental context as this, we would perhaps not expect the future growth of our population to be assured.

However, this population is not, as is normally studied by demographers, a population defined by government officials using counts of the numbers in age-sex groups. This is a population of death. This is a pyramid of a massacred community where, during 11–13 December 1981, US-backed government forces systematic-ally isolated, separated and culled those who were destined to be in this remote part of the Morazan department in the run-up to Christmas. As only one person is thought to have escaped the killing, the pyramid also serves as a tragic statistical memorial to the demography of that place at that time. An international outcry, forensic science, extensive fieldwork and local reconnaissance over the next ten years ultimately led to the compilation and publication of a list of the names and ages of those murdered here (Dammer 1994).

The El Mozote pyramid raises uncomfortable questions for population geographers. Not least among these questions is that surrounding 'what is a population?' What acts made this population? The goal of the Salvadorean authorities to attain discursive leverage by wiping out a complete community rather than practise more generalized violence (a strategy used at a later stage) is an integral part of the population geography of El Mozote. The branding of the entire department of Morazan as 'rebel-held', unfriendly and dangerous to government interests imbued the population with traits justifying (in army commanders' eyes) local genocide. El Mozote was created as a target by the army's use of two inherently spatial strategies: concentration of force (wiping out a local base of support for rebels) and discursive leverage (projecting a symbolic message). Nearly a quarter of a century on, events in Darfur suggest that this geopolitics of population persists.

States also silence political critics by torturing opponents. Inger Agger's account of refugees from Latin America and the Middle East reveals that states use gendered and embodied population tactics to torture opponents. In *The Blue Room* she both describes how a political technology of torture disciplines refugees and how those now in exile could reclaim meaningful lives. While generalized techniques of political torture were reported by male refugees in Sweden (including sleep deprivation), women reported the systematic application of sexualized forms of torture. These drew their power from women's own complicity in the acts committed against them. Women refugees were made to feel shame when they were beaten and raped by guards because they internalized the feelings of guilt derived from failing in their social duty to protect their own (bodies') boundaries.

Agger (1994) documents how these political technologies ultimately sourced their power from the ways that lines, boundaries and borders had been inscribed on bodies through population acts (dating) and performances (virginity) that took place in private and public spaces. But this diagnosis also proceeds alongside intervention, as she constructs a metaphorical house of exiles from a series of linked rooms that each references an experience of sexuality. While many of these women had been socialized to believe that public discretions of women's boundaries were part of the normal course of patriarchal society, strong beliefs in the maintenance of (and ability to prove) virginity meant that acts of rape and incest that occurred in the private sphere of the home represented transgressive behaviour that called into question the women's own actions. These harmful population acts and boundary violations thus perpetrated a sense of guilt and complicity in women, and it was this sexualized weakness that lay at the heart of the political technology of torture that Agger excavates. The end point of Agger's testimonial research method, the Veranda, brings the refugees together into a healing circle of fellowship, where meaning is made of the commonalities of their past experiences of trauma.

States also make use of discourses around health to discipline groups in the name of cultural legitimacy. The projection of geographically informed, racialized discourses onto population groups has been linked to the exclusion of such groups from access to social and economic opportunities in society. The treatment of asylum seekers provides clear examples of this practice. In the Netherlands, asylum seekers arriving from parts of Africa were automatically separated from other immigrants and screened for TB (Van Ewijk et al. 1998). While this did afford such individuals access to medical resources that could, in theory, contribute to their improved well-being (through the diagnosis and treatment of any TB), in practice it served to stigmatize the general class of asylum seekers as those with unhealthy bodies that were in need of state intervention and technology. For the group as a whole, such stigmatization had a greater negative impact than the offsetting biomedical gains that accrued to a few.

The state was able to demonstrate that migrants had been disciplined by the use of technology and surveillance and their bodies and movements controlled for the benefit of society. Concerns with the health of immigrants continue to justify the use of exclusionary tactics, and to fuel resentment toward immigrants who are charged with placing unreasonable demands upon already stretched western health-care systems. Elsewhere, AIDS orphans, returning sex workers and women prisoners-of-war who had been raped faced economic hardship because of exclusionary practices in their former communities that were based on the negative construction of transgressive population acts (disease, sex for money, complicit sex) inscribed upon their unhealthy/unsafe bodies.

Illegal immigrants to South Africa have been stigmatized *as a population group* for political ends (Croucher 1998). The process of state-building was being transformed from the apartheid system based on racial difference and exclusion to one based on a new South African nation where diverse social groups would come to recognize the legitimacy of a common national community. During the 1990s, South Africa had not been isolated from the general increases in international migration which, compounded with its relatively dominant position as an economic power in southern Africa, had meant this shift in state-building unfolded against the context of increasing in-migration, particularly from Mozambique, Angola and Zimbabwe (but also East Africa).

The stigmatization took several forms. First, uncertainty over the exact size of the immigrant population fuelled insecurity and sponsored the idea that the group was a threat. Second, political speeches and media content perpetrated an 'immigrant takeover thesis' that not only called into question any immigrant contributions to the economy, but also suggested that illegal immigrants may be benefiting at the expense of the historically disenfranchised (black) groups. Third, rising immigration had been linked to South Africa's rising crime rate. Fourth, immigrants were also blamed for the spread of diseases in the region, including HIV-AIDS. Thus constructed as an enemy of the state project, immigrants become racialized as the new other. It was by excluding this other through border controls and notions of criminality imbued with mobility that the inclusionary state project could proceed.

Hyndman's (1997) work among refugees in the Horn of Africa illustrates how state discourses operate through previous and contemporary patterns of international governance. Colonially imposed borders continued to cast their long political and economic shadow on the region in the 1990s and lay behind the displacement and impoverishment of Somali refugees along the border with Kenya. Also threatened by political and economic insecurities, Kenya proceeded to implement 'a colonialism of derision', with Somalis arrested and detained without trial for prolonged periods on account of their presence along this sensitive border zone.

However, tactics shifted after civil war and famine in much of southern Somalia in 1991–2 attracted deepening interest from the international community. During this period, the UNHCR allocated $40 million to build three refugee camps in northern Kenya, a figure soon dwarfed by the estimated $1.5 billion budget of the UN peacekeeping force that followed the US 'Operation Restore Hope' mission. Kenya perpetrated a 'colonialism of compassion', under the disciplining gaze of players with interlinked interests, including the UNHCR, the US military, the EU, national governments, tribal leaders, NGOs and refugee groups themselves. Crucially, while the motive and agenda may have shifted from national geopolitics to global compassion, Hyndman suggests that for refugees – whose status was tied to their acceptance of mobility restrictions – the politics of containment continued.

As the cases of Darfur, Rwanda and the Horn of Africa all show, it is often the relations between states that mediate both the international response and the initial treatment of population by a single state. International relations and the packet of rights available to different classes of migrants and residents affects the geopolitics of population. As a sovereign state member of a world system that recognizes the right of states to make their own laws, China's right and need to control its population size is acknowledged and endorsed by the international community. Indeed, China's stance on fertility limitation was in line with prevailing advice from the International Conference on Population and Development pro-gramme in 1974. However, the coercive techniques used, including late-term abortions, female infanticide and forced sterilization, have led many commentators – from inside China and beyond its borders – to condemn the government's human rights record.

The link between the one-child policy and human rights violations lies beneath an increasing number of asylum claims in the USA, Canada and other countries of refuge. How do nations square the circle that is Chinese population policy in practice? Discussions of recent asylum cases involving individuals claiming asylum on the basis that their human rights have been violated by the one-child policy have met with mixed success in Canada and the USA. Courts with different jurisdictions continue to make contradictory judgements about the 'safety' of return to China for those subject to forced sterilization. What the one-child policy illustrates is the deeply problematic nature of the current system of inter-national protection and rights that attempts to balance a respect for sovereign determinacy against the rights of population groups. Political asylum is still a highly individual concept, and the international community has been slow to recognize and support the victims of more generalized and group-based persecution.

Dual citizenship rights are also framed with respect to the evolving pattern of international relations. By selectively granting and denying bilateral citizenship agreements, states jockey and manage the geography of their diasporic populations to further global political objectives. Second only in size to the Chinese overseas community, non-resident Indians (NRIs) comprise a significant diaspora population located around the world (see figure 5.1). Recent Indian legislation – the 2003 Dual Citizenship Agreement – granted the right to participate in Indian politics (voting) and play a greater role in Indian society to selected NRIs living overseas. While on the surface the legislation, and debates surrounding this, presented an image of a single, unified diasporic population, in practice, the Indian state only extended dual citizenship rights to residents in countries where Indians had made outstanding economic gains (for example, the USA) and those countries where Indians had made cultural gains by successfully integrating into a multicultural society (for example, Canada and Australia). Other significant NRI communities – in the Gulf oil states and southern Africa – were excluded from these rights.

Other rights frameworks prioritize the needs of individuals as purposive actors. Recent debate about the global sex trade illustrates one such engagement. The size, rapid growth and involvement of young and vulnerable populations in the global sex trade has led to a series of international discussions about rights for sex workers (Raymond 2002). This is of interest to the field because (im)mobility is often an integral component of participation in the industry, and plays both enabling (return and reintegration) and constraining (captivity, return and ostracization) roles in affecting the lives of sex workers and their communities. Policy responses are varied and include a denial of the presence of the industry, abolishment of the industry, criminalization of sex workers, treating workers as passive victims and liberalization of the industry and legalization of the trade. While the latter response – favoured by authorities in the Netherlands – avoids pushing the industry underground, it has been criticized for ignoring demand factors (and contributing to increased demand by appearing to bring prostitution into the mainstream), and for being insensitive to the fact that increasingly visible sex workers can face higher levels of public stigmatization (Kempadoo and Doezema 1998). However, treating workers as passive victims ignores their rights to enter an industry and escape conditions of dependency. This implies that debates about the rights of sex workers should go beyond a consideration of the apparent individualistic motives to choose/be forced into the trade, and discuss the relationship between mobility and the possibilities for economic and cultural livelihoods in a global community.

Broader discussions of how migration is contributing to new rights regimes link work in the field to debates in political science and international relations (Castles and Davidson 2000). Universal personhood rights are affecting the lives of an increasing number of the world's populations. Thus, while states are still the arbiters of most rights, further work is needed to debate how universal personhood rights regimes enable states to exert power at a distance, and/or enable population groups to achieve social progress. Suggestive work has looked at the changing rights regimes of groups, including the elderly (Ackers and Dwyer 2001) and those with HIV-AIDS (Brown 1997).

Action

Our future places are for us to make. But we cannot make them without inscribing our struggles in space, place, and environment in multiple ways. That process is ongoing and every single one of us has agency with respect to it. The places – material, representational, and symbolic – handed down to us by former generations were also built up by social struggles and strivings to create material, symbolic, and imaginary places to fit their own particular and contested aspirations. A better appreciation of such processes – of the social and political dialectics of space, place, and environment – has much to teach us about how to construct alternative futures. (Harvey 1996: 326)

Harvey's call for visions of futures instructed by geographic materialism coincides with the emergence of a critical human geography project that both problematizes how knowledge is produced and proposes transformations in the relations between the academy and society. Yet, while post-Enlightenment belief systems help undermine the modernist belief in the separation of the research process from political action, Noel Castree reminds us that: 'as geography has become more overtly Leftist – Marxism, feminism, queer theory, postcolonialism, and a plethora of other critical approaches are all now legitimate aspects of the geographic enterprise – the wider world has become less so' (2000: 2091).

For Castree, one critical geography project would 'look to contest the moral and political economy of the higher education system'. In this context, population geography has long been an established part of the introductory geography curriculum, with successive generations of new geography students cutting their teeth on an introductory chapter or module on population issues. National benchmark statements and recently launched high school to college geography curricula demonstrate solidarity with Trewartha's intellectual vision of population geography within human geography. The goals of the US-based People's Geography Project (see figure 5.3 below) acknowledge that the classroom is an important site of politics. At the time of writing, the Project included no indicative syllabus or entry for population geography.

The field's practitioners have been more prominent in contributing to other developments in activism and action-oriented research. Mike Kesby's (2004) work on participatory AIDS research links population, activism and the academy. He writes:

participatory approaches do not dissolve the power-relations endemic to research, nor do they enable researchers to avoid the difficult ethical questions raised in recent post-structuralist debates ... participatory research can at least develop tangible mechanisms through which researchers *and participants* can produce partial, practical resolutions to ethical questions in the arena of the fieldwork praxis itself ... The greatest challenge for social science investigation into HIV in Africa really is to finds ways to help Africans *themselves* move HIV work beyond epidemiology. (228, italics in original)

- **Produce popular accounts (both written and filmed) of the social geography of the United States.** *The goal of these accounts is to help people understand how their lives are caught up in complex relations of power that are fundamentally geographical.*
- **Produce popular, easily understandable, and compelling accounts of contemporary, critical approaches to geographical knowledge.** *The goal of these accounts is to produce alternative visions of what geographical knowledge is and can be than those currently available.*
- **Develop curricula for both K-12 and college-level courses.** *Support young scholars, both pre- and post-doctoral, in their development of new, critical, and, eventually, popular approaches to pressing geographical problems and issues.*
- **Create active linkages with community organizations,** *labor unions, social movements, and so forth both to move geographical knowledge out of the academy and 'into the streets' and to learn from those organizations, unions, and movements about how they actively construct and contest the geographical structures that govern their lives.*
- **Develop an institutional base** *(or bases) to assure not only the short-term success of the People's Geography Project, but its lasting influence in geography and public discourse more widely.*

Figure 5.3 Goals of the People's Geography Project.
Source: www.peoplesgeography.org (accessed April 2004)

In Agger's *The Blue Room*, the collection of exile narratives culminated in a room called the Veranda. It was in the space of the Veranda that Agger symbolically stepped away from her enabling role and left the participants to talk to each other and imagine their own resolutions.

Studying how knowledge and power flow through the contexts of activism and community organizing addressed to population matters stands as another direction of research for the field. In the case of HIV-AIDS, a number of co-operative organizations have begun to make a difference in the lives of many. The Durbar Mahila Samamwaya Committee (DMSC) started as a project to inform sex workers in Calcutta of the risks of HIV-AIDS, but has since developed to protect the rights of this population (Thekaekara 2004). Rather than being ostracized for their work, the act of trading sexual services is recognized as the legitimate basis of this population and this worker co-op. Participation and empowerment of sex workers were established as the building blocks of membership when it was recognized that indebtedness, not ill health, was the major problem facing these women (although ill health triggered further indebtedness to pimps and minders because women could not work). DMSC collects nightly earnings from sex workers and banks them, thereby guaranteeing a measure of financial security. This, in turn, enabled women to take greater control over their lives and to escape stigmatization and criminalization. It also funded more effective educational outreach programmes, with the net result a significant reduction in HIV-AIDS cases. Other more specialized parts of DMSC tackle violence against sex workers, consider the situation of the children of sex workers and forge international links with other sex workers.

While co-operative organizing accompanied the rise of industrial capitalism in northern England over a century ago, DMSC shows that its principles are clearly apposite for the contemporary context. These principles include: voluntary basis of membership, control of strategic direction and finances by members, autonomy and commitments to sustainable community development, educational outreach and cooperation with other co-ops. As producers and enablers of alternative population futures, the field might usefully engage with such co-operative frameworks. Indeed, Rachel Pain's review of action-orientated work in social geography noted that 'engagement with individuals, groups and communities and action beyond the traditional research encounter ... has fully re-emerged across human geography in recent years' (2003: 650).

Back to geography

Transnational geographies and the geopolitics of populations illustrate two (from several) sets of agendas that are responsive to the security and neo-liberal concerns that comprise some of today's external context to the field. Such research takes us back to the book's premise, that the field is made and remade by the ways that internal and external contexts legitimize nations as institutions that link population with social progress.

This chapter has demonstrated how two elements of context contribute to the making of the field. First, in common with many other sub-disciplines in human geography, population geographers are starting to engage with the methodologies and epistemologies of action-oriented research and activism. Continued openness to diversity of approach and ontology will position the field closer to developments in, for example, social geography (Pain 2003).

Second, and following on, new approaches to engagement imply additional partners, not different partners. That is, many practitioners have a long track record of significant interventions in, for example, the design and execution of national and international data-gathering exercises (Rees et al. 2002). While nobody would argue that these instruments are without problems, equally few would deny their place in a functioning democracy. Continuing to inform and shape the direction of such exercises remains a strategic priority for those with the skills so to do. Likewise, collaborations with corporations, NGOs, community groups and other bodies will raise new methodological and epistemological challenges, but has the potential to inform, problematize and implement new visions for society. The fact that states are joined by other prominent players with influential roles in enhancing social progress does not (as some have prematurely suggested) mean the role of the state is finished; if anything, as is illustrated by state management of diaspora, the presence of new players has raised the stakes for states. Population matters and their geographic roots are likely to remain on state agendas for the foreseeable future.

chapter 6
CONCLUSION

Population geography has recently enlarged its traditional concerns with the spatial and demographic organization of society to consider the social and political ways in which populations reflect and influence the circulation of influence and power in society. This 'making' of population geography hints at some futures and, indeed, some challenges for the field, and I introduce these below. In describing how population geography is made, I have emphasized the broader historic and geographic context of change. Such an intellectual history and geography of the field reflects not just 'who said what', or the rise of positivism and, more recently, post-positivism, but asks how multiple layers of contextual influences come to bear on ideas, in this case, ideas about groups of people in particular places. By positioning the field's current 'social make-over' and shift in emphasis in this longer run of changes in topic and approach, a nuanced story emerges about the roles of key individuals, the credibility of academic disciplines, the rise and fall of national schools of thought, changes in philosophies and beliefs and global economic and social transformations.

My selective approach read, in some detail, key research debates and research perspectives to suggest an absence of triggers and smoking guns that changed the field overnight or that inevitably pushed it in one direction (towards spatial demography in the 1960s) or another (towards critical human geography in the 1990s). At particular moments, in particular places, specific research agendas reflect: the calls of individuals (Trewartha, but not Pokshishevskiy); the influence of journals (International Journal of Population Geography, relaunched as *Population, Space and Place* in 2004) and organizations (International Geographical Union Commission on Population Geography); the release of census data and development of methods; and an appetite to engage in public debates, such as segregation and global migration. In short, the focus on the specific ideas and threads and clusters of ideas amplifies the importance of contingency in the making of the field.

Any broader generalizations about the making of population geography should bear in mind this contingency. The field has already shown how it recycles both its concepts (space, environment and place) and its ways of organizing itself administratively (notably, as it moves to a more loosely based, cross-disciplinary and multi-partnered base beyond a recognizable disciplinary core). The field's futures, then, seem as discoverable in its pasts, or in its elsewheres, as they do in the role of any one influence, including approach. I briefly summarize how the book has addressed its goals before turning to some of the general challenges and opportunities that lay ahead for the field's practitioners.

Perspectives

The book articulated how the field deepens our understanding of society and why population matters. I argued that it has done this by asking a set of questions prompted from the overlap of two broad ideas, those relating to geography and those relating to population. As industrialization, imperialism and colonialism fed into globalization, geographic differences in wealth, health, ecological sustainability, cultural security and opportunity seemingly became more entrenched. Before an institutionally organized sub-discipline emerged, key thinkers like Thomas Malthus linked the idea of population with geography to comment on just these issues of wealth, health and ecological sustainability. This same manoeuvre of rubbing population and geography together has sparked a perspective that I see as apposite to debates about sex trafficking, HIV-AIDS, reproductive rights, housing provision, race and economic growth.

During the 1960s and 1970s, much of the field's authority flowed from its proven ability to inform state policy and feed into debates on modernization and the implications of regional and local patterns of population growth. The field took a view of states where governments acted in the public good by managing and influencing social (including population) and economic change. After the 1980s, broader cultural and political changes undermined the confidence that society had in the state to deliver, or at least manage, social progress. Bhopal, Rwanda, Enron and Iraq led many to doubt the extent to which governments could be trusted to deliver social progress. However, the field stayed relevant by continuing to add to its demographic contributions and by exploring social and cultural topics. It did some provocative philosophical thinking about who – besides the state – would take responsibility for social change and progress, and how this might be accomplished.

Changes

Population geography has maintained an interest in how populations are made. But, like all fields of knowledge, population geography has changed and the book has introduced several instances of this. First, the field modified its view on geography. Prior to the rise of positivism and the dominance of spatial frameworks, practitioners had drawn on multiple views of landscapes that ranged from environmentally determined perspectives to more cultural and synthetic readings of places. By the 1990s, critiques of Enlightenment beliefs about knowledge encouraged a joining up of the concepts of space, environment and place. Key features of this expanded take on geography are its emphasis on local context and contingency, and the socially constructed and contested experience of people's daily lives.

Adopting such thinking transformed the field's ideas on population. Population moved from being a demographically defined object that existed in space to a socially constituted process that helped to make space. Geography was implicated in population's formation and vice versa. Research examined how acts, performances, institutions and discourses affected the relationship between populations and those with power and influence. In particular, the actions of states in influencing the social and demographic bases of population have been related back to globalization, issues of maintaining security and neo-liberalism.

Third, population geography shifted its topical emphases to reflect key issues in society, rather than to follow the dictates of a demographic framework. Migration is one such issue that is studied both as a signal demographic event that changes population compositions, exerts demands on infrastructure and contributes to the economic vitality of nations, and as an example of how geopolitical and cultural agendas are advanced by states through their management of and involvement with mobility. This includes analyses of new forms of exclusion based on intersections of pregnancy, race, ethnicity and religion.

Fourth, and most generally, while the field looks beyond demography for its inspirations, it retains an interest in and expertise with the interdependencies between social and demographic factors. Emerging work on constructions taken for granted, like age and gender, inform studies of the implications of rapid fertility decline upon demographic ageing in China. The recent remaking of the field has explored the benefits of methodological plurality and recognized the need to integrate both cultural and material elements into its conceptual vocabulary.

Challenges and opportunities

The field makes itself as layers of context give rise to new opportunities to discuss people, places and power. Through its emerging work on the geopolitics of populations and its discussion of how power flows through transnational societies, the field has reconnected to a cultural heritage while retaining its more recent involvement with economic matters. What it has less successfully addressed is the shifting relationship between knowledge projects (academic disciplines) and states. This close – sometimes intimate – relationship has underwritten a good deal of the field's relevancy and legitimacy over the past 50 years.

Problematizing the relationship between power and social progress should not mean, however, a jettisoning of the field's concerns with relevance, with big issues of the day like the sexual exploitation of children and the widening gap between the rich and the poor. A more culturally informed critique of how states – and other players – affect social progress through populations can only enhance the field's intellectual standing and offer further possibilities for collaboration. Such a critique involves moving beyond method and a concern with technique, with a desire to articulate new visions of alternative futures. As Harvey (1996) noted, 'our future places are for us to make' and, I might add, imagine. In reimagining Enlightenment views of context and spatial representation, Barbara Benish's *Virgin Death* opens up new windows on how we might rethink the challenges of population and geography.

REFERENCES

Abu-Lughod, J. (1964) Urban-rural differences as a function of the demographic transitions. *American Journal of Sociology*, **69**: 476–90.

Abu-Lughod, J. (1975) The end of the age of innocence in migration theory, in **B. M. DuToit and H. I. Safa** (eds), *Models and Adaptive Strategies*. The Hague: Moulton.

Ackers, C. and P. Dwyer (2001) *Senior Citizenship*. Bristol: Policy Press.

Adamchak, D. J. (2001) The effects of age structure on the labor force and retirement in China. *The Social Science Journal*, **38**: 1–11.

Adams, V. (1992) Tourism and Sherpas, Nepal: reconstruction of reciprocity. *Annals of Tourism Research*, 19, 534–54.

Agger, I. (1994) *The Blue Room*. London: Zed.

Agnew, J. (2002) *Making Political Geography*. London: Hodder Arnold.

Agyei-Mansah, S. and A. Aase (1998) Patterns of fertility change in Ghana: a time and space perspective. *Geografiska Annaler*, **80B**: 203–13.

Allen, J. P. and E. Turner (1996) Spatial patterns of immigrant assimilation. *The Professional Geographer*, **48**: 140–55.

Allen, J. P. and E. Turner (2001) Bridging 1990 and 2000 census race data: fractional assignment of multiracial populations. *Population Research and Policy Review*, **20**: 513–33.

Amin, A. (2002) Spatialities of globalisation. *Environment and Planning A*, **34**: 385–99.

Amin, S. (ed.) (1974) *Modern Migrations in Western Africa*. London: Oxford University Press.

Anderson, B. (1991) *Imagined Communities: Reflections on the Origin and Spread of Nationalism*. London: Verso.

Anderson, K. (2002) The racialisation of difference: enlarging the story field. *The Professional Geographer*, **54**: 25–30.

Anselin, L. (1992) Local indicators of spatial association (LISA). *Geographical Analysis*, **27**: 93–115.

Anzaldua, G. (1987) *Borderlands: La Frontera*. San Francisco: Aunt Lute.

Appadurai, A. (1996) *Modernity at Large*. Minnesota: University of Minnesota Press.

Arendt, H. (1966) *The Origins of Totalitarianism*. San Diego: Harcourt Brace.

Arie, S. (2003) Janie's Secret. *The Guardian*, 5 November, G2, p. 2.

Bailey, A. J. (2001) Turning transnational: notes on the theorisation of international migration. *International Journal of Population Geography*, **7**: 413–28.

Bailey A. J., J. D. Sargent, D. C. Goodman, J. Freeman and M. J. Brown (1994) Poisoned landscapes: the epidemiology of environmental lead exposure in Massachusetts children, 1990–1991. *Social Science and Medicine*, **39**: 757–66.

Bailey A. J., R. Wright, A. Mountz and I. Miyares (2002) (Re)producing Salvadoran transnational geographies. *Annals of the Association of American Geographers*, **92**: 125–44.

Baranskiy, N. N. (1956 [1926]) *Economic Geography of the USSR*. Moscow: Geograficheskoy Literatury.

Bauman, Z. (1998) *Globalization*. Cambridge: Polity Press.

Beaujeu-Garnier, J. (1966) *Geography of Population*. New York: St Martins.

Biemann, U. (2002) Remotely sensed: a topography of the global sex trade. *Feminist Review*, **70**: 75–88.

Bilsborrow, R. E. (ed.) (1998) *Migration, Urbanisation, and Development: New Directions and Issues*. New York: United Nations Population Fund and Kluwer Academic Publishers.

Black, R. and V. Robinson (1993) *Geography and Refugees: Patterns and Processes of Change*. London: Belhaven Press.

Blaikie, P. M. (1975) *Family Planning in India: Diffusion and Policy*. London: Edward Arnold.

Bocquet-Appel, J. P., I. S. Rajan, J. N. Bacro and C. Lajaunie (2002) The onset of India's fertility transition. *European Journal of Population*, **18**: 211–32.

Bogucki, P. I. (1988) *Forest Farmers and Stockherders: Early Agriculture and its Consequences in North-central Europe*. Cambridge: Cambridge University Press.

Bogue, D. (1954) The geography of recent population trends in the United States. *Annals of the Association of American Geographers,* **44**: 124–34.

Bongaarts, J. (2002) The end of the fertility transition in the developed world. *Population and Development Review,* **28**: 419–44.

Bonnett, A. (1996) Constructions of 'race', place and discipline: geographies of 'racial' identity and racism. *Ethnic and Racial Studies,* **19**: 864–83.

Bourdieu, P. (1977) *Outline of a Theory of Practice.* Cambridge: Cambridge University Press.

Bowman, I. (1921) *The New World: Problems in Political Geography.* New York: World Book Company.

Boyle, P., K. Halfacree and V. Robinson (1998) *Exploring Contemporary Migration.* Harlow: Longman.

Boyle, P. and K. Halfacree (eds) (1999) *Migration and Gender in the Developed World.* London: Routledge.

Broaded, C. M. (1993) China's response to the brain drain. *Comparative Education Review,* **37**: 277–304.

Brown, L. A. (1994) *Place, Migration, and Development in the Third World.* London: Routledge.

Brown, L. A. and E. G. Moore (1970) The intra-urban migration process: a perspective. *Geografiska Annaler,* **52B**: 1–13.

Brown, M. and T. Colton (2001) Dying epistemologies: an analysis of home death and its critique. *Environment and Planning A,* **33**: 799–821.

Brown, M. P. (1997) *RePlacing Citizenship: AIDS Activism and Radical Democracy.* London: Guilford Press.

Bruhnes, J. (1910) *La Géographie humaine.* Paris: Alcan.

Buijs, G. (1993) *Migrant Women: Crossing Boundaries and Changing Identities.* Oxford: Berg.

Bullard, R. D. (1994) *Dumping in Dixie: Race, Class, and Environmental Quality.* Boulder, CO: Westview Press.

Buller, H. and K. Hoggart (1994) *International Counterurbanization.* Aldershot: Avebury.

Bunge, W. (1971) *Fitzgerald.* Cambridge: Schenkam.

Burgess, E. W. (1924) The growth of the city: an introduction to a research project. *Publications, American Sociological Society,* **18**: 85–97.

Butler, J. (1990) *Gender Trouble.* New York: Routledge.

Caldas, S. J. (1993) Current theoretical perspectives on adolescent pregnancy and child-bearing in the United States. *Journal of Adolescent Research,* **8**: 4–20.

Caldwell, J. C. (1976) Towards a restatement of demographic transition theory. *Population and Development Review,* **2**: 321–66.

Carlson, G. (1966) The decline of fertility: innovation or adjustment process. *Population Studies,* **20**: 149–74.

Carr-Saunders, A. (1936) *World Population: Past Growth and Present Trends.* Oxford: Clarendon.

Carvalho, J. A. M. (1974) Regional trends in fertility and mortality in Brazil. *Population Studies,* **28**: 410–21.

Castles, S. and A. Davidson (2000) *Citizenship and Migration: Globalization and the Politics of Belonging.* New York: Routledge.

Castles, S. and G. Kosack (1973) *Immigrant Workers and Class Structure in Western Europe.* London: Oxford University Press.

Castles, S. and M. J. Miller (1993) *The Age of Migration: International Population Movements in the Modern World.* Basingstoke: Macmillan.

Castree, N. (2000) What kind of critical geography for what kind of politics? *Environment and Planning A,* **32**: 2091–5.

Cebula, R. (1975) Migration, economic opportunity, and the quality of life: an analysis for the US according to race, sex and age. *Annals of Regional Science,* **9**: 127–33.

Chambers, I. (1994) *Migrancy, Culture, Identity.* London: Routledge.

Champion, A. G. (ed.) (1989) *Counterurbanization.* London: Edward Arnold.

Chang, K. A. and L. H. M. Ling (2000) Globalization and its intimate other: Filipina domestic workers in Hong Kong, in **M. Marchand and A. Sisson Runyan** (eds), *Gender and Global Restructuring: Sightings, Sites and Resistances.* London: Routledge.

Chapman, M. (1978) The cross-cultural study of circulation. *International Migration Review*, **12**: 559–69.

Chatterton, P. and R. Hollands (2001) *Changing our 'Toon': Youth, Nightlife and Urban Change in Newcastle*. Newcastle upon Tyne: University of Newcastle Press.

Citizenship (Amendment) Bill (2003) India.

Clark, G. (1983) *Interregional Migration, National Policy, and Social Justice*. Totowa: Rowman and Allanheld.

Clark, G. L. and J. Whiteman (1983) Why poor people do not move: job search behaviour and disequilibrium amongst local labor markets. *Environment and Planning A*, **15**: 85–104.

Clark, W. A. V. (1986) *Human Migration*. London: Sage.

Clark, W. A. V. (1998) *The California Cauldron*. New York: Guilford.

Clarke, J. I. (1965) *Population Geography*. Oxford: Pergamon.

Clarke, J. I. (ed.) (1984) *Geography and Population*. Oxford: Pergamon.

Clarke, J., P. Curson, S. Kayastha and P. Nag (eds) (1989) *Population and Disaster*. Oxford: Basil Blackwell.

Clayton, C. (1977) Interstate population migration process and structure in the United States, 1935 to 1970. *Professional Geographer*, **29**: 177–81.

Cliff, A. D. and P. Haggett (1988) *Atlas of Disease Distributions: Analytical Approaches to Epidemiological Data*. Oxford: Basil Blackwell.

Cliff, A. D., P. Haggett, J. K. Ord and G. R. Versey (1981) *Spatial Diffusion*. Cambridge: Cambridge University Press.

Coale, A. J. (1969) The decline of fertility in Europe from the French Revolution to World War II, in **S. J. Behrman, L. Corsa and R. Freedman** (eds), *Fertility and Family Planning*. Ann Arbor: Michigan University Press.

Coale, A. J. and S. Chen (1987) *Basic Data on the Fertility of China 1940–82*. Hawaii: East-West Centre, Papers of the East-West Population Institute, No. 104.

Cohen, R. (1997) *Global Diasporas: An Introduction*. London: UCL Press.

Coleman, D. A. (2002) Populations of the industrial world – a convergent demographic community? *International Journal of Population Geography*, **8**: 319–44.

Coleman, D. A. and J. Salt (1992) *The British Population: Patterns, Trends and Processes.* Oxford: Oxford University Press.

Compton, P. (1976) Religious affiliation and demographic variability in Northern Ireland. *Transactions of the Institute of British Geographers,* **1**: 433–52.

Connell, J. (1992) Far beyond the Gulf: the implications of warfare for Asian labour migration. *Australian Geographer,* **23**(1): 44–50.

Conway, D. and J. H. Cohen (1998) Consequences of migration and remittances for Mexican transnational communities. *Economic Geography,* **74**: 26–44.

Cooke, T. J. (2001) 'Trailing wife' or 'trailing mother'? The effect of parental status on the relationship between family migration and the labor market participation of married women. *Environment and Planning A,* **33**: 419–30.

Correa, S. (1995) *Population and Reproductive Rights.* Atlantic Highlands: Zed.

Cossman, R. E., J. S. Cossman, T. C. Blanchard, W. L. James and A. Cosby (2004) Mortality rates across time: does persistence suggest 'healthy and unhealthy' places in the United States? in **D. G. Janelle, B. Warf and K. Hansen** (eds), *World Minds.* Boston: Kluwer.

Coward, J. (1978) Changes in the pattern of fertility in the Republic of Ireland. *Tijdschrift voor Economische en Sociale Geografie,* **69**: 353–61.

Craddock, S. (2001) Scales of justice: women, equity, and HIV in East Africa, in **I. Dyck, N. D. Lewis and S. McLafferty** (eds), *Geographies of Women's Health.* London: Routledge.

Craddock, S. (2004) Introduction, in **E. Kalipeni, S. Craddock, J. R. Oppong and J. Ghosh** (eds), *HIV and AIDS in Africa. Beyond Epidemiology.* Malden: Blackwell.

Crang, P., C. Dwyer and P. Jackson (2003) Transnationalism and the spaces of commodity culture. *Progress in Human Geography,* **27**: 438–56.

Cresswell, T. (1999) Embodiment, power and the politics of mobility: the case of female tramps and hobos. *Transactions of the Institute of British Geographers,* **24**: 175–92.

Croucher, S. (1998) South Africa's illegal aliens: constructing national boundaries in a post-apartheid state. *Ethnic and Racial Studies,* **21**: 639–60.

Cutter, S. (1995) The forgotten casualties: women, children and environmental change. *Global Environmental Change,* **5**: 181–94.

Dale, A., E. Fieldhouse and C. Holdsworth (2000) *Analysing Census Microdata.* London: Arnold.

Dammer, M. (1994) *The Massacre at El Mozote.* New York: Vintage.

Das Gupta, M. (1997) 'What is Indian about you?' A gendered, transnational approach to ethnicity. *Gender and Society,* **11**: 572–96.

Demko, G., G. Ioffe and Z. Zayonchkovskaya (eds) (1999) *Population under Duress.* Boulder, CO: Westview Press.

Demko, G. J., H. M. Rose, G. A. Schnell (eds) (1970) *Population Geography.* New York: Mc-Graw Hill.

Deng, F. (1993) *Protecting the Dispossessed: A Challenge for the International Community.* Washington, DC: Brookings Institution.

Derrida, J. (1991) *A Derrida Reader: Between the Blinds* (edited with an introduction and notes by Peggy Kamuf). London: Harvester Wheatsheaf.

Desbarats, J. M. (1975) Contemporary trends in French geography. *The Professional Geographer,* **27**: 7–13.

DHSS (1980) *Inequalities in Health: Report of a Research Working Group.* London: DHSS.

Dobson, M. (1997) *Contours of Death and Disease in Early Modern England.* Cambridge: Cambridge University Press.

Dorling, D. (1995) *A New Social Atlas of Britain.* Chichester: Wiley.

Duncan, S. S. and D. P. Smith (2002) Geographies of partnering and parenting in Britain. *Transactions of the Institute of British Geographers,* **27**: 471–93.

Dwyer, C. (2000) Negotiating diasporic identities: young British South Asian Muslim women. *Women's Studies International Forum,* **23**(4): 475–86.

Dyck, I., N. D. Lewis and S. McLafferty (eds) (2001a) *Geographies of Women's Health.* New York: Routledge.

Dyck, I., N. D. Lewis and S. McLafferty (2001b) Why geographies of women's health?, in **I. Dyck, N. D. Lewis and S. McLafferty** (eds), *Geographies of Women's Health.* London: Routledge.

Dykstra, P. A. and L. J. G. Van Wissen (1999) Introduction, in **L. J. G. Van Wissen and P. A. Dykstra** (eds) *Population Issues: An Interdisciplinary Focus.* New York: Kluwer.

Easterlin, R. A. (1968) *Population, Labor Force, and Long Swings in Economic Growth: The American Experience.* New York: National Bureau of Economic Research.

Eastmond, M. (1993) Reconstructing Life: Chilean Refugee Women and the Dilemmas of Exile, in **G. Buijs** (ed.) *Migrant Women. Crossing Boundaries and Changing Identities.* Oxford: Berg.

Eden, J. A. (1989) Life cycle strategies of female assembly line workers in Malaysia: demographic profiles of a dual work force. *Urban Anthropology*, **18**: 153–85.

Edmondston, B. (1975) *Population Distribution in American Cities.* Lexington, MA, Lexington Books.

Eicher, C. and D. Byerlee (1972) *Rural Employment, Migration, and Economic Development.* East Lansing: Michigan State University, Africa Rural Employment Paper 1.

Elder, G. H. (1994) Time, human agency, and social change: perspectives on the life course. *Social Psychology Quarterly*, **57**: 4–15.

Ellis, M., D. Conway and A. J. Bailey (1996) The circular migration of Puerto Rican women: towards a gendered explanation. *International Migration*, **34**: 31–64.

Ellis, M. and R. Wright (1999) The industrial division of labor among immigrants and internal migrants to the Los Angeles economy. *International Migration Review*, **33**: 26–54.

Evans, S. L. and S. Bowlby (2000) Crossing boundaries: racialised gendering and the labour market experiences of Pakistani migrant women in Britain. *Women's Studies International Forum*, **23**: 461–74.

Farmer, P. (1999) *Infections and Inequalities.* Berkeley: University of California Press.

Fernandez-Kelly, M. P. (1994) Towanda's triumph: social and cultural capital in the transition to adulthood in the urban ghetto. *International Journal of Urban and Regional Research*, **18**(1): 88–111.

Fielding, A. (1986) Counterurbanisation, in **M. Pacione** (ed.), *Population Geography: Progress and Prospects.* London: Croom Helm.

Fincher, R. (1991) *Immigration, Urban Infrastructure and the Environment.* Canberra: Australian Government Publishing Service.

Findlay, A. M. (2004) Population geographies for the 21st century. *Scottish Geographical Journal*, **119**: 177–90.

Findlay, A. M. and E. Graham (1991) The challenge facing population geography. *Progress in Human Geography*, **15**: 149–62.

Foster, H. (2004) Halting the AIDS Pandemic, in **D. G. Janelle, B. Warf and K. Hansen** (eds), *World Minds*. Boston: Kluwer.

Foucault, M. (1977) *Discipline and Punish: The Birth of the Prison*. London: Penguin.

Franklin, S. H. (1958) The age structure of New Zealand's North Island communities. *Economic Geography*, **34**: 64.

Freedman, R. (1979) Theories of fertility decline: a reappraisal. *Social Forces*, **58**: 1–17.

Frey, W. (1996) Immigration and internal migration 'flight' from US metropolitan areas: toward a new demographic balkanisation. *Urban Studies*, **32**: 733–57.

Friedlander, D. (1969) Demographic responses and population change. *Demography*, **6**: 359–81.

Gaile, G. L. and C. J. Willmott (1989) *Geography in America*. Columbus: Merrill Publishing.

Gattrell, A. C. (2002) *Geographies of Health*. Oxford: Blackwell.

George, P. (1959) *Questions de Géographie de la Population*. Paris: Presses Universitaires de France.

Gesler, W. (1993) Therapeutic landscapes: theory and a case study of Epidauros, Greece. *Environment and Planning D: Society and Space*, **11**: 171–89.

Geyer, H. and T. Kontuly (1993) A theoretical foundation for the concept of differential urbanization. *International Regional Science Review*, **15**: 157–77.

Ghosh, B. (2000) *Managing Migration*. Oxford: Oxford University Press.

Gilbert, A. (1998) The coping capacity of Latin American cities, in **R. E. Bilsborrow** (ed.), *Migration, Urbanisation and Development: New Directions and Issues*. Norwell, MA: United Nations Population Fund and Kluwer Academic Publishers.

Gober, P. (1994) Why abortion rates vary: A geographical examination of the supply of and the demand for abortion services in the United States in 1988. *Annals of the Association of American Geographers*, **84**: 23–250.

Goldstein, S. (1976) Facets of redistribution: research challenges and opportunities. *Demography*, **13**: 423–34.

Gordon, I. (1991) Multi-stream migration modelling, in **J. Stillwell and P. Congdon** (eds), *Migration Models: Macro and Micro Approaches*. London: Belhaven.

Goss, J. and B. Lindquist (1995) Conceptualising international labor migration: a structuration perspective. *International Migration Review*, **24**: 317–51.

Graham, E. (1995) Singapore in the 1990s: can population policies reverse the demographic transition? *Applied Geography*, **15**: 219–32.

Green, A. E. (1997) A question of compromise? Case study evidence on the location and mobility strategies of dual career households. *Regional Studies*, **31**: 641–57.

Greenhalgh, S. (1995) *Anthropology and Demographic Inquiry*. Cambridge: Cambridge University Press.

Greenhalgh, S. and J. Li (1995) Engendering reproductive policy and practice in peasant China: for a feminist demography of reproduction. *Signs*, **20**: 601–41.

Greenwood, M. J. (1981) *Migration and Economic Growth in the United States*. New York: Academic Press.

Greenwood, M. J. and J. R. Ladman (1978) An economic analysis of migration in Mexico. *Annals of Regional Science*, **12**: 4–16.

Gregory, D. (1996) *Geographical Imaginations*. Oxford: Blackwell.

Grigg, D. B. (1980) Migration and overpopulation, in **P. White and R. Woods** (eds), *The Geographical Impact of Migration*. London: Longman.

Grigg, D. B. (1995) The nutritional transition in Western Europe. *Journal of Historical Geography*, **21**: 247–61.

Grimes, S. (1999) From population control to 'reproductive rights': ideological influences in population policy. *Third World Quarterly*, **19**: 373–93.

Haggett, P. (1990) *The Geographer's Art*. Oxford: Basil Blackwell.

Haines, M. (1977) Fertility, nuptiality and occupation: a study of coalmining populations and regions in England and Wales in the mid-nineteenth century. *Journal of Interdisciplinary History*, **8**: 245–80.

Hajnal, J. (1965) European marriage patterns in perspective, in **D. Glass and D. Eversley** (eds) *Population History*. London: Arnold.

Halfacree, K. H. (1994) The importance of the rural in the constitution of counterurbanization: evidence from England in the 1980s. *Sociologica Ruralis*, **34**: 164–89.

Halfacree, K. H. (1995) Household migration and the structure of patriarchy: evidence from the USA. *Progress in Human Geography*, **19**: 159–82.

Halfacree, K. H. (2004) Untying migration completely: de-gendering or radical transformation? *Journal of Ethnic and Migration Studies*, **30**: 397–414.

Hall, R. (1993) Family structures, in **D. Noin and R. Woods** (eds), *The Changing Population of Europe*. Oxford: Blackwell.

Hardill, I. and S. MacDonald (1998) Choosing to relocate: an examination of the impact of expatriate work on dual career households. *Women's Studies International Forum*, **21**: 21–9.

Harris, J. and M. P. Todaro (1970) Migration, unemployment and development: a two sector model. *American Economic Review*, **60**: 126–42.

Harris, N. (1995) *The New Untouchables*. London: Taurus.

Hart, J. F. (1960) The changing distribution of the American Negro. *Annals of the Association of American Geographers*, **50**: 242–66.

Hartshorne, R. (1939) *The Nature of Geography*. Lancaster, PA: The Association.

Harvey, D. W. (1974) Population, resources and the ideology of science. *Economic Geography*, **50**: 256–77.

Harvey, D. (1982) *The Limits to Capital*. Oxford: Basil Blackwell.

Harvey, D. (1985) *The Urbanization of Capital*. Oxford: Blackwell.

Harvey, D. (1996) *Justice, Nature, and the Geography of Difference*. Oxford: Blackwell.

Hawthorn, G. (ed.) (1978) *Population and Development, High and Low Fertility in Poorer Countries*. London: Cass.

Henry, L. (1976) *Population: Analysis and Models*. London: Edward Arnold.

Hettner, A. (1927) *Die Geographie*. Breslau: Ferdinand Hirt.

Hicks, W. W. (1974) Economic development and fertility change in Mexico, 1950–1970. *Demography*, **11**: 407–21.

Hofstee, E. (1968) Population increase in the Netherlands. *Acta Historiae Nederlandica*, **3**: 43–125.

Holloway, S. and G. Valentine (eds) (2000) *Children's Geographies*. London: Routledge.

Hondagneu-Sotelo, P. (1994) *Gendered Transitions*. Berkeley: University of California Press.

Hondagneu-Sotelo, P. and E. Avila (1997) 'I'm here but I'm there': The meanings of transnational Latina motherhood. *Gender and Society*, **11**: 548–71.

Hooson, D. J. M. (1960) The distribution of population as the essential geographical expression. *The Canadian Geographer*, **17**: 10.

Hornby, W. F. and M. Jones (1980) *An Introduction to Population Geography*. Cambridge: Cambridge University Press.

Huang, S., P. Teo and B. S. A. Yeoh (2000) Diasporic subjects and identity negotiations: women in and from Asia. *Women's Studies International Forum*, **23**(4): 391–8.

Huang, S. and B. S. A. Yeoh (1996) Ties that bind: state policy and migrant female domestic helpers in Singapore. *Geoforum*, **27**: 479–93.

Hugo, G. (1994) The turnaround in Australia: some first observations from the 1991 census. *Australian Geographer*, **25**: 1–17.

Hunter, J. M. (1967) Population pressure in a part of the West African savanna: A study of Nangodi, Northeast Ghana. *Annals of the Association of American Geographers*, **57**: 101–14.

Hunter, P. R. (1997) *Waterborne Disease: Epidemiology and Ecology*. Chichester: John Wiley.

Huntington, E. (1924) *Civilization and Climate*. New Haven, CT: Yale University Press.

Hussain, A. (2002) Demographic transition in China and its implications. *World Development*, **30**: 1823–34.

Iredale, R. (2001) The migration of professionals. *International Migration*, **39**: 7–26.

Jackson, R. H. and R. L. Layton (1976) The Mormon village: analysis of a settlement type. *The Professional Geographer*, **28**: 136–41.

Jarvis, H. (1999) Identifying the relative mobility prospects of household employment structures 1981–1991. *Environment and Planning A*, **31**: 1031–46.

Jones, E. F. (1971) Fertility decline in Australia and New Zealand 1861–1936, *Population Index*, **37**: 307–38.

Jones, H. R. (1981) *A Population Geography*. London: Harper & Row.

Jones, R. (1989) Causes of Salvadorean migration to the United States. *Annals of the Association of American Geographers*, **79**: 183–94.

Jowett, A. (1987) India: feeding the world's second largest nation, in **A. M. Findlay and A. Findlay** (eds), *Population and Development in the Third World*. London: Methuen.

Kalipeni, E., S. Craddock, J. R. Oppong and J. Ghosh (eds) (2004) *HIV and AIDS in Africa. Beyond Epidemiology*. Malden: Blackwell.

Kant, I. (1987 [1791]) *The Critique of Judgement*. Translated by Werner S. Pluhar. Indianapolis: Hackett Publishing.

Kaplan, D. H. (1994) Population and politics in a plural society: the changing geography of Canada's linguistic groups. *Annals of the Association of American Geographers*, **84**: 46–67.

Kates, R. W. (1987) The human environment: the road not taken, the road still beckoning. *Annals of the Association of American Geographers*, **77**: 525–34.

Kayastha, S. and P. Nag (1989) The Bhopal disaster, in **J. Clarke, P. Curson, S. Kayastha and P. Nag** (eds) *Population and Disaster*. Oxford: Basil Blackwell.

Kempadoo, K. and J. Doezema (1998) *Global Sex Workers*. London: Routledge.

Kesby, M. (2004) Participatory diagramming and the ethical and practical challenges of helping Africans help themselves, in **E. Kalipeni, S. Craddock, J. R. Oppong and J. Ghosh** (eds) *HIV and AIDS in Africa. Beyond Epidemiology*. Malden: Blackwell.

King, R. (1976) The evolution of international labour migration movements concerning the EEC. *Tijdschrift voor Economische en Sociale Geografie*, **67**: 66–82.

King, R. (ed.) (1986) *Return Migration and Regional Economic Problems*. London: Croom Helm.

King, R., A. M. Warnes and A. M. Williams (1998): Special issue: international retirement migration in Europe. *International Journal of Population Geography*, **4**: 87–200.

King, R., J. Connell and P. White (eds) (1995) *Writing Across Worlds. Literature and Migration.* London: Routledge.

Kirk, D. (1971) A new demographic transition? in *Rapid Population Growth: Consequences and Policy Implications.* Baltimore: Johns Hopkins Press.

Kirk, D. (1996) Demographic transition theory. *Population Studies*, **50**: 361–87.

Kobayashi, A. (ed.) (1988) Focus: Asian migration to Canada. *The Canadian Geographer*, **32**: 351–61.

Kofman, E. (1999) Female 'birds of passage' a decade later: gender and immigration in the European Union. *International Migration Review*, **33**: 269–99.

Kojima, Y. (2001) Theoretical implications of the mail order bride phenomenon. *Women's Studies International Forum*, **24**: 199–210.

Koser, K. and H. Lutz (eds) (1998) *The New Migration in Europe: Social Constructions and Social Realities.* Basingstoke: Macmillan.

Koser, K. and J. Salt (1997) Research Review 4: The Geography of Highly Skilled International Migration. *International Journal of Population Geography*, **3**: 285–304.

Kosiński, L. A. (1970) *The Population of Europe: A Geographical Perspective.* Harlow: Longman.

Kosiński, L. A. (1984) The roots of population geography, in **J. Clarke** (ed.) *Geography and Population.* Oxford: Pergamon.

Kraly, E. (1997) International migration statistics: issues of refugee movements, asylum, and gender, in **J. Fairhurst et al.** (eds), *Migration and Gender.* Pretoria: Department of Geography for IGU Commission on Gender and Geography and IGU Commission on Population Geography.

Kuijsten, A. C. (1996) Changing family patterns in Europe: a case of divergence? *European Journal of Population*, **12**: 115–43.

Kumar, A. (2000) *Passport Photos.* Berkeley: University of California Press.

Landry, A. (1934) *La Révolution Démographique: Études et essais sur les Problèmes de la Population.* Paris: Payot.

Lansing, J. B. and E. Mueller (1967) *The Geographic Mobility of Labour.* Ann Arbor, MI, Survey Research Center.

Lawson, V. A. (2000) Arguments within geographies of movement: the theoretical potential of migrant's stories. *Progress in Human Geography,* **24**: 173–89.

Lawton, R. (1959) Irish Immigration to England and Wales in the mid-Nineteenth Century. *Irish Geography,* **4**: 35–54.

Learmonth, A. (1988) *Disease Ecology: An Introduction.* Oxford: Basil Blackwell.

Lechner, M. (2001) The empirical analysis of East German fertility after unification: an update. *European Journal of Population,* **17**: 61–74.

Lee, E. S. (1966) A theory of migration. *Demography,* **3**: 47–57.

Lefebvre, H. (1991) The Production of Space. Oxford: Blackwell.

Lessinger, H. (1995) *From the Ganges to the Hudson.* Needham Heights: Allyn and Bacon.

Liaw, K.-L., W. H. Frey and J.-P. Lin (2002) Location of adult children as an attraction for black and white elderly primary migrants in the United States. *Environment and Planning A,* **34**: 191–216.

Loescher, G. (1993) *Beyond Charity: International Cooperation and the Global Refugee Crisis.* Oxford: Oxford University Press.

Lowry, I. (1966) *Migration and Metropolitan Growth.* Los Angeles: University of California Press.

Mabogunje, A. L. (1970) Systems approach to a theory of rural-urban migration. *Geographical Analysis,* **2**: 241–60.

Mabogunje, A. L. (2004) Geography in the Nigerian public policy domain: The impact and influence of American geographers. *GeoJournal,* **59**: 63–7.

Macklin, A. (1994) On the inside looking in: foreign domestic workers in Canada, in **W. Giles and S. Arat-Koc** (eds), *Maid in the Market: Women's Paid Domestic Labour.* Toronto: Fernwood Press.

MacLeod, C. and K. Durrheim (2002) Racializing teenage pregnancy: 'culture' and 'tradition' in the South African scientific literature. *Ethnic and Racial Studies,* **25**: 778–801.

Mahler, S. (1999) Engendering transnational migration: A case study of Salvadorans. *American Behavioral Scientist,* **42**: 690–712.

Malthus, T. (1798) *An Essay on the Principle of Population, as it Affects the Future Improvement of Society*. London: J. Johnson.

Marston, S. (2000) The social construction of scale. *Progress in Human Geography*, **24**: 219–42.

Mason, K. O. (1997) Explaining fertility transitions. *Demography*, **34**: 443–54.

Massey, D. (1990) Social Structure, Household Strategies, and the Cumulative Causation of Migration. *Population Index*, **56**(1): 3–26.

Massey, D., J. Arongo, G. Hugo, A. Kouaouci, A. Pellegrino and J. E. Taylor (1999) *Worlds in Motion*. Oxford: Clarendon Press.

Matthews, H., M. Limb and B. Percy-Smith (1998) Changing worlds: the microgeographies of young teenagers. *Tijdschrift voor Economische en Sociale Geografie*, **89**: 193–202.

Mattingly, D. J. (2001) The home and the world: domestic service and international networks of caring labor. *Annals of the Association of American Geographers*, **91**: 370–86.

Mayer, J. D. and M. S. Meade (1994) A reformed medical geography reconsidered. *The Professional Geographer*, **46**: 103–6.

McCollum, A. (1990) *The Trauma of Moving*. Newbury Park: Sage.

McGinnis, R. M. (1977) Childbearing and land availability, in **R. Lee** (ed.), *Population patterns in the past*. New York: Academic Press.

McHugh, K. E. and R. C. Mings (1996) The circle of migration: attachment to place in aging. *Annals of the Association of American Geographers*, **86**: 530–50.

McLafferty, S. and B. Tempalski (1995) Restructuring and Women's Reproductive Health: Implications for Low Birthweight in New York City. *Geoforum* **26**: 309–23.

Meadows, D. H., D. L. Meadows, J. Randers and W. Behrens III (1972) *The Limits to Growth*. New York: Universe.

Meillassoux, C. (1972) From reproduction to production: a Marxist approach to anthropology. *Economy and Society*, **1**: 93–105.

Meinig, D. W. (1965) The Mormon culture region: strategies and patterns in the Geography of the American West, 1847–1864. *Annals of the Association of American Geographers*, **55**: 191–220.

Meir, A. (1986) Demographic transition theory: a neglected aspect of the nomadism-sedentarism continuum. *Transactions of the Institute of British Geographers*, **11**: 199–211.

Melezin, A. (1963) Trends and issues in the Soviet geography of population. *Annals of the Association of American Geographers*, **53**: 144–60.

Meslé, F. and J. Vallin (1998) Evolution et variations géographiques de la surmortalité masculine: du paradoxe français à la logique russe. *Population*, **53**: 1079–101.

Mincer, J. (1978) Family migration decisions. *Journal of Political Economy*, **86**: 749–73.

Mitchell, J. C. (1959) Labor migration in Africa south of the Sahara. *Bulletin of the Inter-African Labor Institute*, **6**: 12–47.

Mitchell, K. (1997) Different diasporas and the hype of hybridity. *Environment and Planning D: Society and Space*, **15**: 533–53.

Miyares, I., R. Wright, A. Mountz, A. J. Bailey and J. Jonak (2003) The interrupted circle: truncated transnationalism and the Salvadoran experience. *Journal of Latin American Geography*, **2**: 74–86.

Mohanty, C. T. (1991) Under Western eyes: feminist scholarship and colonial discourses, in **C. T. Mohanty, A. Russo and L. Torres** (eds) (1991) *Third World Women and the Politics of Feminism*. Bloomington: Indiana University Press.

Monk, J. (1981) Social change and sexual differences in Puerto Rican rural migration, in **O. H. Horst** (ed.) *Papers in Latin American Geography in Honor of Lucia C. Harrison*. Muncie, IN: Conference of Latin Americanist Geographers.

Morokvasic, M. (1991) Fortress Europe and migrant women. *Feminist Review*, **39**: 69–84.

Morrill, R. (1990) Regional demographic structure of the United States. *Professional Geographer*, **42**: 38–53.

Morrill, R. L. (1965) The negro ghetto: alternatives and consequences. *Geographical Review*, July 1965: 221–38.

Moss, P. and I. Dyck (1996) Inquiry into environment and body: women, work, and chronic illness. *Environment and Planning D: Society and Space*, **14**: 737–53.

Mountz, A. and R. Wright (1996) Daily life in the transnational migrant community of San Agustin, Oaxaca and Poughkeepsie, New York. *Diaspora*, **6**: 403–28.

Mukherji, S. (1997) Underdevelopment and migration of women for employment in India, in **J. Fairhurst et al.** (eds), *Migration and Gender*. Pretoria: Department of Geography for IGU Commission on Gender and Geography and IGU Commission on Population Geography.

Murray, M. A. (1962) The geography of death in England and Wales. *Annals of the Association of American Geographers*, **52**: 130–49.

Murray, M. A. (1967) The geography of death in the United States and the United Kingdom. *Annals of the Association of American Geographers*, **57**: 301–14.

Myers, D. (1990) Introduction: The emerging concept of housing demography, in **D. Myers** (ed.), *Housing Demography: Linking Demographic Structure and Housing Markets*. Madison: University of Wisconsin.

Myers, G. C., R. McGinnis and G. Masnick (1967) The duration of residence approach to a dynamic stochastic model of internal migration: a test of the cumulative inertia. *Eugenics Quarterly*, **14**: 121–6.

Newbold, K. B. (1996) Determinants of elderly interstate migration in the United States, 1985–1990. *Research on Aging*, **18**: 451–76.

Nijkamp, P. (1976) *Spatial Mobility and Settlement Patterns: An Application of a Behavioural Entropy*. Luxemburg, Austria: International Institute for Applied Systems Analysis Publication RM-76-045.

Noin, D. (ed.) (1991) *Where Is Population Going?* Paris: International Geographic Union, Commission on Population Geography.

Noin, D. and R. Woods (eds) (1993) *The Changing Population of Europe*. Oxford: Blackwell.

Notestein, F. W. (1945) Population: the long view, in **T. W. Schultz** (ed.), *Food for the World*. Chicago: Chicago University Press.

Noyes, J. K. (2000) Nomadic fantasies: producing landscapes of mobility in German Southwest Africa. *Ecumene*, **7**: 47–66.

Nyíri, P. (2001) Expatriating is patriotic? The discourse on 'new migrants' in the People's Republic of China and identity construction among recent migrants from the PRC. *Journal of Ethnic and Migration Studies*, **27**: 635–53.

Ogden, P. E. (1998) Population geography. *Progress in Human Geography*, **22**: 105–14.

Omran, A. (1983) The epidemiological transition theory. *Journal of Tropical Pediatrics*, **29**: 305–16.

Ong, A. (1995) Making the biopolitical subject: Cambodian immigrants, refugee medicine and cultural citizenship in California. *Social Science and Medicine*, **40**: 1243–57.

Openshaw, S., A. W. Craft, M. Charlton and J. M. Birch (1988) Investigations of leukaemia clusters by use of a geographical analysis machine. *The Lancet*, **i**: 272–3.

Orellana, M. F., B. Thorne, A. Chee and W. Lam (2001) Transnational childhoods: the participation of children in processes of family migration. *Social Problems*, **48**: 572–91.

Pain, R. (2003) Social geography: on action orientated research. *Progress in Human Geography*, **27**: 649–57.

Pain, R., G. Mowl and C. Talbot (2000) Difference and the negotiation of 'old age'. *Environment and Planning D: Society and Space*, **18**: 377–93.

Park, R. E., E. W. Burgess and R. D. McKenzie (1925) *The City*. Chicago: University of Chicago Press.

Pavlík, Z. (1964) *Nastín populačniho vývoje svĕta*. Prague: Cĕskoslovenska Akademia Vĕd.

Peach, G. C. K. (1966) Factors affecting the distribution of West Indians in Great Britain. *Transactions of the Institute of British Geographers*, **38**: 151–63.

Peach, G. C. K. and G. Glebe (1995) Muslim minorities in western Europe. *Ethnic and Racial Studies*, **18**: 26–45.

Peters, G. L. and R. P. Larkin (1979) *Population Geography*. Third Edition. Dubuque: Kendall/Hunt.

Peterson, W. (1958) A general typology of migration. *American Sociological Review*, **23**: 256–65.

Philo, C. (2001) Accumulation populations. *International Journal of Population Geography*, **7**: 473–90.

Plane, D. A. (1992) Age composition change and the geographical dynamics of interregional migration in the US. *Annals of the Association of American Geographers*, **74**: 244–56.

Plane, D. A. and P. A. Rogerson (1991) Tracking the baby boom, the baby bust and the echo generations: how age composition regulates US migration. *The Professional Geographer*, **43**: 416–30.

Plaza, D. (2000) Transnational grannies: the changing family responsibilities of elderly African-Caribbean-born women resident in Britain. *Social Indicators Research*, **51**: 75–105.

Pokshishevskiy, V. V. (1962 [1960]) *Soviet Geography: Accomplishments and Tasks.* Washington, DC: American Geographical Society.

Portes, A. (1996) Transnational communities: Their emergence and significance in the contemporary world system, in **R. P. Korzeniewicz and W. C. Smith** (eds), *Latin America in the World Economy*. Westport, CT: Greenwood Press.

Pooley, C. (1977) The residential segregation of migrant communities in mid-Victorian Liverpool. *Transactions of the Institute of British Geographers*, **2**: 364–82.

Pooley, C. (1979) Residential mobility in the Victorian city. *Transactions of the Institute of British Geographers*, **4**: 258–77.

Potts, L. G. (2003) Global trafficking in human beings: assessing the success of the United Nations protocol to prevent trafficking in persons. *The George Washington International Law Review*, **35**: 227–40.

Pratt, G. (1997) Re-placing race: reactions to 'Brown skinned white girls'. *Gender, Place and Culture*, **4**: 363–6.

Pratt, G. (1999) From registered nurse to registered nanny: discursive geographies of Filipina domestic workers in Vancouver, B.C. *Economic Geography*, **75**: 215–36.

Prothero, R. and M. Chapman (eds) (1985) *Circulation in Population Movement: Substance and Concepts from the Melanesian Case.* London: Routledge and Kegan Paul.

Pulsipher, L. M. (1993) 'He won't let she stretch she foot': Gender relations in traditional West Indian households, in **C. Katz and J. Monk** (eds), *Full Circles: Geographies of Women over the Life Course*, New York: Routledge.

Rafiq, N. (1991) Female child mortality in Bangladesh: the discrimination against women at the root. *Oriental Geographer*, **35**: 21–31.

Ratzel, F. (1882) *Anthropo-Geographie*. Stuttgart: Engelhorn.

Ravenstein, E. (1885) The laws of migration. *Journal of Royal Statistical Society*, **48**: 167–227.

Raymond, J. G. (2002) The New UN Trafficking Protocol. *Women's Studies International Forum*, **25**: 491–502.

Rees, P. (1997) The second demographic transition: what does it mean for the future of Europe's population? *Environment and Planning A*, **29**: 381–85.

Rees, P. and A. Convey (1984) Spatial population accounting, in **J. Clarke** (ed.) *Geography and Population*. Oxford: Pergamon.

Rees, P., D. Martin and P. Williamson (eds) (2002) *The Census Data System*. Chichester: Wiley.

Reher, D. (1998) Family ties in western Europe: persistent contrasts. *Population and Development Review*, **24**: 203–34.

Rengert, A. C. (1981) Some sociocultural aspects of rural out-migration in Latin America, in **O. H. Horst**, *Papers in Latin America Geography in Honor of Lucia C. Harrison*. Muncie, IN: Conference on Latin Americanist Geographers.

Richmond, A. H. (1994) *Global Apartheid*. New York: Oxford University Press.

Riddell, J. B. (1981) Beyond the description of spatial pattern: the process of proletarianization as a factor in population migration in West Africa. *Progress in Human Geography*, **5**: 370–92.

Rogers, A. (ed.) (1992) *Elderly Migration and Population Redistribution: A Comparative Study*. London: Belhaven Press.

Rogers. A. and F. J. Willekens (1986) *Migration and Settlement: A Multiregional Comparative Study*. Dordrecht: D. Reidel Publishing Company.

Rogerson, P. A., J. A. Burr and G. Lin (1997) Changes in geographic proximity between parents and their adult children. *International Journal of Population Geography*, **3**: 121–36.

Rose, G. (1993) *Feminism and Geography: The Limits of Geographical Knowledge*. Cambridge: Polity Press.

Rose, H. (1969) *Social Process in the City: Race and Urban Residential Choice.* Washington, DC: Association of American Geographers Resource Paper 6.

Rosenberg, M. W. (1998) Research review 5: medical or health geography? Populations, people and places. *International Journal of Population Geography,* **4**: 211–26.

Rossi, P. H. (1955) *Why Families Move.* New York: Free Press.

Rowland, D. T. (1979) *Internal Migration in Australia.* Canberra: Australian Bureau of Statistics, Census Monograph Series.

Rowles, G. D. (1986) The geography of aging and the aged: toward an integrated perspective. *Progress in Human Geography,* **10**: 511–39.

Ruddick, S. (2003) The politics of aging: globalisation and the restructuring of youth and childhood. *Antipode,* **35**: 334–62.

Rudzitis, G. (1993) Non-metropolitan geography: migration, sense of place, and the American West. *Urban Geography,* **14**: 574–85.

Sachs, P. (1993) Old ties: women, work, and ageing in a coal-mining community in West Virgina, in **C. Katz and J. Monk** (eds), *Full Circles: Geographies of Women over the Life Course.* New York: Routledge.

Said, E. (1978) *Orientalism.* London: Routledge and Kegan Paul.

Samers, M. (1997) The production of diaspora: Algerian emigration from colonialism to neo-colonialism (1840–1870). *Antipode,* **29**: 32–53.

Sassen, S. (1991) *The Global City: New York, London, Tokyo.* Princeton, NJ: Princeton University Press.

Semple, E. (1911) *Influences of Geographic Environment.* New York: H. Holt & Co.

Sen, A. (1990) More than 100 million women are missing. *New York Review of Books,* **20**: 61–6.

Shaw, E. B. (1938) Population distribution in Newfoundland. *Economic Geography,* **14**: 239–54.

Shaw, R. P. (1975) *Migration Theory and Fact: A Review and Bibliography of Current Literature.* Philadelphia: Regional Science Research Institute.

Silvey, R. M. (2000) Diasporic subjects: gender and mobility in south Sulawesi. *Women's Studies International Forum,* **23**: 501–15.

Sjaastad, L. A. (1962) The costs and returns of human migration. *Journal of Political Economy,* **70** (supplement): 80–93.

Skeldon, R. (1992) International Migration Flows within and from the East and Southeast Asian Region: A Review Essay. *Asian and Pacific Migration Journal,* **1**: 19–63.

Skeldon, R. (1995) The challenge facing migration research: a case for greater awareness. *Progress in Human Geography,* **19**: 91–6.

Skeldon, R. (1997) *Migration and Development.* Harlow: Longman.

Smith, G. C. (1998) Residential separation and patterns of interaction between elderly parents and their adult children. *Progress in Human Geography,* **22**, 368–84.

Smith, M. P. and L. E. Guarnizo (eds) (1998) *Transnationalism from Below.* New Brunswick, NJ: Transaction Press.

Smyth, I. (1994) 'Safe Motherhood', Family Planning and Maternal Mortality: An Indonesian Case Study. *Focus on Gender,* **2**: 19–28.

Snow, J. (1965) *Snow on Cholera.* New York: Hafner.

Sobotka, T. (2002): Comments on 'The empirical analysis of East German fertility after unification: an update'. *European Journal of Population,* **18**: 203–8.

Stewart, J. Q. (1947) Empirical mathematical rules concerning the distribution and equilibrium of population. *Geographical Review,* **37**: 461–85.

Stolnitz, G. J. (1965) Recent mortality trends in Latin America, Asia and Africa: review and reinterpretation. *Population Studies,* **19**: 117–38.

Stouffer, S. A. (1940) Intervening opportunities: a theory relating mobility and distance. *American Sociological Review,* **5**: 845–67.

Susser, I. and Z. Stein (2004) Culture, sexuality, and women's agency in the prevention of HIV/AIDS in Southern Africa, in **E. Kalipeni, S. Craddock, J. R. Oppong and J. Ghosh** (eds), *HIV and AIDS in Africa. Beyond Epidemiology.* Malden: Blackwell.

Swindell, K. (1979) Labor migration in underdeveloped countries. *Progress in Human Geography,* **3**: 239–59.

Thekaekara, M. M. (2004) Sex workers with attitude. *New Internationalist,* **368**: 20–1.

Thompson, W. S. (1929) Population. *American Journal of Sociology*, **34**: 959–75.

Thrift, N. (1999) Steps to an ecology of place, in **D. Massey, J. Allen and P. Sarre** (eds) *Human Geography Today*. Cambridge: Polity Press.

Tien, H. Y. (1984) Induced fertility transition: the impact of population planning and socio-economic change in the People's Republic of China. *Population Studies*, **38**: 385–400.

Tilly, C. (1978) *Historical Studies of Changing Fertility*. Princeton, NJ: Princeton University Press.

Trewartha, G. T. (1953) The case for population geography. *Annals of the Association of American Geographers*, **43**: 71–97.

Trewartha, G. T. (1969) *A Geography of Population: World Patterns*. New York: Wiley.

Trewartha, G. T. (ed.) (1978) *The More Developed Realm: A Geography of its Population*. Oxford: Pergamon Press.

Trewartha, G. T. (1979) *The Less Developed Realm: A Geography of its Population*. New York: Wiley.

Trewartha, G. T. and W. Zelinsky (1954) The population geography of Belgian Africa. *Annals of the Association of American Geographers*, **44**: 135–45.

Tsui, A. and D. Bogue (1978) Declining world fertility: trends, causes and implications. *Population Bulletin*, **33**(4).

Twine, F. W. (1996) Brown skinned white girls: class, culture, and the construction of white identity in suburban communities. *Gender, Place and Culture*, **3**: 205–24.

Tyner, J. (1994) The social construction of gendered migration from the Philippines. *Asia and Pacific Migration Journal*, **3**: 589–612.

UNAIDS/WHO (2002) *Projected population structure with and without the AIDS epidemic, Botswana, 2020* (electronic document). http://www.unaids.org

Underhill-Sem, Y. (2001) Maternities in 'out-of-the-way' places: epistemological possibilities for retheorising population geography. *International Journal of Population Geography*, **7**: 447–60.

Underhill-Sem, Y. (2004) The fertility of mobility: impulses from Hawaii. *GeoJournal*, **59**: 55–8.

United Church of Christ (1987). *Toxic Wastes and Race in the United States: A National Report on the Racial and Socio-economic Characteristics with Hazardous Waste Sites.* New York: United Church of Christ, Commission for Racial Justice.

US Census Bureau (2004) *Mean Center of Population for the United States: 1790 to 2000* (electronic document): http://www.census.gov/geo/www/cenpop/meanctr.pdf

Valentine, G. (1995) Out and about: geographies of lesbian landscapes. *International Journal of Urban and Regional Research,* **19**: 96–111.

Valentine, G. (2001) *Social Geographies.* Harlow: Prentice Hall.

Van de Kaa, D. J. (1987) Europe's second demographic transition. *Population Bulletin,* **42**: 1–57.

Van de Walle, E. (1978) Alone in Europe, in **C. Tilly** (ed.) *Historical Studies of Changing Fertility.* Princeton, NJ: Princeton University Press.

Van Ewijk, M. and P. Grifhorst (1998) Controlling and disciplining the foreign body: a case study of TB treatment among asylum seekers in the Netherlands, in **K. Koser and H. Lutz** (eds) (1998) *The New Migration in Europe: Social Constructions and Social Realities.* Basingstoke: Macmillan.

Van Hear, N. (1998) *New Diasporas.* London: UCL Press.

Van Wissen, L. J. G. and P. A. Dykstra (eds) (1999) *Population Issues: An Interdisciplinary Focus.* New York: Kluwer.

Vidal de la Blache, P. (1922) *Principes de géographie humaine.* Paris: Armand Colin.

Waldorf, B. (1994) Assimilation and attachment in the context of international migration: the case of guest workers in Germany. *Papers in Regional Science,* **73**: 241–66.

Walter, B. (1998) Challenging the Black/White binary: The need for an Irish category in the 2001 Census. *Patterns of Prejudice,* **32**: 73–86.

Walter, B. (1999) Inside and outside the Pale: diaspora experiences of Irish women, in **P. Boyle and K. Halfacree** (eds) (1999) *Migration and Gender in the Developed World.* London: Routledge.

Warnes, A. M. (ed.) (1982) *Geographical Perspectives on the Elderly.* Chichester: Wiley.

Warnes, A. M. and R. Ford (1995) Housing aspirations and migration in later life: developments during the 1980s. *Papers in Regional Science*, **74**: 361–87.

Wasserman, E. (1999) Environment, health, and gender in Latin America: trends and research issues. *Environmental Research*, **80**: 253–73.

Weeks, J. R. (1999) *Population*. Belmont, CA: Wadsworth.

White, P. (1993) Ethnic minority communities in Europe, in **D. Noin and R. Woods** (eds) (1993) *The Changing Population of Europe*. Oxford: Blackwell.

White, P. (1998) The settlement patterns of developed world migrants in London. *Urban Studies*, **35**: 1725–44.

White, P. and P. Jackson (1995) (Re)theorising population geography. *International Journal of Population Geography*, **1**: 111–23.

Willis, K. and B. Yeoh (2000) Gender and transnational household strategies: Singaporean migration to China. *Regional Studies* **34**: 253–64.

Winchester, H. P. M., L. Kong and K. Dunn (2003) *Landscapes*. Harlow: Pearson.

Wolpert, J. (1965) Behavioural aspects of the decision to migrate. *Papers and Proceedings, Regional Science Association*, **15**: 159–69.

Wolpert, J. (1966) Migration as an adjustment to environmental stress. *The Journal of Social Issues*, **22**: 92–102.

Woods, R. (1982) *Theoretical Population Geography*. London: Longman.

Woods, R. (1984) Spatial demography, in **J. I. Clarke** (ed.) *Geography and Population: Approaches and Applications*. Oxford: Pergamon.

Woods, R. (2000) *The Demography of Victorian England and Wales*. Cambridge: Cambridge University Press.

Woods, R. and P. Rees (1986) *Population Structures and Models: Developments in Spatial Demography*. London: Allen & Unwin.

Wright, R. A., M. Ellis and M. Reibel (1997) The linkage between immigration and internal migration in large metropolitan areas in the United States. *Economic Geography,* **73**: 234–54.

Wright, R. A., S. Houston, M. Ellis, S. Holloway and M. Hudson (2003) Crossing racial lines: geographies of mixed race partnering and multiraciality in the United States. *Progress in Human Geography*, **27**: 457–74.

Wrigley, E. A. and R. S. Schofield (1981) *The Population History of England, 1541–1871. A Reconstruction.* Cambridge: Harvard University Press.

Zelinsky, W. (1966) *A Prologue to Population Geography.* Englewood Cliffs: Prentice-Hall.

Zelinsky, W. (1971) The hypothesis of the mobility transition. *Geographical Review,* **61**: 219–49.

INDEX

abortion 137–8, 146
Abu-Lughod, J. 88, 97
adult child–parent proximity 132, 151, 153
age of equalization 85
age–sex composition see composition
age–sex distributions 83–5
aging, as a social process 151
Albania – source of child trafficking 43–5
Anderson, K. 156
Anzaldua, G. 170, 176
apartheid system (South Africa) 57, 139, 156, 182
Arendt, Hannah 18
assimilation, concept of 49, 58, 121
asylum seekers
  and exclusion 182
  and livelihoods 163
  and migration systems 126
  political significance of 108
'axiom of cumulative inertia' 99
axis of evil 168

baby boom/baby bust cycles 56, 131, 159
Bauman, Zygmat 168
Beaujeu-Garnier, Jean 51, 67–70, 73, 99, 103
behavioural approach 61, 98–9, 129–32
below replacement population 109
Berlin Wall, the 53
biographical approach 83, 102, 134
Black, R. 122
Black Report, The 141
Bogue, Donald 72
Bourdieu, Pierre 110, 119
Boyle, Paul 161
Brown, L.A. 99, 159
Bruhnes, J. 35, 65, 68
Bunge, W. 62, 104
Burgess, E.W. 31
Bush, George 6, 168

Caldwell, J.C. 90
caring 124–5, 148, 161, 163, 173–4,
Castles, Stephen 97, 122, 168, 185
census
  as a data source 29, 66, 68, 70, 86, 101, 114, 119, 151

origins of 17, 24
centre of gravity
  centroid calculation 74
  of US population 75
Champion, A.G. 135
Chapman, M. 94, 100, 128
Chatterton, Paul 152
China – population policy 38–42, 184
children and childhood 151–2
  and the family 6, 124, 173, 174
  and fertility 37–41
  and migration 96, 125
  and the sex trade 43–5, 125
citizenship 106
  dual-citizenship 170, 184
  and the state 127–8
Clark, W.A.V. 121, 154–5, 159
Clarke, John 51, 77–9, 81
Coale, A.J. 89, 136
cohorts 31, 116, 159
colonialism 20, 28, 50, 53, 111, 113, 117
Commission on Global Aging 157
commuting 47, 131
composition
  age–sex 81, 83–5, 155–6
  topics and approaches to 148–56
conception 137–8, 140
contraception 37, 47–9, 52, 89–90, 146
Conway, Dennis 161
counterurbanization 25, 112, 121, 128, 134, 135
Craddock, S. 48, 147
Croucher, S. 156, 182
cumulative causation 125, 171

data
  cross-sectional 92
  on gender, and its meaning 163
  importance of quantitative 24, 71–2, 117, 164
  literature as a source of 134
  longitudinal 130, 134
  partners in collection 188
  shortages of population data 74, 103
dating 156, 181
deconcentration 150, 154

221